GLOBAL UNIVERSITY PRESIDENT LEADERSHIP

This book unlocks mysteries surrounding university presidents. Presidents have a large and growing influence on world and academic affairs. Yet until now, little has been revealed about how they enact their roles, how they capture motivation and academic energy, and their views on higher education.

This book sheds light on these critical topics, revealing insights from in-depth interviews with presidents of nineteen globally focused universities from thirteen countries. The book presents the interview transcripts and surrounds these with interpretative commentary. Underpinned by leadership theory and framed by analysis, the book provides glimpses into how top leaders think, how presidents manoeuvre through their careers, how leaders form and run productive teams, and opportunities for research and innovation. Common themes and challenges are identified. The presidents reflect on university landscapes, strategic outlooks, the formation of executive teams, online teaching, funding, industry engagement, sustainability, grand challenges, and interdisciplinarity.

This book is for professionals and scholars who are interested in education, universities, public policy, science and humanities, and global affairs.

Hamish Coates is a Tenured Professor at the Institute of Education Tsinghua University, Director of the Higher Education Research Division, and Deputy Director of the Tsinghua University Global Research Centre for the Assessment of College and Student Development.

Zheping Xie is Deputy Director of the Policy Research Office and an Associate Professor at the Tsinghua University Institute of Education.

Wen Wen is Deputy Secretary of the Tsinghua University Centre for Asian Studies and an Associate Professor at the Institute of Education Tsinghua University.

Asian Higher Education Outlook

Series Editors

Zhong Zhou, Tsinghua University, China.
Hamish Coates, Tsinghua University, China.
Shi Jinghuan, Tsinghua University, China.
Chuanjie Zhang, Tsinghua University, China.

List of titles:

For more information about the series, please visit www.routledge.com/Asian-Higher-Education-Outlook/book-series/AHEO

GLOBAL UNIVERSITY PRESIDENT LEADERSHIP

Insights on Higher Education Futures

Hamish Coates, Zheping Xie and Wen Wen

LONDON AND NEW YORK

Cover image: © Getty Images

First published 2022
by Routledge
2 Park Square, Milton Park, Abingdon, Oxon OX14 4RN

and by Routledge
605 Third Avenue, New York, NY 10158

Routledge is an imprint of the Taylor & Francis Group, an informa business

British Library Cataloguing-in-Publication Data
A catalogue record for this book is available from the British Library

Library of Congress Cataloging-in-Publication Data
Names: Coates, Hamish, author. | Xie, Zheping, author. | Wen, Wen, 1981- author.
Title: Global university president leadership : insights from Tsinghua interviews / Hamish Coates, Zheping Xie, and Wen Wen.
Description: First Edition. | New York : Routledge, 2022. | Series: Asian Higher Education Outlook | Includes bibliographical references and index. | Identifiers: LCCN 2021037458 (print) | LCCN 2021037459 (ebook) | ISBN 9781032163758 (Hardback) | ISBN 9781032163758 (Paperback) | ISBN 9781003248286 (eBook)
Subjects: LCSH: Educational leadership--Cross-cultural studies. | Education, Higher--Administration--Cross-cultural studies. | College presidents--Interviews. | Globalization.
Classification: LCC LB2806 .G5458 2022 (print) | LCC LB2806 (ebook) | DDC 378.1/01--dc23
LC record available at https://lccn.loc.gov/2021037458
LC ebook record available at https://lccn.loc.gov/2021037459

ISBN: 978-1-032-16376-5 (hbk)
ISBN: 978-1-032-16375-8 (pbk)
ISBN: 978-1-003-24828-6 (ebk)

DOI: 10.4324/9781003248286

Typeset in Bembo
by SPi Technologies India Pvt Ltd (Straive)

CONTENTS

PART 3
Guiding insights   **221**

FIGURES

ABOUT THE AUTHORS

Hamish Coates Professor Hamish Coates is a Tenured Professor at Tsinghua University's Institute of Education, Director of the Higher Education Research Division, and Deputy Director of the Tsinghua University Global Research Centre for the Assessment of College and Student Development. He was Professor of Higher Education at the University of Melbourne, Founding Director of Higher Education Research at the Australian Council for Educational Research, and Program Director at the LH Martin Institute for Tertiary Leadership and Management. He concentrates on improving the quality and productivity of higher education.

Zheping Xie Associate Researcher Zheping Xie has a PhD in political science and has post-doctoral experience in education. She is an Associate Professor of Education at the Institute of Education, and Deputy Director of Policy Research Office at Tsinghua University. She serves as an Academic Board Member for Undergraduate Education Committee of Tsinghua University, Board Member of the Aalborg Centre for Problem Based Learning in Engineering Science and Sustainability, Jury of UNESCO International Literacy Prize, and Advisory Board Member of the Chinese National Commission for UNESCO. She was a Visiting Fellow at the London School of Economics and Political Science in 2014. Between 2014 and 2020, she served on the jury for UNESCO's Prize for Girls and Women's Education. She has published over twenty papers, six books, and several book chapters on education and international cooperation. Her current research focuses on education and global governance

Wen Wen is currently an Associate Professor in higher education at Tsinghua University's Institute of Education and Vice Director of the university's Centre for Asian Studies. She participated as a Fulbright Scholar at Harvard University and a Visiting Scholar at the Center for International Higher Education at Boston College in 2019–2020. Dr Wen's research interests include sociology of education, comparative and international higher education, and education policy. Her latest research examines how university organization and higher education development are shaped by political, social, and economic dynamics in the globalized era. She has authored and co-authored over one hundred publications in the aforementioned research area. Her articles have appeared in the top journals of higher education. She is currently on the editorial boards for Studies in Higher Education and has served on many others.

PREFACE

University leadership keeps growing in importance. As our collective experiences affirm, the world expects universities to make greater contributions to knowledge and to society. University leaders play an ever more important role in steering institutions through uncertain terrain and enabling talented people to learn and discover.

University presidents have a large and growing influence on knowledge and world affairs. Yet too little is known about these people, how they execute their roles, and their personal views on higher education. This book sheds light on these critical topics.

The book stems from research which Tsinghua University President Qiu Yong sponsored in 2019 to interview the presidents who visit the university. It reveals insights from these in-depth interviews and surrounds these with interpretative commentary. We are delighted that this book has been co-created with so many distinguished university presidents, who together explore this significant topic.

Underpinned by leadership theory and framed by analysis, the book provides glimpses into how top leaders think, how presidents manoeuvre through their careers, how leaders form and run productive teams, and opportunities for future research and innovation.

Reading this book invites us to share experiences on how we deliver effective leadership. It deepens our understanding of how we can be transformative as individuals, and through our executive teams and colleagues. To help us construct universities for the future, let's identify challenges confronting higher education and the value we seek to make.

This book is for readers with a mature or growing interest in education, universities, public policy, the role of science, and global affairs. We welcome you to the conversation.

Hamish Coates, Zheping Xie, and Wen Wen
Institute of Education Tsinghua University

ACKNOWLEDGEMENTS

The authors are very grateful to Academician Professor Qiu Yong, president of Tsinghua University, for supporting this project.

This project was also supported by an editorial board consisting of Sun Haitao, Li Jinliang, Shi Zhongying, and Qin Chuan.

We would like to extend our sincere thanks to the presidents interviewed and to colleagues who helped arrange interviews and follow-up work. Without the presidents, this book and related research would be impossible to complete.

Thank you to colleagues from Tsinghua University's Institute of Education for their support of this book. In particular, we offer thanks to Shi Zhongying, Liu Lu, Hong Xi, Luo Yan, Wu Shengnan, Gao Xi, Zhou Jingbo, Liu Ruixi, Zhang Juan, Yang Qingyuan, and Xie Haixia.

The authors are grateful to Taylor & Francis Group for permission to use material from this article: Liu, L., Hong, X., Wen, W., Xie, Z., & Coates, H. (2020). Global university president leadership characteristics and dynamics. *Studies in Higher Education*, *45*(10), 2036–2044.

This project has received strong support from the Policy Research Office of Tsinghua University, the International Cooperation and Exchange Office of Tsinghua University, and News Centre of Tsinghua University. We are very grateful to Sun Haitao, Li Jinliang, Qin Chuan, Wang Hui, Ling Yun, Liu Nannan, Zhong Ziwei, and Li Xiaoxu.

The authors are eternally grateful to their families and colleagues for helping them understanding education, universities and leadership.

PART 1
Framing perspectives

1

UNIVERSITY PRESIDENT VOICES

Introduction

While universities may have always had international characteristics, in recent decades, certain universities have emphasized their global perspective and role. Globally focused universities can be characterized by a deeply international vision or perspective, geographic and cultural dispersion, international renown, playing a national flagship role, being research-intensive, and often (though not always) being 'world-class.' Mohrman et al. (2008, 5), for instance, identified such institutions as having a "global mission, research intensity, new roles for professors, diversified funding, worldwide recruitment, increasing complexity, new relationships with government and industry, and global collaboration with similar institutions."

Reviewing the website of any such university reveals a large, complex organization requiring substantial leadership. Enormous value is produced therefore by studying university leadership and leaders. Indeed, much has been written about university leadership and management. Research and commentary have adopted various perspectives, such as internal governance, organizational culture, and gender (e.g. Coates, 2017; Coate et al., 2018; Huang, 2017; Scott et al., 2010) and about presidents' opinions of universities (Bosetti & Walker, 2010). Yet very little research has sought to reveal the characteristics and work of university presidents. Anglospheric research exists (e.g. ACE, 2007; Bosetti & Walker, 2010; Bryman, 2007; Scott et al., 2008; Shattock, 2013), but there is little research outside this context (e.g. Huang, 2017; Sirat et al., 2012) and even less about presidents from across the world.

This is a notable gap. Indeed it is somewhat strange that relatively little is known about important aspects of global university presidents. There is particular value in studying university presidents given their enormous authority, expertise, and prominence.

DOI: 10.4324/9781003248286-2

To address this lacuna, this book contributes initial insights from a study of the nature, perspectives, and work of globally influential university presidents. The study rests on interviews conducted with a selection of university presidents who have visited Tsinghua University. It presents interviews with nineteen presidents, touching on leadership, Chinese higher education, and global developments. As the 2020 pandemic has shown, these presidents play a hugely important role, not just in their universities or countries but also in the world. This book helps reveal their voices.

Tsinghua University launched the University President Interviews (UPI) project in 2019. This project absorbs the experience and best practices of university leaders, promotes understanding and cooperation with partners, and builds insight into global higher education. By combining minds, experiences, and practices from around the globe, this project plays a role in serving social advancement, intellectual well-being, and international cooperation. The project is a continuation of work launched before Tsinghua's 2011 centennial. Presidents are keen to engage and contribute to a unique global leadership resource.

It is helpful to provide a little detail on the research approach. As a leading university (ARWU, 2019; Yang et al., 2020), Tsinghua is visited by many people who run global universities. They are typically referred to as 'presidents,' 'rectors,' 'vice chancellors,' or 'principals.' As part of the visit preparation, the UPI team requests that the visiting president participates in a one-hour interview. A semi-structured interview schedule is used, which includes around twenty questions about presidents and executive teams, the president's university, Tsinghua University, Chinese higher education, and global higher education. Not all questions are asked, other questions may arise as the dialogue proceeds, and presidents typically talk associatively, which is encouraged as a means of giving life to the points being made. After signing a consent form, the interviews are conducted in English, recorded, transcribed, and then translated into Chinese. A total of nineteen interviews have been conducted. The bilingual transcripts are returned for review and revision by each president, often multiple times. The proofed data is used in a range of ways. The full transcripts are distributed to Tsinghua's senior leaders. The transcripts are subjected to qualitative analysis for scholarly research.

Listening to presidents' voices

There is substantial research and practical value in studying university presidents and their leadership. Such work shifts the study of university presidents out of the secretive ethers and into the zone of scientific research. This research contributes insights that help current presidents understand their peers and their work, can help deepen international engagement and collaboration among top universities, can inform the development of future presidents, and can serve as conceptual and empirical foundations for future international research. Indeed, finding out about global university presidents is becoming more important given the changing political economy of higher education in many countries whereby the locus of power and responsibility is shifting from systems to institutions, emphasizing the work of university leaders (Badillo-Vega et al., 2019; Shattock, 2013). It is particularly the case, of course, that the people presiding over the world's top universities are operating in ways which might be characterized as 'post-systemic.'

There is particular value in going beyond received or public information about university presidents and engaging in deep qualitative analysis. Presidents have specific executive and academic authority, rendering distinguishing individual value in these people. Their privileged position gives them unique information and insight. Studying their candid stories in their own voices takes analysis well beyond sanitized information available from university websites or third-party analyses. It also helps move beyond observational studies into leadership traits and characteristics (e.g. Bolden, 2014) and unpack instead the lived experience of presidential leadership. Of course, leadership is always distributed in large research universities; there are limitations with the 'great man' [sic] perspectives on leadership, and arguments have even been advanced that formal leadership roles are inflated or redundant (Bolden et al., 2015; Davis & Maldonado, 2014; Hoffman et al., 2011). Such angles, however, do not discount the value generated in exploring the insights of very senior members of the world's higher education community.

Focus of the interviews

Careful research underpins the choice of interview topics. This research focused on leaders, leadership, university governance, encounters with Chinese higher education, and global developments (Croucher et al., 2019; Liu et al., 2020). The interviews touch on these specific topics:

- The president
- The university leadership team
- The president's university
- Tsinghua University
- Chinese higher education
- Global higher education

Questions about the president as a person are included based on research which affirms the uniquely important role they play. While leadership in any major university is highly devolved and distributed, presidents' personal characteristics remain important. Often presidents are selected because of who they are and what they have done. Their personal characteristics are significant. At the same time, presidents often have unique insight into higher education, their universities, and their roles. The interviews then asked presidents how they invest their energy as a leader, how their disciplinary background shapes their leadership, and about key steps into their presidency.

No president leads alone. These days, leadership teams are incredibly important. To get insight into the important but rarely researched role played by leadership teams, presidents were asked how they build and manage such teams; how they manage competing priorities associated with performance, operations, people, and innovation; how they juggle the internal and external; and who controls university financial affairs and university academic affairs.

Of course, presidents have many unique insights into their own universities. Presidents are asked about important university cultures and traditions, distinguishing initiatives and reforms being planned, big institutional challenges, important national contributions, balancing financial and non-financial interests, and innovative and emerging social contributions. Insights on these matters are important. They help prise open the university's daily life, aspirations, and anxieties and get beneath corporate publications or websites.

The presidents visit Tsinghua University for many reasons, including personal connections, university-level meetings, and broader academic events. Their views on Tsinghua and its nature and future are keenly sought. Presidents are asked what interests them most about Tsinghua, how Tsinghua can best contribute to global higher education, and what challenges are likely to shape Tsinghua's future. The responses provide important insight into how globally relevant stakeholders view Tsinghua.

The presidents come to Tsinghua with varying histories of visiting and engaging with China. Chinese higher education has developed rapidly in recent decades, and while certain visiting presidents have been actively engaged, others have had far less direct contact. During interviews, they are asked to report their main impressions of, and the big challenges facing, Chinese higher education.

Finally, presidents are asked to report on global higher education, though this topic tends to arise throughout the interviews. They are asked what is distinctive about global universities, about the main contributions of research universities over the next thirty years, about specific reforms to undergraduate education, about best strategies for boosting productivity of university innovation and research, productive changes to doctoral education, and salient characteristics of future leadership.

The timing of these interviews is important and must be clarified to help make sense of the transcripts. Interviews were conducted mostly in the second half of 2019. Of course, 2020 has been the most disrupted period in higher education's recent history. These interviews thus reveal insights from top university leaders at what may be considered the peak of higher education's pre-pandemic era. The insights touch on presidents' concerns and opportunities before the pandemic crisis and serve as a plinth for analyzing contemporary developments and future progress.

Structure of this book

This book presents interview transcripts from university presidents. As background, the next chapter documents important contexts and concepts. Interviews with nineteen presidents are then presented. Each chapter begins with a first section which introduces the president, the university, and the interview. The transcripts are presented, edited to help with readability and to present the most interesting insights.

This book can be read and used in a range of ways. It can be read from start to finish, providing a whirlwind tour of the thoughts and experiences of higher education leaders. Interviews can be read one by one. The book provides a wealth of 'data' which can be read to inform a host of subsequent research endeavours.

Converting an interview into a book-ready transcript is not a straightforward task. Thoughts and words manifest differently when presented for the ear rather than the eye. Even highly accomplished public speakers communicate differently when they are talking, especially in the context of a discursive interview which is roaming around complex and creative ideas. While the interviews deployed a reasonably uniform script, the interviewers encouraged the presidents to talk freely and associatively.

Many editorial decisions have been made in rendering the interview transcripts into this book. The basic process has been sketched above in terms of production and validation of the transcription. There are many more micro-steps, of course, both in terms of converting the verbatim transcript into a readable transcript and then refining the transcript to make it informative, interpretable, and enjoyable. This work takes time and has engaged dozens of people. Rather than detail all editorial designs, methods, criteria, and changes, we alternatively declare at the outset that the transcripts will contain semantic obscurities and linguistic errors. For these, we apologize but note that it is such imperfections which spotlight the life and subtlety of the topics at hand.

We hope you enjoy the words and ideas of these leaders. We hope that the book helps you improve your understanding and experience of higher education.

References

American Council on Education (ACE). (2007). *The American college president study 2017*. Washington, DC: American Council on Education.

ARWU (2019). Academic ranking of world universities: Tsinghua University. Accessed from: http://www.shanghairanking.com/World-University-Rankings/Tsinghua-University.html

Badillo-Vega, R., Krücken, G., & Pineda, P. (2019). Changing analytical levels and methods of leadership research on university presidents. *Studies in Higher Education*, *46*(4), 677–689. DOI: 10.1080/03075079.2019.1647417

Bolden, R. (2014). *What is leadership?* Accessed from: http://www.leadershipsouthwest.com

Bolden, R., Jones, S., Davis, H., & Gentle, P. (2015). *Developing and sustaining shared leadership in higher education*. London, Melbourne: Leadership Foundation for Higher Education & LH Martin Institute.

Bosetti, L., & Walker, K. (2010). Perspectives of UK vice-chancellors on leading universities in a knowledge-based economy. *Higher Education Quarterly*, *64*(1), 4–21.

Bryman, A. (2007). Effective leadership in higher education: A literature review. *Studies in Higher Education*, *32*(6), 693–710.

Coate, K., Howson, K.C., & Yang, Y.T. (2018). *Senior professional leaders in higher education: The role of prestige*. London: King's College London.

Coates, H. (2017). *The market for learning: Leading transparent higher education*. Dordrecht: Springer.

Croucher, G., Wen, W., Coates, H., & Goedegebuure, L. (2019). Framing research into university governance and leadership: Formative insights from a case study of Australian higher education. *Educational Management Administration & Leadership*, *48*(2), 248–269.

Davis, D.R., & Maldonado, C. (2014). Shattering the glass ceiling: The leadership development of African American women in higher education. *Advancing Women in Leadership*, *35*(1), 48–64.

Hoffman, B.J., Woehr, D.J., Maldagen-Youngjohn, R., & Lyons, B.D. (2011). Great man or great myth? A quantitative review of the relationship between individual differences and leader effectiveness. *Journal of Occupational and Organizational Psychology*, *84*, 347–381.

Huang, F. (2017). Who leads China's leading universities? *Studies in Higher Education*, *42*(1), 79–96.

Liu, L., Hong, X., Wen, W., Xie, Z., & Coates, H. (2020). Global university president leadership characteristics and dynamics. *Studies in Higher Education*, *45*(10), 2036–2044.

Mohrman, K., Ma, W., & Baker, D. (2008). The research university in transition: The emerging global model. *Higher Education Policy*, *21*(1), 5–27.

Scott, G. Coates, H., & Anderson, M. (2008). *Learning leaders in times of change: Academic leadership capabilities for Australian higher education*. Sydney: Australian Learning and Teaching Council.

Scott, G., Bell, S., Coates, H., & Grebennikov, L. (2010). Australian higher education leaders in times of change: The role of pro vice chancellor and deputy vice chancellor. *Journal of Higher Education Policy and Management*, *32*(4), 401–418.

Shattock, M. (2013). University governance, leadership and management in a decade of diversification and uncertainty. *Higher Education Quarterly*, *67*(3), 217–233.

Sirat, M., Ahmad, A.R., & Azman, N. (2012). University leadership in crisis: The need for effective leadership positioning in Malaysia. *Higher Education Policy*, *25*(4), 511–529.

Yang, J., Wang, C., Liu, L., Croucher, G., Moore, K., & Coates, H. (2020). The productivity of leading global universities: Empirical insights and implications for higher education. In: Broucker, B., Borden, V., Kallenberg, T., & Milsom, C. (Eds.), *Responsibility of higher education systems. What? How? Why?* (pp. 224–249). Leiden: Brill.

2
STUDYING UNIVERSITY PRESIDENTS

Introduction

This chapter articulates the contexts, characteristics, and concepts which underpin the interviews that follow. It draws on selected interview quotes, using these to articulate the guiding perspectives which underpinned the empirical research.

Drawing from data collection prior to and during the interviews, the chapter starts by looking at the 'preparation' of university presidents, including how they develop and transition into their roles. Attention then turns to the characteristics of presidents' executive leadership teams. The conceptual framework underpinning the analysis of leadership is then given life with reference to quotes sampled from the interviews. Summary remarks then lay exploratory foundations which help in reading the interview transcripts and prising open the substantial world of presidents who lead global universities.

Leadership preparation

Analyzing context data revealed much about the characteristics of people who reach the presidency, what they have studied, their working years, and appointment processes. This analysis worked from an analytical framework validated by Croucher et al. (2019). Drawing from an Australian case study, this framework sets up a means to study key demographic and context characteristics of university leaders. Application in the current research brings out the characteristics of the interviewed presidents.

Most presidents are in their sixties (average age sixty-two), with a small number in their fifties, and one aged over seventies. Over 80 per cent are male, and the same percentage share their nationality with their university. Just over half have a background in humanities or social sciences. Only a fifth took their doctorate

DOI: 10.4324/9781003248286-3

from the same university which they lead, with just under half undertaking doctoral study outside their home country. All presidents had held their doctorate (or equivalent terminal degree) for twenty years, with most over thirty years. Most had worked for thirty-two years, with most spending sixteen years at their current university and sixteen years at other institutions. Just over half assumed their presidency from a prior dean or head role, very few entered from outside the academy, and just under half came through from prior vice or full presidential posts. Most presidents were appointed, though voting remains common, and there are many intricate processes and sequences. The presidents interviewed had typically held their role for five to six years.

Themes emerged about how personal backgrounds shaped leadership. Most broadly, the presidents discussed whether 'leadership characteristics' are innate or acquired. The presidents did identify certain dispositions and orientations towards leadership.

> [W]hen I was appointed, it was obviously an international search, and I told my mother, she said, "I'm not surprised." I said, "Why not?" She said, "Because you were always so bossy as a child. You always tried to organize everybody."
>
> (Nancy Rothwell, University of Manchester)

The interviews probed how disciplinary background shapes presidential leadership. A few presidents suggested certain disciplines tended to prepare people for leadership. As these presidents spoke to the benefits of their own disciplines, it would appear to be the process of reflection rather than any discipline itself which readies people for presidential leadership. Conversely, nearly all presidents explicitly doubted the affordance of the discipline, even pinpointing the limitations of disciplinary epistemologies. These insights align with prior research which has affirmed the importance of more generalizable competencies (Freeman & Kochan, 2013). This resembles the prestigious scholarly epistemology which Goodall (2009) contests is essential for effective university leadership. Of course, most presidents are successful scholars.

> Well, I think there's a reason that you particularly see lawyers and engineers as university presidents. The thing that lawyers and engineers have in common is a need to engage with the realities of the world to some extent.
>
> (David Leebron, Rice University)

> So my discipline, rather oddly, made me think of it as more structural than it was, whereas in fact personal interactions, personal difference, personal credibility, matters an awful lot, especially with government ministers.
>
> (Steve Smith, University of Exeter)

Together, while these perspectives imply that no specific personal or disciplinary background prepares people for presidential leadership and that a certain amount of epistemological reconfiguration or loosening may be required, the process of reflecting on leadership development seems useful. Indeed, this was affirmed in a tranche of observations about the generic rather than disciplinary imperatives instilled by prior academic work. Chiefly, the presidents emphasized how their backgrounds helped them learn how to help bright people work together to address grand challenges. Finding balance and harmony within the university came across as very important.

> I used to do lectures at universities around the world [for]…a very diverse international organization…. Very knowledge intensive, and you have to develop a certain management style so that you make sure that they come along.
>
> (Shigeo Katsu, Nazarbayev University)

> So because of my discipline I had to do a lot of research at grassroots level, and also you need to look at the social behaviour of people. You need to understand, you have to connect with, people.
>
> (Lakshman Dissanayake, University of Colombo)

As this analysis conveys, the interview material reveals much about the preparations for leadership. Whether or not leadership capabilities are innate is impossible to discern, but certain orientations and predispositions do seem useful. Though disciplines equip people with different skills, no one specific discipline prepares people for presidential leadership, and disciplinary perspectives may even shape epistemological structures which require renovation. The generic capabilities developed through discipline mastery seem to matter for leadership, such as solving practical problems and leading a big research team. The process of reflecting on leadership development seems to play a useful role in preparing people for the role of president. In summary, preparation for global university presidency involves leadership orientation, scholarly excellence, generalized competencies, and reflective development.

Steps into the presidency

Analyzing career profiles reveals people's steps into presidential roles. Drawing inspiration from studies like Huang (2017), ACE (2017), and Liu et al (2019), Figure 2.1 presents a career trajectory map which profiles the number of years spent in different roles by each of the interviewed presidents (P1 to P19), as well as the average (AV). While the most common immediate prior role is vice president, a number entered from headships or deanships, and four had experience outside universities. These early results illuminate three paths – namely, scholarly, dual-sectoral, and industry (Figure 2.1).

The interviews probed steps into the presidency. While the traditional view is that linear promotion processes float the best faculty to the top (Cohen & March, 1974), the reality seems far more complex and involves people shifting through a variety of roles, institutions, and industries (Coates & Goedegebuure, 2012).

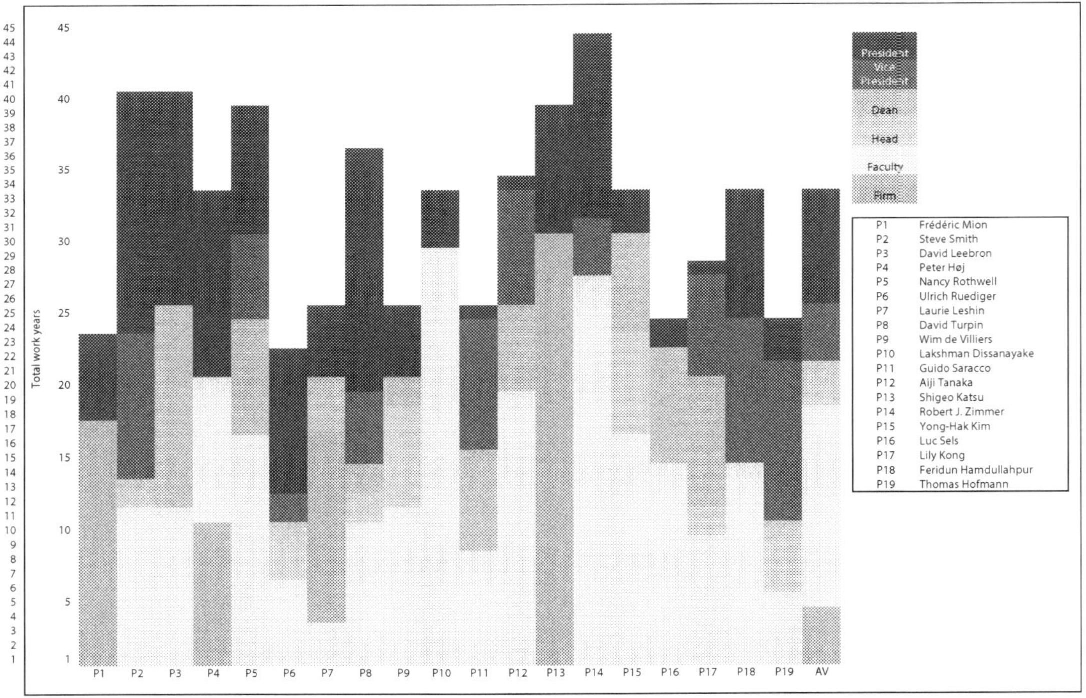

FIGURE 2.1 Presidents' career trajectory map

Legend:
- President
- Vice President
- Dean
- Head
- Faculty
- Firm

- P1 Frédéric Mion
- P2 Steve Smith
- P3 David Leebron
- P4 Peter Høj
- P5 Nancy Rothwell
- P6 Ulrich Ruediger
- P7 Laurie Leshin
- P8 David Turpin
- P9 Wim de Villiers
- P10 Lakshman Dissanayake
- P11 Guido Saracco
- P12 Aiji Tanaka
- P13 Shigeo Katsu
- P14 Robert J. Zimmer
- P15 Yong-Hak Kim
- P16 Luc Sels
- P17 Lily Kong
- P18 Feridun Hamdullahpur
- P19 Thomas Hofmann

Name	Frédéric Mion	Steve Smith	David Leebron	Peter Høj	Nancy Rothwell	Ulrich Ruediger	Laurie Leshin	David Turpin	Wim de Villiers	Lakshman Dissanayake	Guido Saracco	Aiji Tanaka	Shigeo Katsu	Robert J. Zimmer	Yong-Hak Kim	Luc Sels	Lily Kong	Feridun Hamdullahpur	Thomas Hofmann	Average
	P1	P2	P3	P4	P5	P6	P7	P8	P9	P10	P11	P12	P13	P14	P15	P16	P17	P18	P19	AV
Total work years	23	40	40	33	39	39	22	25	36	33	25	34	39	44	33	24	28	33	24	32
President	6	17	15	13	9	9	10	5	17	4	5	1	9	13	3	2	1	9	9	8
Vice President	0	10	10	0	6	6	2	0	5	0	9	8	0	4	7	0	7	7	11	3
Dean	0	0	14	0	8	8	0	4	0	0	7	6	0	0	0	8	9	0	0	4
Head	0	2	0	0	0	0	4	0	2	0	7	19	0	0	7	0	0	0	5	3
Faculty	0	11	1	10	16	16	6	3	7	6	8	0	30	27	16	14	11	14	12	12
Firm	17	0	0	10	0	0	0	13	0	29	0	0	0	0	0	0	0	0	0	4

This complex landscape puts greater weight on presidential appointment processes which are becoming more important to productivity (Sirat et al, 2012). As most presidents are appointed from within the academy, most emphasized the need to race up the ranks into leadership. While very few presidents have worked outside the sector, many emphasized the value of such service.

> I was first a single researcher, elbowing up to become as fast as possible associate and then full professor. Then I was going abroad, and I was developing my own publication record…and then I became the Head of the Department of Applied Sciences and Technology.
>
> (Guido Saracco, Politecnico di Torino)

> Throughout my career, I've sat on quite a number of committees, and chaired a lot of committees. I've been on the councils of charities, of government funding.
>
> (Nancy Rothwell, University of Manchester)

The interviewees emphasized the importance of what can be referred to as political skills. Such skills are the capability to maximize and leverage relationships in order to achieve organizational, team, and individual goals (Ferris et al, 2005). Interviewees identified the need for political leadership within the university, within the community and country, and globally. Presidents' political leadership manifested formally via internal election processes, via national contributions, and through contribution to international dialogue. But presidents also expressed the value of diplomacy and discretion.

> I decided when I finished my period as the head of my second department mandate to get outside and lead a research centre…. After two years there it was sort of, let me say, a final destination to become a candidate for rectorship.
>
> (Guido Saracco, Politecnico di Torino)

The interviews conveyed a need for and excitement with ongoing learning. Overall, however, it seems reasonable to conclude that many presidents are delightfully surprised by the role. There was recognition, indeed, that the job almost by definition perpetually eludes understanding. This echoes Birnbaum's (1979, 383) perspective that presidents are "intuitive scientists who rely on their background and experience as much as upon data to reach judgements and make predictions about relationships such as cause and effect."

> And I convinced my university and I'm now very happy with what I do. After my election, the next surprise, I would say, after being astonished by the culture that was present in other departments from mine, was that as rector, I became an important person for the rest of the city, maybe also the rest of the country.
>
> (Guido Saracco, Politecnico di Torino)

In summary, the interviews reinforced key means of stepping into the presidency. Working one's way up the academic and disciplinary ranks is important, but more important is swift and deliberate manoeuvring through leadership roles. Experience outside the university is important, either through prior roles or through service contributions. Formal and implicit political skills are important in the university, country, and internationally, as is a continuous growth mindset. Overall, stepping into the presidency involves academic pedigree, leadership experience, political skills, and continuous growth.

Leadership dynamics

The interviews touched on the presidents' executive leadership teams. As global universities have expanded, there has been a proliferation of executive and managerial roles, and these teams have grown to form a very substantial and intimate facet of each president's leadership (Croucher et al, 2019; Shattock, 2013; Shepherd, 2017). These teams are the senior managerial decision-making bodies which are vital in helping presidents develop policy and catalyze action. Such teams can be defined as people who are directly connected to presidents, often through line reporting arrangements, and have university-wide portfolios derivative of the president's role.

The interview data affirmed the importance of achieving team balance. This includes diverse disciplinary and professional backgrounds, contrasting personalities and interests, complementary experiences and expertise, and diverse demographics.

> You need to have a diversified portfolio of people with talents and skills. The key thing is they work together and get along. You hope they don't always agree.... I'm very fortunate. I think the team that I've got right now is one of the best I've ever worked with. I'm extraordinarily proud of them. Putting those teams together, I think, is the biggest challenge any leader faces.
>
> (Wim de Villiers, Stellenbosch University)

Contextual data reveals considerable variation in team characteristics. These range from five to twenty in size. On average, around 60 per cent of team members are male. They are also around 60 per cent occupied by academics, although there are teams with no academics and also teams with no professional staff. Just over half of the teams are appointed by the president, although over a third are not and are instead appointed by the council or through another method such as voting. In terms of the overall functions of the team, as determined through a review of university-specific documentation, most emphasis is placed on advising presidents, routine administration, and supervising reforms. The teams in just over half the universities emphasize strategic planning, with decision-making forming part of the agenda in under half. Decision-making, it seems, falls often to presidents. In terms of actual roles, most teams have personnel who perform what appear to be core roles that target operations, academics, finance, and human resources. A focus on international matters and on students is also evident. Under half of the universities had legal and information technology people in the executive leadership team. Clearly, teams have grown to play core roles in how presidents run global universities.

Leadership styles

This research investigated leadership styles. This analysis was framed by Quinn's Competing Values Framework (CVF; Quinn & Rohrbaugh, 1983). The CVF has established prominence as a mechanism for understanding leadership in complex environments such as universities (Cameron et al, 2006). The CVF has a structural dimension defined in terms of control and flexibility and a focus dimension defined in terms of internal and external focus. Together these dimensions map out four management models: rational goal model, internal process model, human relations model, and open systems model (Figure 2.2). Quinn (1988) linked leadership styles with these models which effective leaders should be able to deploy.

The open systems model emphasizes an innovative and broking style of leadership. The interviews convey that presidential leadership often involves such innovation and brokering. Specifically, this goes to lobbying governments, building public perception of the value of higher education, contributing to policy development and implementation, working with other universities, and fundraising and revenue generation.

> We have gained a lot in this year for our reputation.… I proposed a plan for making a strategic plan for the town where our campus is. A plan referencing new manufacturing, outer space, merging with companies. That strategic plan with the town itself was not there one year ago.
>
> (Guido Saracco, Politecnico di Torino)

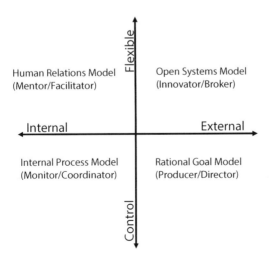

FIGURE 2.2 Competing Values Framework (CVF)

The rational goal model emphasizes leadership styles focused on producing and directing. The interviewees put great emphasis on designing the broad environments and platforms within which the university operates as well as clarifying priorities. This stretches across the full range of senior leadership activities, such as strategy design, goal setting, financial management, and more ceremonial engagements. Administrative skills are especially valued in both the producer and director roles because presidents best serve the needs of rational goals.

> I invest most of my time in thinking, planning, strategizing about how we can make the university a more advanced university that students, staff, faculty, will basically benefit from that more advanced study.
>
> (Feridun Hamdullahpur, University of Waterloo)

The internal process model focuses on monitoring and coordinating leadership styles. The coordinator role values the coordination of activities and encapsulates more of a strategic planning role compared to the monitor role. Most closely aligned with typical forms of general management, this very much involves a focus on controlling and reforming institutional systems.

> My personal philosophy is to spend as little time as possible in managing that involves micromanaging, and spend most of my time in building, strategizing, and innovating. But there are times that, for a variety of reasons again, I spend more of my time in managing than I would like to.
>
> (Feridun Hamdullahpur, University of Waterloo)

The last model, the human relations model, focuses on mentoring and facilitating styles of leadership. This leadership style evidently plays out in terms of education-related work ranging from undergraduate to doctorate. While much of any presidential role may seem to involve talking, the interviewees emphasized active listening. There is clear investment in ongoing communication, often multilevel and sometimes in completely open fora. As part of this more curatorial form of leadership, the presidents emphasized the core role of selecting the right people for subordinate roles.I find that a great deal of my time is spent listening to people, whether it be students, academic staff, or other kind of staff at Sciences Po.

> (Frédéric Mion, Sciences Po)

> There is a very important role for the president, internally, setting the strategic direction of the institution and communicating the key messages of the institution internally, right down through the organization, from the vice presidents to the deans. Four times a year, I meet with all new faculty and staff when they first join the university and talk about the university, what our goals are, and how they can help us get there.
>
> (David Turpin, University of Alberta)

It is clear presidents actively curate their leadership styles and forms of engagement. The results align with previous research on presidential leadership styles (Tan et al, 2015; Neumann & Neumann, 1999). This previous research clarifies the importance of matching styles with contexts. To round out this consideration of global university presidents' leadership dynamics, the interviews probed the tactical toolkit deployed to navigate between these styles. Most obviously, presidents used formal structures such as meetings to negotiate and develop different leadership stances. Executive assistants clearly play a role in following up on ideas and actions. One president mentioned the important but still nascent role that technology could play, looking well beyond broadcast announcements and enabling much broader digital forms of leadership.

> But ideally, I like to spend at least, if you want a hypothetical ratio, thirty percent of my time in management and seventy percent of my time in strategizing, planning, and building.
>
> (Aiji Tanaka, Waseda University)

> I would say probably forty percent would be on senior management issues…. [P]robably of the rest about a third would be internal communications and engagement. About a third regional, working with regional government, local companies, partners. About a third…meeting with ministers in government or travelling.
>
> (Nancy Rothwell, University of Manchester)

> It's better that somebody says, oh, I think we're running out of fuel and should land now to refuel rather than running out of it before we reach the final destination. So that's a culture we try to have.
>
> (Peter Høj, University of Queensland)

The interviews confirm that global university presidents are adept at engaging in a diverse range of leadership styles, which also reveals the increasing complexity of global universities. Presidents are involved in many forms of lobbying and brokering with a wide range of stakeholders, affirming the importance of dealing with myriad uncertain externalities. They play an important role in coordinating external circumstances, engaging in the strategic design of their university, building plans, and engaging and communicating with large numbers of staff and stakeholders. They work on internal control systems, being the executive authority at the university, although they clearly tried to delegate such work and limit the extent to which they needed to step in to solve problems. This appeared to be an area in which presidents' responses varied, apparently based on experience, expertise, backgrounds, university change contexts, and characteristics of the senior executive team. Much of the presidents' interest and energy appears to be expended in mentoring and facilitating people within the university. They particularly emphasized the education, as opposed to the research, facet of such leadership. Varying forms of communication are deployed, from executive coaching to public communication. Presidents use a range of formal administrative, interpersonal, managerial, and technological tactics to navigate different leadership styles. The concept of balance and harmony arose often.

Foundation insights and launch perspectives

This chapter has revealed initial insights from an ongoing research project being conducted to analyze the complex and shifting roles and functions of presidents of global universities. Figure 2.3 articulates a framework which summarizes the narrative. It captures the key themes which emerged from the previous qualitative coding and discussion. The framework also extends a means for understanding the preparations, characteristics, and dynamics of the global university presidency (Figure 2.3).

As suggested from the previous analysis, throughout the preparation for leadership, steps into presidency, and leadership characteristics to leadership dynamics, there is much variance and diversity. While there is no stereotypical 'global university president,' several commonalities emerged, such as political awareness and skills, great emphasis on education and talent cultivation, and adept communication skills.

Overall, this chapter has charted exploratory foundations which help in using the interview transcripts to prise open the mysterious world of presidents who lead global universities. It has started to frame themes, models, and characteristics which service foundations for subsequent analyses. The conceptual and empirical insights will evolve as more interviews are conducted. Larger samples will also enable deeper interpretation of concepts such as presidents' characteristics, executive team constitution, and global universities' developmental strategies. There is surely no algorithm for global university presidencies but exploring salient development and characteristics will shed light on the development of global universities. It also highlights the important role played by the presidents of these important institutions.

FIGURE 2.3   Global university president analytical framework

References

Birnbaum, R. (1979). Leadership and learning: The college president as intuitive scientist. *Review of Higher Education, 9*(4), 381–395.

Cameron, K.S., Quinn, R.E., DeGraff, J., & Thakor, A.V. (2006). *Competing values leadership: Creating value in organizations.* Northampton, MA: Edward Elgar.

Coates, H., & Goedegebuure, L. (2012). Recasting the academic workforce: Why the attractiveness of the academic profession needs to be increased and eight possible strategies for how to go about this from an Australian perspective. *Higher Education, 64*(6), 875–889.

Cohen, M.D., & March, J.G. (1974). *Leadership and ambiguity: The American college president.* New York: McGraw-Hill.

Croucher, G., Wen, W., Coates, H., & Goedegebuure, L. (2019). Framing research into university governance and leadership: Formative insights from a case study of Australian higher education. *Educational Management Administration & Leadership, 48*(2), 248–269. doi:10.1177/1741143219893101

Ferris, G.R., Treadway, D.C., Kolodinsky, R.W., Hochwarter, W.A., Kacmar, C.J., Douglas, C., & Frink, D.D. (2005). Development and validation of the political skill inventory. *Journal of Management, 31*(1), 126–152.

Freeman, S., & Kochan, F. (2013). University presidents' perspectives of the knowledge and competencies needed in 21st century higher education leadership. *Journal of Educational Leadership in Action, 1*(1), 1–21.

Goodall, A.H. (2009). *Socrates in the boardroom: Why research universities should be led by top scholars.* Princeton, NJ: Princeton University Press.

Huang, F. (2017). Who leads China's leading universities? *Studies in Higher Education, 42*(1), 79–96.

Liu, P., Wang, X., & Liang, X. (2019). Understanding university president leadership research in China: A review. *Frontiers of Education in China, 14*(1), 138–160.

Neumann, Y., & Neumann, E.F. (1999). The president and the college bottom line: The role of strategic leadership styles. *International Journal of Educational Management, 13*(2–3), 73–79.

Quinn, R.E. (1988). *Beyond rational management: Mastering the paradoxes and competing demands of high performance.* San Francisco: Jossey-Bass.

Quinn, R.E., & Rohrbaugh, J. (1983). A spatial model of effectiveness criteria: Towards a competing values approach to organizational analysis. *Management Science, 29*(3), 363–377.

Shattock, M. (2013). University governance, leadership and management in a decade of diversification and uncertainty. *Higher Education Quarterly, 67*(3), 217–233.

Shepherd, S. (2017). Why are there so few female leaders in higher education: A case of structure or agency? *Management in Education, 31*(2), 82–87.

Sirat, M., Ahmad, A.R., & Azman, N. (2012). University leadership in crisis: The need for effective leadership positioning in Malaysia. *Higher Education Policy, 25*(4), 511–529.

PART 2

University president interviews

3

PROFESSOR FRÉDÉRIC MION, DIRECTOR OF THE SCHOOL OF POLITICAL SCIENCES IN PARIS, FRANCE

Interview background

Frédéric Mion, the former director of the Paris School of Political Sciences, visited Tsinghua University in April 2019. He exchanged views with the Tsinghua University's party secretary, Chen Xu, on further strengthening cooperation. On 15 April 2019, associate researcher Xie Zheping of the Institute of Education at Tsinghua University interviewed Director Mion.

Frédéric Mion, male, French, born in 1969, lawyer and educator, graduated from the French National School of Administration. He has served as a member of the French State Council. As a member of the Attali Commission, he participated in writing the "European Higher Education Model" report. He also served as an advisor to the French minister of education, and as deputy minister of the General Council in charge of the French Civil Service. He taught public law courses at the Paris Institute of Political Sciences (Sciences Po). He served as director of Sciences Po from 2013 until 2021.

Sciences Po was founded in 1872 and is located in Paris, France. It is a world-renowned school of political and social sciences and has trained dozens of leaders for France and the world. The political and international relations disciplines of Sciences Po are ranked as world leading. In the 2020 QS World University Rankings, the school rose from third in 2019 to second behind Harvard University. In addition, the school's social policy and management, sociology, law, and other disciplines are also among the best in Europe and the world. Sciences Po enjoys an extensive network of colleges and universities around the world, such as Columbia University, Oxford University, and Princeton University. The school's Institute of Sustainable Development and International Relations currently has in-depth cooperation with Tsinghua University in the field of green economy.

DOI: 10.4324/9781003248286-5

FIGURE 3.1 Director Frédéric Mion and Associate Researcher Xie Zheping

The interview involved discussions about the director and his personal background, leadership team, the director's university, Tsinghua University, Chinese higher education, and global higher education. Key points touched on managing working time and listening to colleagues, how to make and communicate institution-wide decisions, managing cooperation, and understanding emerging developments in higher education (Figure 3.1).

The interview

Interviewer: Where do you invest most of your energy as a leader?

Director: I think when I look, a lot of the time is not necessarily time that I allocate freely because there are lots of meetings I need to attend and so on and so forth. But in those moments when I have more leeway on what I can do, I find that a great deal of my time is spent listening to people, whether it be students, academic staff, or other kind of staff at Sciences Po. And I find that listening to people is key in several ways. First of all because it's proven to be a great source of inspiration for ideas for the university, ideas as to what we need to do. To give you just one example. We're all aware that the climate issue is a major issue for all universities in many, many ways, and that was something I had very strongly in mind. But it is only through dialogue with students over the past few months I realized that for them the issue was not just pressing but absolutely essential. Then I decided that we should speed up our action on anything that has to do with the climate, both in terms of research and training, and the way we operate our institution. So by listening to people of all categories, you first of all get inspiration regarding what you need to do, and also, I think that will help build consensus, which is of course essential as well. In a leadership position, you have to show the way, but you also have to be able to create the conditions that will enable people to feel truly mobilized by the action you're trying to launch. And so creating consensus is a large part of what a leader needs to do, and that also involves a lot of listening beforehand. It seems to me to be an essential thing.

Interviewer: What do you think is the biggest challenge for you as a university president?

Director: The biggest challenge is obviously taking those decisions that are right for our institution at a moment when I feel that competition in the world of higher education and research has never been stronger. And it's now the competition that plays out at a global level, and so you have a sense that the decisions you're making have an impact not simply on the life of the students and staff you're working with but possibly on the trajectory of your institution in this world of very fierce competition. So that enhances the sense of responsibility that weighs upon my shoulders. And you know, on a day-to-day basis that question of how Sciences Po will be positioned five, ten years from now, because of actions and decisions we're taking now, that is something that I find to be extremely challenging.

Interviewer: Yes, I fully understand. And then another question regarding the global universities. Sciences Po is very specially organized. You have a central campus in Paris and also six campuses all around France. I don't know what the logic is behind such distribution. If you have enough space, will you consider taking those six campuses back to Paris?

Director: It is a very good question, and I will answer it truthfully. I think those campuses came into being because of the space question, because of the lack of space in Paris. So I think that my predecessor was a man of vision, even a genius. But in all fairness, the reason why those campuses came into existence was that he wanted the institution to grow. He wanted to take in more students, more staff, and there simply wasn't the capacity in terms of space in Paris. That was the structure of it. That was the beginning. But interestingly, that constraint with space led to the creation of those campuses which then, in fact, proved to be very valuable for the institution in other ways. First of all, because it gave us, for the first time in our history, a connection with the country at large, and not simply the city of Paris. We all know that, at least in the West, the political, the administrative, the economic leaders are being fiercely criticized. They are really under trial, and one of the criticisms they incur is that they are too Parisian, at least in France, too disconnected from the rest of the country. And so having campuses that are located in smaller cities around the country has proven to be a very important thing for us. That's one thing.

Second thing is that those campuses, which as you know are strictly undergraduate campuses, have been a wonderful springboard or starting ground for students who come from around the world at a very young age. Because these are undergraduates, so we take them in at age seventeen or eighteen, their families are often a little afraid to have to see them go and go far away at so early an age. And those campuses are of a size such as to enable us to, in fact, know those students much better, be far closer to them, in their daily lives. And it enables us also to have classes that really form very strong bonds. That is to say, the students create a true sense of common belonging. And so, based now on nearly twenty years of experience of those campuses, I can see the benefits for Sciences Po have been incredible, and they've been, again, being totally honest, unexpected in the sense that they were not exactly foreseen when we first created those campuses. So based upon that, I can tell you in truth that we are very happy to have those campuses, and I would not for any reason want to do away with them, even if suddenly Paris became a much more accessible place. Of course, there are costs to having campuses outside of Paris because operating divisions of your own universities that are far away from the centre is more complicated, but it's proved to be an invaluable addition to our experience.

Interviewer: Yeah, it is a very special arrangement. You can compare it to more and more universities having overseas campuses. In the same sense, Sciences Po has domestic branch campuses which are yet internationally oriented.

Director: That's a very, very wise way of putting it. And we chose deliberately not to have international campuses because we feel that we are not in a position to impose our model on foreign countries, in countries such as China, which now has an amazing number of top-tier universities. What sense would it make for Sciences Po to open a campus in Beijing or in Shanghai? You know, the offer there is incredibly rich. There is so much more to gain for us from partnerships with institutions such as Tsinghua. There are world-class universities that can teach us as much as we can bring them, so foreign campuses are something we will not consider.

Interviewer: Thank you very much. Back to the routine questionnaire. What specific cultures and traditions are important for Sciences Po?

Director: Well, within Sciences Po, there are two or three things that are key in terms of the institutional culture. First of all, multidisciplinarity at all levels of training. We feel that it is important to exchange disciplinary viewpoints in order to enable our students to gain a true understanding of the complexity of the world. That is the first thing. The second thing is being open to the world. And so the internationalization that has been going on for at least twenty years, and even a little more, is also very central to the way we see ourselves as having to learn from the rest of the planet and having to teach our students to be aware of what's happening out there. The third thing, in terms of culture, is mixing at all times. Mixing theory, that is to say, science with practice, because we aim at training young people who will take up positions of leadership in the world five, ten, twenty years from now. And we want them to be able to gain knowledge but to be able to act upon the knowledge that they gained, and so within the classroom, we are trying to mix those approaches. That is to say, to have academics and practitioners teach our students.

Interviewer: Very good points. What is your main impression of Chinese higher education? And also, what do you think universities like Tsinghua can contribute to global higher education?

Director: First of all, maybe I'll make one clarification: my understanding of the system is biased because universities that I know are the very best in the country. But having said that, I am amazed, truly amazed, at the speed with which those universities have changed in the past twenty years. And even more so, as you know, my last trip to China was five years ago, the change that has occurred in those five years is already staggering to me. So there's an amazing ability of those universities to embrace the evolutions on the planet, which as far as I can tell is unmatched by any other universities I've seen elsewhere in the world. Even the very rich universities, in the West and in America, and so on and so forth, do not have the ability to transform themselves quite so quickly. And I think that's what great universities such as Tsinghua can bring to the global conversation: it is the specific viewpoint of a great university which is in fact at the heart of the fastest-changing country on the face of the planet but also a country which is gradually assuming the position of global leadership. And so I think it's very interesting for us to get that perspective that only a university located here at the heart of Beijing – where so much power is concentrated, economically, politically, culturally – can contribute to the planet.

Interviewer: Maybe the last question. What do you see as the main, enduring contributions of research universities over the next thirty years?

Director: I think we have a responsibility which is greater now than ever in our history. That responsibility is to train young women and young men who will have to lead the planet in all fields of activity – public, private, all sectors – at a moment when for the first time we know that the very future of the planet is at stake and at risk. And so the contribution we have to make is one which is almost a question of life and death. If we do our work right, if we train those young people well, then chances are, you know, our species will continue living on a planet that will make life possible. If we make the wrong choices, if we don't face up to our responsibilities in the way we should, then we would fail not just those students but the whole world.

Interviewer: I think Tsinghua shares something in common with Sciences Po, although we are so different. Because time is limited, the last question is just a small comment about your university and my university. Sciences Po was established in 1872. That year is also the year the first group of Chinese students went abroad to study. The first president of my university was in that group.

Director: There are moments in history such as this! That's really interesting. In fact, the first Chinese students came to Sciences Po in 1876, so only four years after our founding. One of them who went on to become a big and principal servant for the Qing Dynasty was the brother of the founder of Fudan University.

4

PROFESSOR SIR STEPHEN SMITH, VICE CHANCELLOR OF THE UNIVERSITY OF EXETER, UNITED KINGDOM

Interview background

Sir Stephen Smith, the former vice chancellor of the University of Exeter, visited Tsinghua University in April 2019 and attended the first China-United Kingdom Higher Education Humanities Alliance Youth Student Forum. On 18 April 2019, Professor Hamish Coates of the Institute of Education at Tsinghua University interviewed Sir Stephen.

Sir Stephen Smith, male, British, born in 1952, is an international relations scientist with a PhD from the University of Southampton. As a well-known international relations specialist, he has written fifteen monographs, published more than one hundred academic papers, and delivered more than one hundred lectures in more than 170 universities in twenty-two countries. Sir Stephen served as the vice chancellor of the University of Exeter from 2002 to 2020 and was appointed by the British government as the United Kingdom's first International Education Champion in June 2020, a role that promotes the internationalization of higher education in which the UK is a leader. In addition, he has served as a researcher at the Royal Society of Arts, chairman of the Professional Admissions Program Support Committee, and chairman of the Federation of British Universities. He was awarded an honorary fellow by Aberystwyth University and the Global Leadership Award by the University of South Florida.

The University of Exeter was formally established in 1955. The main campus is located in Exeter, United Kingdom. It is a member of the Russell University Group, the European University Association, and the Commonwealth University Association. The university currently has more than 20,000 students and more than 2,000 teachers and researchers. The University of Exeter has the world's top research level in many disciplines, including social sciences, medical research, engineering, anthropology, and sports science. In the 2021 QS World University

DOI: 10.4324/9781003248286-6

FIGURE 4.1   Vice Chancellor Sir Stephen Smith and Professor Hamish Coates

Rankings, the University of Exeter is ranked 164. The University of Exeter has established cooperation with many universities in mainland China, Hong Kong, and Taiwan. Among them, the Department of Earth Sciences of Tsinghua University has maintained a very close cooperative relationship in the field of earth sciences. The two universities have also successfully developed doctoral degrees and other joint training projects.

The interview covered the vice chancellor and his personal background, leadership team, the vice chancellor's university, Tsinghua University, Chinese higher education, and global higher education. Key points touched on generating successful global partnerships, being relevant to local communities, winning the trust of people, tactics for learning leadership on the job, and engaging with global universities (Figure 4.1).

The interview

Interviewer: So why don't we start with you and your disciplinary background. How does that affect your time in higher education and your sense of where higher education is now in your university or with your leadership of universities?

Vice Chancellor: I'm essentially an international relations person, and I never thought of becoming a leader in higher education. That wasn't the aim, like other people. And I had a decision to make. I was elected president of the world body in my field, and the same month, I got offered the vice chancellor of Exeter. So that was a bit of a "which way am I goanna go?" kind of thing. The interesting thing is that being an international relations person made me enormously aware of how policies get made in politics. One of my special areas was on a whole series of foreign policy mistakes and fiascos, and how the decisions made in Britain went wrong. So I came into it with what you might call a structured model of decision-making. As I've been vice chancellor, that model has been eroded by the extent to which you realize decision-making draws on broad personal relationships. And having worked for four prime ministers in Britain, I have seen the way in which ministers have standing or don't have standing, have influence or don't have influence, how officials can do or cannot do things. You realize that forming good working relationships and trust is central. Actually, that's informed – it almost sounds glib – but that's informed all our international relationships as a university. The work you have to do is build trusting relationships with partners you're working with. Be explicit about your interest. They can be explicit about theirs. You work out where the overlap is, and you move together on that. So my discipline, rather oddly, made me think of it as more structural than it was, whereas in fact personal interactions, personal difference, personal credibility, matters an awful lot, especially with government ministers. They don't trust you. They do not trust you. End of story. I am still the editor of three big books we do with Oxford University Press, but I'm not going to lie and pretend I still can do the research for them; I edited them. Most of vice chancellors in Britain now last just about four years. I've done seventeen, so you find that your ability to do the research has gone because you're working unorderly hours.

Interviewer: You might not have been on the ground in government, working with regards international relations, but surely your work was quite international. All of a sudden, you're managing an institution. So you have to spend a lot of time in one spot. How did you manage that transition?

Vice Chancellor: Well, two things. One, you suddenly realize the international connections of this institution. And being an international relations person, you realize it doesn't just go up to the state and across and down again. There are all sorts of societal links. And you also realize the importance of international cooperation. I don't mean in a silly liberal way, but I mean you have to build understanding between peoples and between societies, which aren't just governments. And you have to work out, you have to understand, that a university only really exists in international ecosystem. The job of being a head of a university in Britain is partly what you do in the institution.

The least important thing I do is to chair meetings. I've chaired a lot of meetings. But frankly, pretty much anyone can do that. It's more the links with governments, governments in London, travelling internationally, dealing with personnel issues, people from different cultures. So if you stayed in the office five days a week, you wouldn't be doing the job, or rather you'd be doing the least important bits of the job. Universities now are fiercely competitive places. We live in fiercely competitive international research environment, competing for staff, students, resources, break-throughs, equipment, etcetera. You've got to be a part of, a player in, that.

Interviewer: You obviously have a deep knowledge of government from your research field, but also your broader leadership engagements with government in the UK and beyond. Do you think that's an area where university leaders need to be stronger in terms of understanding the nature of government? Usually, university leaders come up through the ranks, not in from the government or in from the corporate sector. Can you see that changing in the years to come?

Vice Chancellor: They do come up through the ranks. Well, I think you put your finger on it, but I think actually it depends on the way we want to go into it. Let me make the basic points; then we can follow up.

I think there can be a lot of naivety in universities across the world that research is for truth: truth is unvarnished and just let them give me the money and then go with it. In Britain, I'm sure in every single country in the world, universities have to earn the trust of populations. And just because you think you have to be world leading doesn't mean that anyone is ready to fund it, you know. And so to be candid, it is all a battle for resources, and I suspect that's the same whichever country you are working in. It's absolutely no good sitting there saying, "I am pure, I am wonderful. Let me get on with it. Give me the money and leave me to it." That's not going to get you anywhere.

Interviewer: So do you think that has implications for the PhD as a leadership training ground before people join faculty and while they are faculty? What would you do differently?

Vice Chancellor: Well, the one thing I wish I had known, which I have realized, is the brute economics of running a university. I mean, no one trains you to be a vice chancellor or university president. There is no training. And nor is there a manual that you take down from the shelf: you know, *Crisis with Student Protest: Volume I.* You know, you get insights, but the major insight you get is learned on the job. There's quite a lot of commonality between the leaders of universities in the UK and abroad. But again, you have to trust each other, because if I approach you as another university leader and say, my goodness, I think I'm gonna lose one of my research teams. Well, you might well decide, "We'll take that." I mean trust matters, and I don't think it comes up in training.

Universities UK International is the body that represents all British universities. It does training and mentoring when you're appointed. There is a leadership program you can go on. The need to compete on a world scale for research – I mean, it's no good anymore being okay. You know, if you're a scientist and your kind of okay, why would we fund that? It's that pressure, and the decisions we have to make as university leaders about what to invest in and what to disinvest in.

Interviewer: I'll come back to some of those points later on. My colleague, Ulrich Teichler, has called it a research destruction system, not a research creation system.

Share with me your initial impressions of Tsinghua, and it may take you back a few years. How has it changed?

Vice Chancellor: My initial impressions were of an incredibly prestigious, high status, elite meritocracy. But when I first encountered it – I'll get the language wrong, and I apologize – Tsinghua was beginning to get to grips with the world of international research and education. I wouldn't say "inward looking" because that's patronizing, but it was very much what came out at the top of Tsinghua was very much what bubbled up from inside. Now you see an unbelievably success-ful university. I mean, up eight places in QS this year, up eight places in this year: seventeenth and twenty-fifth in the world. My goodness, the rise is extraordinary. And of course, this is the key point: it's not accidental, and it's not about money – it is in part about money, but it's about getting the analysis, it's about understanding the rules of the game you're playing.

And Tsinghua has blossomed really during the last fifteen years, from being not just good and not just productive but to being a real player on the world stages. I say that with absolute humility. I mean it is outstanding. But I would say if you took it back twenty years ago, it wouldn't be defined, to use a soccer analogy, as a player in the world champions league of research. Now, absolutely it is that. I mean everyone beats at Tsinghua's door. If there is one university in China you would do work with, it's Tsinghua. So it's got a positional good element. And by the way, you could come to British universities and find the same things. It's not about China. It's about universities waking up to the fact that the best research is now international, is done with co-authorship, co-publication, co-investment. Tsinghua was playing very much as a university of China and for China, and now it's the university of the world and for the world. That is how I put it.

Interviewer: Excellent. I think you've touched on this to some extent: where do you invest your time as a leader within your university? How much do you spend being inside the office and travelling around?

Vice Chancellor: The office keeps a diary of all of this and then puts it up elec-tronically. So basically, I spend probably one or two nights a week in London because that's where the power is; that's what the meetings are.

Interviewer: That's on behalf of your university and on behalf of the sector?

Vice Chancellor: On behalf of my university and this sector, both. We said fifty-fifty on that. So for example, a lot of our wealthy alumni are in London, and I meet them there. The journalists are in London. I tend to meet them there for dinner or drinks or whatever. Civil servants, ministers, our offices for both the Russell Group of elite universities and Universities UK are in London. All of that is there. Our chair of governors lives in London, and I meet her there. So I'm there a lot.

But it's really important that you're not seen as being away from the university. I pride myself on being in contact through email, whatever: not twenty-four-seven, but certainly sixteen hours a day, basically. So although I'm in London,

I'm often between meetings, chatting away on email or on the phone to my office. And frankly, most people don't know whether I'm in Exeter, or whether I'm in London, or wherever I am. I am trying to restrict international travel, probably four big international visits a year. I can't do more. And they tend to be for one week because you can't get out of the cycles of meetings. Every Monday morning at the key meetings, eight-thirty, every Monday morning, I meet the Registrar of the Administration, and the Provost of the university is with me. And then I meet my senior team at ten o'clock for two hours. We meet every Monday morning, and that's absolutely key. The other thing I do is half-yearly meetings with academics. I've just come of the back off twenty-six meetings with academic departments. I do that twice a year, visiting every department: question and answer, open sessions. Now, when I go back, I've got five big public lunchtime meetings for anyone in the institution, different buildings, different campuses. The format is twenty minutes of "where are we?" and forty minutes of Q&A.

Interviewer: So the students see you walking around the campus?

Vice Chancellor: Yes, and I meet the students a lot. The Students Guild, Students Union, in Exeter is very involved in the governance of the university. So I'll see the Student Union president – we have got two presidents, one for the Cornwall Campus and one for the other campuses. I probably see them something like once a week. I mean it's quite an integrated system. The job – and the office are brilliant at it – is balancing the diary. That's always it.

Interviewer: Time is something you struggle to make more of. What are the specific challenges, do you think, facing the university when you get back?

Vice Chancellor: So, the overarching, the biggest challenge is Brexit, and it leads to a whole series of other challenges because the government's got no bandwidth. It can't do anything at the moment. There is not agreement on anything, no decisions on anything.

Interviewer: So where does the leadership of the higher education sector come from in that instance?

Vice Chancellor: In that instance, I'm afraid an awful lot of pressures the leadership responds to is media, and that's a virulent campaign in British universities. We've been very well funded for many years. I mean, Britain as you know has had ten years of austerity, lots of government departments have been cut by about thirty per cent of their funding. Universities have increased their funding massively. We've been invested in. And now we are being paid back for having done rather well. The press is full of stuff every day about our universities. So the big challenge, other than Brexit, the big challenge is how do we make sure the University of Exeter stays in that group of universities in Britain that is competing on the world stage. The two words I use, they are the mantra at Exeter, research power.

Interviewer: Do you do that by specialization or by building the balance sheet?

Vice Chancellor: It's basically the strength times the quality of the activity of research. You can do it by grant income. You can do it by our seven yearly reviews of research power of research quality. But basically, you can say that eighty-five per cent of the research funding in Britain goes to twenty-five universities. There are 136 universities, but the money is very skewed. When I went to Exeter, it was in terms of research power about thirtieth. Now it's about twentieth and it's actually improving quite nicely. So we expect it to be, in a couple of years, about sixteenth, and we think that's stable to be funded for research. The nightmare is that, candidly, the cost of getting that right is you've got to keep investing very large sums in very, very, very, very expensive science.

Interviewer: Investing in core fields. But also you mentioned disinvesting before.

Vice Chancellor: Yeah, we were famous for that. If you google me, one of the things you'll see immediately is that we were the first university in Britain to make decisions to close unsuccessful departments. We closed three departments back in 2005.

Interviewer: Unsuccessful on some sort of viability grounds but with their broader intellectual rationales still in place, or students could study those things elsewhere in the UK, or…

Vice Chancellor: Yes, they can certainly study those things elsewhere. The big one we closed is chemistry, although we now have more chemists than we did. But they are just in another department: medical. They were not able to compete, either in quality student recruitment or in research, and if you're going to invest in chemistry, if you're spending a lot of money on kit, you've got to make sure the product is good. And it wasn't. We've had two House of Commons Select Committee inquiries into us for closing as we are the first top university to close a big science department. We've become known as an institution that was quite ruthless, but of course, our research income has grown elevenfold since then. I mean we have just taken off because rather than using it to subsidize our loss activities, we put it into very strong areas in the university. The big challenge for us is research power. The other big challenge, and this may not travel internationally, is that the student body in the UK is giving rise to some quite significant worries for us about mental health. We are spending a lot of money supporting the welfare of our students. That's a UK, I think that's a Western world, phenomenon. And I think when I go back what I should be worried about is the exam season coming up, you know.

Interviewer: Because the pressure on students or broader social factors, or…

Vice Chancellor: Well, it's obviously partly the pressure.

Interviewer: A cohort issue with particular student factors, or…

Vice Chancellor: Oh no, it's more isolation. It's isolation, it's social media. It's a bit glib to criticize social media, but it's a big difference, a big piece of the problems we're having in Britain is things that I might have done or said when I was eighteen and nineteen in the pub late at night weren't recorded, you know. Looking back, I'm glad not everything I did was recorded. What I mean is now people communicate with each other on WhatsApp or whatever. It's on Facebook. It's there forever, and you get people doing stupid things. We've had a lot of referrals – 2,606 students referred themselves to our mental health board out of 24,000: one in eight or one in nine. Twenty years ago, doesn't mean there were no problems, but…. So that worries, and that's across the UK.

Interviewer: Well, there's a serious problem.

Vice Chancellor: Yes, and I think a quarter of those students had come to university with a pre-existing medical diagnosis of mental and health problems. There is a lot of work going on in Britain about it. We think it's partly the effect of social media, everyone saying what a great time they're having posting pictures of themselves, feeling great and hanging out with friends, and if you're lonely on your own…. So that's an issue. Student welfare is genuinely worrying, with also the humility of realizing that we're not their parents, we can't do everything for them. But we are worried, you know.

Interviewer: Yes. Can I go from that quite serious issue to more education matters? You've talked about research power. I don't know, you would probably know: Does education contribute more to the world than research, all things considered? Not in terms of papers but from fifty years of income returns and the like. The UK has pioneered some new measures in the field. Do you think we might be coming off the back of twenty years of bibliometric rankings to look at a more balanced view of the education contribution of the university?

Vice Chancellor: You're quite right, and of course the great thing we do isn't the research output, it is the skills we'll give to our students.

Interviewer: So how do you tell that story in the UK or the global context?

Vice Chancellor: On the UK, we've started, the government has started, to assess the quality of teaching through the Teaching Excellence Framework (TEF). The trouble is it doesn't actually measure teaching. It measures outcomes, which to be fair could be to do with the social class inputs of the students concerned. But what has happened? The key point that you are leading to is that, in the UK, it is now far more realized that you've got to look at the quality of education, and there is a view from the government that some students are not getting a good deal. And they look at a number of measures. TEF is one. The other big one that's coming up, it's probably the dominant one at the moment, is the LEO (Longitude Educational Outcomes). It's earnings data. You can now trace your earnings through, if they are connected – the student records to the tax receipt records. So they can say you went to the University of Exeter, did this course, graduated with this degree (whether with or without these entry qualifications), and this is what you are now earning. There's a very problematic finding from those data, which is for twenty-three universities, you earn less ten years after graduation than if you have the same entry grades and didn't go to university. So the Treasury is saying to us, why do we invest in this? On the international stage, our friends at the Times Higher Education would love to develop a measure of teaching, but they can't. The big issue actually is how do you compare the experience of a student here with one at Exeter? They might be brilliant, both of them, but in very different ways. How do you measure it unless there's a curriculum inspection, and then what about the cultural issue in that?

So you are absolutely right: at universities in Britain, the debate now is far more about a group of students who are not being well served at the bottom-ranking universities. I mean social class is still a very big predictor of the grades you get before you go to university. We monitor all that. I chair the Universities and Colleges Admissions Service in Britain, and we look at all of that, you know. Your social class is still a very strong predictor of your entry grades. But the point is, the government is now trying to reduce the balance exactly the way you described, but it is struggling to find the measures to do it because the earnings you end up getting might reflect your social capital, and, in fact, your parents can get you an internship in this bank or that, you know? And also if you're from a poor background, you probably aren't going to get the grades to go to top universities. But nonetheless, literally as we speak, we're waiting for the government report on the future of higher education funding. And we expect we'll try moving some students out of HE into further higher education.

Interviewer: So what are a few big things you think a university in the UK can do to continue to demonstrate its public value? Not just the media but people who don't like or don't know about higher education.

Vice Chancellor: It's really interesting. I'll give you the positive answer and then the worrying. The positive answer is we all absolutely have to spend a lot more time on trying to make sure that we're open to people regardless of socioeconomic circumstances. So in Exeter, we spend twelve and a half million pounds a year – which is roughly one hundred million RMB – on bursaries. So we spend a lot of money supporting students from poor backgrounds to come. The first thing I think we have to do is to try and make sure it's open for everyone. Secondly, we have to realize we are anchored institutions in our cities and regions. So we sponsored the local schools in a multi-academy trust. So we put a lot in there. We fund the theatre.

Interviewer: Big part of the community.

Vice Chancellor: Yes, big part of the community, even down to Chinese New Year. We got three thousand local people coming out to the campus to celebrate Chinese New Year. The downside, and this is really difficult to work through but here it goes: we are seen as part of the elite, which is one of the big issues in the UK. Whereas evidence and facts and knowledge, research, were once seen as neutral, now there is a pushback. Comes out as Brexit because all universities are in favour of remaining, all of them. We are then seen as being part of a liberal elite that benefits from this system.

Interviewer: How to be elite open and to everyone at the same time is a challenge.

Vice Chancellor: Yes, and there's a few who say, "You would say that, wouldn't you?" You see what I mean, that we benefit from the current system? It goes back to an earlier comment that universities are seen as very much up for attack. The bankers ten years ago. And now we, you know, are now all out on the front page of the *Daily Mail* recently; it was not a pleasant experience, because I supported staying in the EU, you know. They paint us as the kind of "remaining universities" as if we are not located in the populations we are part of because many of them are very concerned about the EU, wanted to leave. So that's shown that it's not about bringing forward evidence people can make judgements on. It is that our own activity is the activity of an elite.

Interviewer: Just to keep moving quickly. We'll go back to Tsinghua and maybe in the same breath time to talk about China. What do you think this institution should be contributing to Beijing, to China, to Asia?

Vice Chancellor: Firstly, I think, it goes back to an earlier comment, but just from a different angle. The rise of Tsinghua and the rise of Chinese universities represents actually a really quite fundamental shift. I think Tsinghua and other leading universities are part of a future for China that is part of a global community – a future that is something separate to Chinese economic and political interests. I think in that sense, again not being glib, that the extent to which Tsinghua can engage in the champions league of research and help design solutions to the world's problems, there's almost another world in which Tsinghua is contributing to global issues. In other words, I think, it's a world-ranking university that happens to be in Beijing; it's not a Beijing university that happens to be in a world-ranking system. That's how I put it.

Interviewer: What question do you ask of Tsinghua?

Vice Chancellor:: Ok. The question I ask is how can we at Exeter – and wearing my UK hat, how can we in the UK – link more effectively with Tsinghua for the better education of our students of both countries? But actually, for me crucially, to make sure that our top researchers are able to work together. That to me is the gold standard. So the question is, how can we remove any barriers to cooperation? And you, Tsinghua, how can you help us by supporting your top people to work with us in every area where we're very strong? So it's can we play together? That is the question we ask.

Interviewer: I'm more familiar with the Australian case than the British case. But this twenty or so years of students going back and forth: do you think there's been enough put into distributing those relationships across different levels of staff, even professional staff back offices, so that people can build those deep relationships you talked about? What concrete steps do you think could be taken? Bearing in mind that maybe we won't be flying around to take education courses twenty years from now, what do you think we do?

Vice Chancellor: I agree with that. Well, one of the things we do with the partners we work with, increasingly, is have significant professional service interactions. Actually, that strikes us as very, very clever. Because if colleagues here, colleagues at other universities around the world, can come to see how we operate, we come to see how they operate, then it's much more than just a leader. I mean, if a leader changes, the focus changes. So we're trying to build more organic relations with not just academic staff and students but systems.

5

PROFESSOR DAVID LEEBRON, PRESIDENT OF RICE UNIVERSITY, UNITED STATES

Interview background

Rice University president David Leebron visited Tsinghua University in May 2019 and attended the signing ceremony for the establishment of the Tsinghua University-Rice University Joint Research Center for Human Capital and Sustainable Innovation. On 20 May 2019, Professor Hamish Coates of the Institute of Education at Tsinghua University interviewed President Leebron.

David Leebron, male, American, born in 1955, is a historian and PhD graduate of Harvard University. He became the seventh president of Rice University in 2004 and formulated the Vision for the Second Century, aiming to develop Rice University into a world-class research university. President Leebron has served as the dean of Columbia University School of Law, taught at UCLA and New York University School of Law, and was a visiting researcher at the Max Planck School of Comparative Law and International Justice in Hamburg, Germany. He received an honorary doctorate from Nankai University in 2008.

Rice University is located in Houston, Texas, United States. It is a world-renowned top private research university and a member of the American University Association. It is known, along with Stanford University, California Institute of Technology, Massachusetts Institute of Technology, and other twenty-five universities, as one of the New Ivy League colleges. According to the 2021 comprehensive ranking of American universities published by the *U.S. News & World Report*, Rice University ranks sixteenth in the United States. Rice University is well-known for its engineering, architecture, and other fields, and its sophisticated small-class teaching model. In 2009, Rice University and Tsinghua University signed a university-level cooperation memorandum and carried out a number of exchanges and cooperation projects in various aspects, such as teacher-student exchanges and academic seminars.

DOI: 10.4324/9781003248286-7

FIGURE 5.1 Professor Peter Rodriguez, President David Leebron, and Professor Hamish Coates (from left to right)

The interview focused on the president's personal background, leadership team, the president's university, Tsinghua University, Chinese higher education, and global higher education. The interview touches on the division of time between social and intellectual facets of leadership, internal and external engagements, institutional standards and integrity, the importance of quality online education, and the role of rankings in nudging institutions to improve (Figure 5.1).

The interview

Interviewer: Where do you spend most of your time as a leader?

President: There are things I do which are a little in the weeds and peculiar to the institution. I spent time on things like reviewing honour counsel cases, which isn't a lot of time, but it gives you, I think, in any position in any different institution, there are things that are a little peculiar to what the leadership responsibilities might be. I try to spend my time primarily on two things, not always successful. One is on the broad set of external relations with the university. So that's alumni engagements, some political engagements, some sort of media things. State-based engagement? Some of it is national, like alumni. Our alumni are all over the country. And then there is the kind of strategic working with people to determine strategies for implementing our strategic plan for the university.

Interviewer: Is that focused on buildings, or programs, or revenue, or…?

President: Buildings are subsidiary in the sense that you never build a building just to have a building. You might build a building to…like a number of years ago, we did a big student expansion. You might build a building because of our commitment to some area, like engineering, that we need to grow and expand. But also a lot of it is working with deans. We have a great group of deans. I was a dean when I came to Rice. There are a lot of places where deans function as maybe what people would call middle management. I try to avoid that. The Business School is what's called a tub on its own bottom; it's much more independent. That's generally not true about Rice. But I think the most important thing a leader of an organization structured like Rice, and most universities, does is to recruit and empower the leaders, support them when they need support, and not micromanage them.

Interviewer: Internally, but externally you're quite focused on the relationships and the engagements?

President: Yes, I think for the broader visibility of the university. And we try, sometimes with success and sometimes not, to get the parts of the university to be on brand and on message. They consult with us. We had some little bumps along the road in that particular regard. And some parts, like the School of Architecture, want their own aesthetic sense in their branding. Our colours are blue and grey. The School of Architecture was branded with pink for some period. They had to stand out.

Interviewer: The first part is about your leadership, as you probably picked up. Can I ask you, does your background as an international relations lawyer, or that zone of the world, does that flavour your leadership? Do you think if you were an engineer or economist you would go about it differently?

President: Well, I think there's a reason that you particularly see lawyers and engineers as university presidents. The thing that lawyers and engineers have in common is a need to engage with the realities of the world to some extent. There is a famous quote attributable to Yogi Berra, which most likely he never said: "In theory, practice and theory are the same. In practice, they aren't." I think there is this sort of dialog between what it is we want to do, what the realities are, how we respond to those realities, how do we build processes, how do we build institutional structures, how do we find a different way of doing something when something doesn't work…. Those are the kinds of things lawyers do. It's a very kind of practical orientation. I think what lawyers and engineers in academia have is this ability to bring together the kind of theoretical qualities – and some of them very academic qualities, the importance of thought at some level – with a sense of practical realities, and how do you get people to work together? I mean, you could have in the academy great scholars of cooperation and collaboration who themselves are incompetent of that. That's what I think lawyers and engineers, and many others, bring from different disciplines. I think lawyers and engineers are a little disproportionately represented. I think that's kind of the reason for that in the US context, and yes, US leaders of higher education.

If I look at the top universities in the United States, the Association of American Universities, and counted the number of lawyers in that group and the number of engineers in that group, you would find comparatively fewer folks out of the humanities. I think you find comparatively few business school deans because with business schools I think there's a suspicion they don't appreciate the full breadth of the academy, which I think, by the way, is a bad suspicion. Often folks in the university don't realize how, academic, intellectual, or theoretical, much of the work is in business schools, law schools, and other professional schools in the university setting.

Interviewer: How about the big challenges for Rice?

President: In many ways, when somebody puts Rice and challenge in the same sentence, one's mind goes a little bit to the question of size. We are the smallest wide-spectrum elite research university in the United States. Well, we grew thirty per cent, so I wouldn't call it "a little bit" in percentage terms: it's one of the larger amounts over a short period of time in percentage terms you've seen in a university. But in many other universities, growing the student population by a thousand wouldn't be seen as a huge amount. It actually ended up a thousand in the undergrad population, and another thousand or so in the graduate populations. So from about five thousand to seven thousand. But that's a significant change, and we may or may not grow more in the future. Our goal is, to use the cliche, to punch beyond our weight. We have another disadvantage. We don't have a medical school, so we don't have that adding to our research visibility. You look at a lot of universities with which we compete; if you took away their medical school, they wouldn't be any more productive in research dollars than Rice. I think our challenge is maintaining our relative position, at least advancing both domestically and internationally. When I say "wide-spectrum," we're not like MIT or Caltech or even Carnegie Mellon, in a sense. We have this incredible School of Music, great architecture, great business school. Yes, that's the challenge! How do you do both of those things in a relatively small package?

One of the ways we do it is, like in engineering, being much more focused on the cutting edge, than sort of traditional engineering. There are aspects say of energy engineering, like using nanotechnology, where we're among the best. But even though we're in Houston, we don't spend a lot of faculty slots on traditional aspects of petroleum engineering, and that's how we have to be kind of careful about what priorities we choose. We have a student-faculty ratio of about six to one, and a lot of people think that's driven because we want very intimate classes. I think what drives that student-faculty ratio is the breadth of what we do in this somewhat small place.

Interviewer: Do all the faculty teach? Full professors teach?

President: Everybody teaches. We have a real historic commitment. Our current mission statement begins: "As a leading research university with a distinctive commitment to undergraduate education." There are others like that. Princeton has a similar model. The difference at Princeton is they have an endowment now of something around twenty-five billion dollars, and our endowment is about six billion dollars. We're trying to do a similar thing that Princeton is doing with a quarter of the endowment assets. I shouldn't complain. That makes us a comparatively rich university. We're about number six or number seven in the country in endowment per student.

Interviewer: Can you keep the same academic model going into the future? Or do you need to reengineer that?

President: I think things will need to change. I think a lot of universities think of online education as something optional and interesting to do and kind of an expansion at the edge. My view was that for us online education had to be one of the highest surplus values because of our relatively small size. We're now into the second strategic plan since I've been at Rice. In the first strategic plan, we asked how could we increase our impact and visibility. The answer was in large part of a thirty per cent expansion of the student body, and most of that expansion is outside Texas, so across the United States and internationally. We went from twenty international students per entering undergraduate class to over a hundred international students per entering class. Given our size, that's a pretty significant commitment.

Now, when we did our recent strategic plan, we looked around at the world. We said, well, actually there are different ways to extend our reach and impact. And so we've put as a priority developing online degree programs. For example, we have one in place now at the Business School, and a second will launch in the fall in computer science. Well, they're fully online with opportunities, I would say, to come to campus and participate. But they're fully online, and both of them are at, or close to, the price point of the residential programs. And the commitment, and this is just to the quality of the Rice faculty. When the faculty approved this, what they wanted to know, I would say it was, "Okay, we're willing to consider online, but only if it is the same quality, quality of engagement, quality of education." Consequently, Rice does not have an online program that is very passive, not very engaged, where you sit and listen to lectures, you take tests; that's not what this is supposed to be.

Interviewer: So may I ask if you've done it for a scale motive, principally? Have you done it to grow the brand, or to grow the political footprint of the university?

President: We hope it'll grow scale. A lot of things that are happening which go to your earlier question about the disruption of higher education. It's being unbundled in various kinds of ways, and these very discrete packages universities have had – which is buy a degree or buy nothing at all – are in the process of going away, whether it's buy a course if you want a course, or buy a sequence if you want to sequence, buy a certificate of something. I think when you engage in these things, you're producing both know-how and materials that can be repackaged in different ways.

I think if I look at computer science, what you're ultimately going to find is degrees that can be broken down. Some students are going to come in not as degree candidates. They're not going to fork over tuition revenue for anything other than the segment that they want to apply to that purpose. So I'm telling people that today we have 7,000 students. That doesn't count another 10,000, let's say, in continuing studies; that is, all older non-degree students. I want to be able to go around the world and say at some point we have 20,000 students or 30,000 students. The Business School is already observing that some of these students are hungry for a sense of identification and affiliation. From my point of view, this is more valuable to us as a small university than it is to some big university. It's going to be a very competitive environment.

Interviewer: Your university will have traditionally focused on, reasonably, the school-leaver cohort, apart from the doctoral students. You're looking beyond that?

President: Most of our undergraduates are entering somewhere between the ages of seventeen and nineteen, with a few exceptions. Undergraduate education is being disrupted much less, I think, than some of the graduate education. There are people who think everything in the world is being disrupted. That's not true. Not everything in the world is being disrupted. Luxury is being disrupted much less than commodity. And service and experiential things are being generally disrupted less than goods distribution, for example. Some kinds of services are commodities, right? You get in an Uber or Lift, that's become kind of a commodity. But if you're going off to a luxury resort, that's something that people are going to pay for. What you see in education today, and we see this pretty forcefully in some of the markets we look at, is a bit of a flight to quality. If you look at the obstacles international students are facing in the United States right now, our international applications in a lot of our programs are actually up substantially. I think the ones that are down are ones where the value of the education is closely connected to a residential opportunity. But if you're looking further down list of perceived quality, or the quality of the experience, you're seeing a real fall-off in applications and success. But where we sit in the market – and this year we had 27,000 undergraduate applications for 945 places – we're not seeing a decline in demand. But I think that's in part because people are saying if it's lower in quality it becomes more of a commodity. Then you ask the question, is it worth paying fifty thousand dollars of tuition as compared to, say, a low cost online program? People are looking at the value they get out of an education like Rice and they're saying it's still worth it in terms of the return on investment, the personal engagement experience.

Interviewer: So the online offer is more to extend your footprint rather than to commoditize the service?

President: Yes, we'll lose if we commoditize. When I first got to Rice and we started making some changes, some people said as a criticism that I was trying to turn Rice into Harvard. And my response was, actually, "I'm just not that stupid," right? That is, if I thought I was going to compete with Harvard by being Harvard, that's a dumb thing for us to try to do. How do we compete with Harvard or a lot of other institutions? We compete by being different. If you're an undergraduate coming to Rice, that's a completely different experience in the sense of dedication of the faculty. Because your classes are taught by a full professor. Not only that, you want to make an appointment with a full professor? Not only is the full professor generally going to meet you; the full professor is going to be happy to meet you. That's what we're trying to offer. Like any other enterprise, we have to recognize what our competitive strengths are that put us in more competition with other schools.

Interviewer: Can I ask you how you signpost that contribution in an incredibly globalized marketplace? Not just the Texas marketplace or the US market for higher education, but what is your distinctive way of demonstrating your contribution to various communities globally?

President: I think globally it's hard. It's one of the things we like about China; I mean the word of mouth in China. We don't have to advertise in China. The network spreads information about our students' experience, and whether students are from Beijing or Xiamen or Xi'an, we find that information gets out more efficiently than any other place we operate. That's in part, one because we have a lot of students in China, but two, the social networking is just frankly more effective in China. Some of it is through mechanisms like WeChat. And then I do think, unfortunately in some respects, the rankings are important. The way I always thought about it is rankings are the corporate equivalent of earnings per share. They're certainly not perfect predictors of anything. But I spent some time in law practice. Earnings per share was the first thing people looked at when they were thinking of performance. Now eventually they look at a lot of other things, but people look at those rankings so if we're saying we're number fifteen or so in *U.S. News & World Report*, that's a huge help for us. Our small size makes it a little difficult to compete in the international rankings because, again, unlike say Caltech, we're not focused in the same way Caltech is. But we have to pay attention to that, and it's really delivering the student experience. I think some of the rankings that are qualitative have ended up in many ways helping us, like the Princeton Review that talks about the quality of the education and the interaction of students, and student happiness and things like that. And then we engage in marketing with appropriate websites and materials, and we tour the country with other schools. We do all this much better, I would say, than we did a decade ago.

China has been a particular success for us, but I would say also around the United States. If you went back say fifteen years or so, we had somewhere around 7,500 applications, and at least half of them were from Texas. Now you go to 27,000 applications, and of those 27,000 applications, only 7,000 are from Texas, that's 20,000 people. Now, this is largely about undergraduates, and if you have a college-age student in the United States, and a lot of other places, the number one question of parents with seventeen-year-olds in high school is where is your son or daughter applying to college? Every applicant is leveraged in terms of information, so I would say it's not different from a business: you're looking at who is consuming your goods, getting that word out. The Business School gets engaged in more advertising than the university as a whole. Do you see top-end universities engaging in very little advertising? The exceptions tend to be business schools and schools of continuing studies.

Interviewer: So what are your impressions about the role of Tsinghua in China and your insights into Tsinghua as it is now? Bottle those two things together.

President: Tsinghua was always one of China's outstanding universities. But I think what we've seen, I would say particularly in the last five years or so, is Tsinghua take a clear position among the best universities in the world. I think that in significant part because, I think some focus I would say, of Tsinghua, is around engineering and related areas, even though it's become a fairly wide-spectrum university. I also think there's a kind of innovative entrepreneurial spirit and very strong connections with both government and business in China. When you look at things like the science park and what Tsinghua has for entrepreneurial students, for example, I think it's clear that Tsinghua was really trying to figure out how to unleash that spirit in its students and train that, and foster it, and encourage it. I think that's put Tsinghua really on the cutting edge in many, many respects. That makes it an ideal partner for Rice University. But whatever the exact rankings say, I think whenever people are thinking about the best universities globally, Tsinghua is in that group.

It's been amazing from my first visit to China, my first interaction with universities in China, which probably was in 1983. I've seen several phases to go. When I first came to China, candidly, the universities weren't very good, but they wouldn't acknowledge they weren't very good in 1983. Maybe they thought they were very good, but they weren't. Then I think China went through a period where really the universities acknowledged that they weren't where they wanted to be and looked around and started engaging in a lot of learning about what makes a great university. Importantly, they had the incredible support of the government in order to transform these universities. We're a little bit jealous of the amount of money that the government is putting into universities in China. I think it's a smart decision. It's a competitive decision. The US ought to be worried about that, which is not to say there's anything wrong with it. It's a great thing that China's putting money into higher education and research. In the US we need to look around and say, in my view, it's time to renew that commitment. I think now China has entered a new phase where there are still areas of improvement in higher education, but it's now reached a level of achievement. But again, there's things along the way: for a while, the way China was incentivizing was just to encourage publication, right? Whatever outlet, whatever quality, just publish, publish, publish. That's actually not the way, ultimately, to raise a university's performance. I don't really know this, but my sense is that this is being looked at a little more carefully now. How do you secure truly distinctive, quality research? But what I think China has understood is that exceptional talent is vital. Creativity is what's vital at the end of the day, and having the facilities and equipment, particularly in science and engineering, is vital, and so that's where we see a lot of resources. But I would say, even compared to ten or fifteen years ago, some of these investments are only really getting started. This is a different quality of university. And again, just to bring it back to our mission here, we just couldn't be more happy to have this opportunity to build a joint research centre with Tsinghua, and I personally hope this is the first of a number between us.

Interviewer: So can you tell us a little bit about that?

President: This is a joint centre focused on Chinese companies in Chinese business leadership, which makes it very unusual. I will say that whenever I see something like this started, my hope is always that you started at some very clearly defined place. You achieve excellence and impact. And then when you've got that, you figure out what's the next thing you do, a little like a corporate enterprise. It's focused on how we build human capital, how that human capital is able to train and contribute to innovation and creativity, and how enterprises need to be led and managed in order to foster this quality of sustainable innovation.

Interviewer: Ok. So can I go from there back to investment in universities? In Tsinghua, there are a lot of opportunities arising from that investment, which will flow on for many decades to come, some great new partnerships. What are the challenges amid all of that for not just Tsinghua, if you could start there, but maybe for universities overall? What are the challenges to our capacity to take that kind of thinking into the real world of commerce and business, and broader challenges? How do we address those challenges?

President: I think universities do have this unique position and capacity to build collaborative endeavours, even if our governments are having conflicts and deep disagreements. Universities have been a kind of fifth or sixth estate, something in which even state universities have been recognized as having some independent role in creating a kind of global mindset in which we work together to address and think about common problems. I do worry about the barriers that the political states can sometimes put in front of that, whether that's barriers about the transmission of information and collaborating in certain fields, or the movement of peoples. As I pointed out earlier today, Rice's student population is about twenty-five per cent international. Our faculty is about one-third international, not counting people who got their first undergraduate degree in the United States. That makes us an international institution, and this is our lifeblood in a sense for becoming the excellent institutions that we want to be. I think there's a second part of your question.

Interviewer: Do you think universities are doing enough to express that leadership contribution?

President: No, I don't. I would hope all over the world that universities would speak out forcefully about the importance of this aspect of their vision. I think in some countries it's harder than other countries to speak out. But I am worried about the increasing barriers that are being placed in various aspects. And there are hard issues, frankly, around intellectual property domestically, and we have to get people to respect intellectual property and figure out how to build these collaborations. But there's a second part, if I understand your question, which is assuming all this great work that's done at universities, how does it have impact in the world? I worry about less than I used to. The universities have evolved from the model of the Middle Ages, which was somehow partially founded on monasteries, isolated entities where people got themselves apart from the cares of society. That was kind of the model of the university, to now really just engage much more in this real world. And that's mostly a good thing. But it also could be a bad thing. If you look at what's happening in industry, timeframes have become shorter, and industry, which used to do some basic research, now does basically no basic research. Getting industry to do things where the time horizon is more than ten years is more or less impossible. What you don't want to happen in universities is for them to say everything that we do needs to have an application. What we can envision, as I like to put it, is that universities are necessarily founded upon a kind of faith. Some universities are founded upon a religious faith, but I think all universities are founded upon the faith that the advancement of knowledge is the foundation of the advancement of human progress, and we need to continue to invest in that. It's one of the things that I've seen in China, that watching from a distance seems very smart to me. As I've observed China, it has not limited its investment. It has increased investment in universities, not just to things that are applied or things that have a competitive advantage in the short term. China is also investing in fundamental research, and I think it's vitally important that universities continue to do that.

That said, this ability to move much faster from the idea formulation or insight into application for human benefit is a real value to society. We see that across a whole range of fields, the collaboration that exists between industry and universities to speed that transition from ideas. We just have to be careful in this process that universities continue to fulfill this very fundamental notion of examining, criticizing, and discovering human knowledge. If we stop doing that, we won't produce the things. I sometimes give the example that I was in what turned out to be a very bad skiing accident a couple of years ago and was taken immediately to a clinic where I had an MRI and CAT scan. They discovered something was seriously wrong with me and that I needed more assistance. Well, so that MRI or CAT scan was not discovered because people said, how do we invent something that sees inside the human body? It came about because people were fundamentally curious about nature and physics and molecules and magnetic resonance, and things like that. And out of the advancement of knowledge, then somebody said, what might be the practical application of this? And we have to recognize that this world moves in both directions there. And universities, and almost universities alone, are equipped to look at questions out of curiosity and then out of that curiosity, say, what can we do with this knowledge?

Interviewer: What question would you ask of Tsinghua at this stage?

President: I think the question I might ask is, how are you encouraging your students to think outside the box, to develop innovation and ambition that's different, to question the world around them? And you know, Chinese society does not have a long history of questioning things in a way. Where in the United States, one might say our whole history is questioning things, going back to even before, in some ways, the American Revolution. I think at the end of the day, if you said, "What's the biggest advantage of American society?" I would say this questioning of things, human liberty and freedom, and then, third, I think I would say an openness to the world, right? In some ways, you can almost say, we became a large superpower early on that was open to the world, and this is what concerns me about the attitude toward immigration in the United States now. I think what we've seen is this openness to the world and our engagement has really helped that. So I think for Tsinghua, the last thing I want to say is it's not just me as an American that's asking this question. Earlier I told the story of having China's former vice minister of education in my home, who said to me, don't bother trying to catch us on teaching substantive knowledge. You're wasting your time because you can't catch us on that. But we're trying to figure out how we instil creativity and innovation in our students. I think, and I can see from today, China is making a lot of progress, but I think I would still keep asking Tsinghua that question.

In 1983, I think was the first time I went around speaking at some universities, and in terms of meeting leadership at universities, that didn't really happen so much until 1996 or afterwards when I became dean. But even going just back to the sort of late 1990s, the quality of the university leadership that I've seen in China is just remarkable on every front that I've seen in terms of the difference between now and then. The international experience that I see reflected in Chinese university leadership today, the ambition of creativity. The competition within China among universities, which I think is a very kind of a healthy thing, is one of the factors that's really positioning China so well. My interpretation, might be wrong, is even though the universities are under the authority of the central government, I think China's been able to find a way both to encourage a kind of competition and creativity within the university, and a systemic strategy that looks at all of the universities and passes out some responsibilities among the universities. I wouldn't necessarily say maybe that's the best system for the US. People say the best thing about the American university system is there is no system, and that's probably true. I think what I've seen among the Chinese leadership is a real ability to bring their international experiences, which so many of them have, into the Chinese university system.

Interviewer: I can go right back to the start and ask you, what are the sort of things that you wish you had known before you became a university president?

President: The university is complicated. There may be more things I wish I'd learned before I became dean of the Law School in some ways. And I think that the complexities almost go back to one of the topics of the joint centre. Just the complexities of human beings and how if you just treat all human beings as completely rational, incentive-driven, you're going to make a lot of mistakes. And the necessity of trying to understand what each person's motivations are, what their fears and anxieties are, what makes them feel successful, how you help empower them. I think that's a huge part of what we do in these enterprises. I would say I moved from a law school world where so much of the strategy is just better faculty, better students. In universities, particularly a smaller university, you have to make choices about what you're going to pursue with strategy, and those choices are determined by a lot of both internal and external influences. I think that strategy is a little like dealing with human beings. You have to deal with the reality that you have in some respects.

I mean I can look at something that fifteen years ago I tried to promote at the university, and I couldn't do it because there wasn't leadership that said, "This is what we want to do."

Twelve years later or so, the same thing arose, and then there was leadership that was ready to take on that responsibility. So you might have a great idea, but if you don't have the right people in a university setting in particular where you can't just fire people you don't think are quite producing, you have to figure out how to use the talents you have to the best ability. If you give a typical, let's say, humanities professor ten thousand dollars a year, that's a huge thing. If you're recruiting a top-tier, nano-science professor, the bidding in the US in terms of a start-up package starts at two million dollars. Making careful choices about that, and how you strategize between existing talent resources and incremental new talent resources, that in some ways is one of the most important things you do. And I sometimes say I've learned there's sort of two kinds of people who come to me: the ninety-ten people and the ten-ninety people. Basically, let's say the ten-ninety people come and say, "I'll put up ten per cent if you go and find ninety per cent of what I need." I have a whole university full of those folks. I can't provide them with such extensive resources. But then there are the ninety-ten people who come and say, "If you can help me get started with ten per cent of this, I'm going to do the other ninety per cent." And that's where you want to make your investment. So it's a long answer to your question.

Interviewer: Well, if I'm understanding I think you are saying investing, understanding the complexities of people as they are as messy human beings, and knowing how to somewhat cut through and make a strategic investment on behalf of the university.

President: And to add to that, particularly in universities where you have tenure systems and other things, how do you leverage what you have and take that into a new kind of strategic strength? I think that's one of the most important things, whether it's the school level or the university level, how do you do that? And so when I can find the ninety-ten people, I want to invest in them every single time because that's what's scarce. It's human talent. This is back to the centre. What's talented? What's scarcity at the university? Ultimately, it's talented people who are willing to make the time and invest themselves in something that's not just a return to themselves but a return to the good of the school and the university. I hope that's all helpful.

6

PROFESSOR PETER HØJ, VICE CHANCELLOR AND PRESIDENT OF THE UNIVERSITY OF QUEENSLAND, AUSTRALIA

Interview background

The former vice chancellor and president of the University of Queensland (UQ), Peter Høj, visited Tsinghua University in July 2019 and had a meeting with Tsinghua University's party secretary Chen Xu about further deepening the cooperation between the two universities. On 2 July 2019, Wen Wen, an Associate Professor of the Institute of Education at Tsinghua University, interviewed President Høj.

Peter Høj, male, Australian, born in 1957, biochemist, genetic scientist, botanist, PhD, graduated from the University of Copenhagen. He served as vice chancellor and president of the UQ from 2012 to 2020. Prior to serving as the president, Professor Høj served as a professor of basic viticulture at the University of Adelaide, an executive director of the Australian Wine Research Institute, chief executive officer of the Australian Research Council, and vice president of the University of South Australia. In 2017, he served as chairman of the Group of Eight in Australia. In 2015, Professor Høj received the Outstanding Individual of the Year Award from the Australian Medical Research Future Fund Advisory Committee.

Founded in 1909, the UQ is the first comprehensive university in Queensland, Australia, and one of the largest and most prestigious research universities in Australia. It is a member of the Australian Group of Eight and the Pacific Rim University Alliance. The university currently has more than 50,000 students, of which about one-third are international students; there are more than 6,000 faculty members. The UQ ranks forty-sixth and thirty-sixth in the 2021 QS World University Rankings and the 2021 *U.S. News & World University* Rankings, respectively, and the biology, engineering, and business fields are all ranked first in the world. The university has a long history of cooperation with Tsinghua University. As early as 1989, the first university-level cooperation agreement was signed.

DOI: 10.4324/9781003248286-8

FIGURE 6.1 Vice Chancellor Peter Høj and Associate Professor Wen Wen

The interview concentrated on the vice chancellor and his personal background, leadership team, the vice chancellor's university, Tsinghua University, Chinese higher education, and global higher education. The vice chancellor talked about balancing excellence across an institution's disciplinary portfolio, the necessity for comprehensive development and boundary-crossing within an institution, understanding government and industry, and the importance of challenging students to explore new technologies and complex ideas and to be creative (Figure 6.1).

The interview

Interviewer: I'm very glad to interview you as the president of one of the leading universities in the world. So actually I have three questions to ask. One is about your university, and one about yourself, and one about Tsinghua University or China's higher education in a general sense.

Ok. So the first question is about your university because according to my knowledge, the University of Queensland (UQ) is one of Australia's most comprehensive and leading universities. And we also know that almost all the universities around the world now are keen to become world-class universities and to have an increasingly higher ranking. So my question to you, as the president of UQ, is that there might be many areas to work on to make the university number one. There are many areas and many aspects so you must select your priority. What is your priority for UQ, and how do you make decisions like which areas you should work on?

Vice Chancellor: You're absolutely right that UQ is one of the top three universities in Australia. For most universities, you want to be good across the board; however, often you have to decide in which discipline area you really want to be the top university, and for UQ at the moment, we focus very much on the life sciences, so that's where we're the best in Australia. However, as you say, we want to be a comprehensive university, so the number one thing I think for a comprehensive university is to make sure that none of your areas fall below world-class and that the vast majority are above world-class. If you want a comprehensive university, you need to ensure that everything is world-class. We have in Australia an assessment of universities made by government each year, and you can get a rating of well above world-class, above world-class, at world-class, or below and very much below. UQ is ranked in about ninety-five different disciplines, and in all of them, we are at world-class or above. But the majority of them are in well above world-class and above. We have only five out of ninety-seven areas that are world-class; the other ninety-two areas are above world-class or well above world-class.

Going forward, our aim would be to never have anything that's at world-class. It all has to be above world-class or well above world-class. So at the moment, seven per cent is at world-class, and we want to move that up to the other ninety-three per cent that are well above world-class. If you want to be comprehensive, everything has to be very good, and that judgement has to be made by independent ratings. I think that's the advice to anybody who wants to be comprehensive, and then you have to say, why does the university want to be comprehensive? And that is because the students of today will go out to a very complex world where many different decision points have to draw on economics, on the law, on technology, on social systems. The biggest problems in the world today are multifactorial. They can't be solved with technology alone. They can't be solved with money alone. If you want to be a university that can really make transformational change in society, you need to be very comprehensive, so you pull all the disciplines together. For example, there's no point finding a technical solution to a problem, if society's norm said we would never do that. In such cases, we have to understand what is it about these norms that stopped a technological solution being acceptable. That's definitely one thing I would say: that we are trying to work that way.

Another thing that we know very well is that virtually no university in the world can afford to do things without international collaboration because when the good people find the good people, they do things faster. And if you can't do things fast these days, you will get beaten. To be a top-ranked university, you have to be very good, but you also have to be fast, and sometimes that means that you had to pick a component of your capability that is actually better somewhere else than in your university and put it together. So be comprehensive and make sure you are not having any of your comprehensive disciplines below world-class – and recognize that international collaboration is important to having a world-class university. The other thing that I think is changing – and this is certainly how we are operating – is that we have a strong strategic plan.

If you were to read our strategic plan and summarize it in one word, that word is "partnerships." It's partnerships between disciplines, internally, it's partnerships with other universities externally, but it's also partnerships with government and industry. Because the other thing I predict will change in higher education is that the old days where an academic does some research and says I hope this can be used for something – that is changing. Now we have to codesign the problem to be solved with people from outside universities, and once we know what the problem to be solved is, then the university will say, "Um, we can't solve this because there's some fundamental knowledge we don't have." So we have to do fundamental research in, for example, these areas of physics, in this area of education, in this area of the law. It's still fundamental, but it's inspired by the end goal you want to solve, and that end goal is the first thing you design. Of all the problems in the world that we want to solve, which one do we want to work on? Is it food security or climate change? How do they interact? And then you work back and do your fundamental research. That's how we are going to attack our future.

The other thing that we are very clear on is that the world is measuring university quality too much based on research alone. We also need to have much better measures for graduate success. I still believe that the most important output for universities is graduates who can go out and make greater contributions to society because of the education we gave them. That education will only be a top education if the students are educated in an environment where knowledge is created, where big difficult questions are asked. It is in such environments they then see how one goes about asking and solving big questions. We also believe that students increasingly should become partners in some of those activities. One of the things I think many universities have to think about, and we certainly are, is how we should teach students in the twenty-first century because the students in the old days graduated into very stable societies, very stable job structures. Many people would have thought, "I have graduated as an engineer, I will have a good career." We have to teach students that in the twenty-first century, you never really graduate. The world is changing so fast that you will have to pick up new skills all the time. If I were to put it in one way, we want our students to understand that they never really stop learning and that they have to be entrepreneurial; they have to become better masters of their own destiny. To put it differently: a very good university should have the ambition that these students become disrupters rather than disrupted by new technology. They use many opportunities – new technology, machine learning, artificial intelligence, synthetic biology, whatever it is, big data, all of that – all the new knowledge and technology gives unprecedented opportunities to think about new ways of putting together, good companies, good job prospects. This is not just me saying this. This is what our students think as well. Indeed, when we surveyed seven thousand students at UQ, more than half of them came back and said their ambition was to start their own enterprise. I asked one of them, why do you want to do that? He said, "Well, it's a very uncertain world. If I'm going to lose my job, I want to sack myself. I don't want somebody else to do it to me."

So I think, therefore, that the old ways of teaching students have to be looked at very carefully because in the old ways of teaching, the students were very passive. They would sit and listen to the professor, try to take down notes, and remember exactly what the professor said. Now we're moving towards a situation where students themselves have the opportunity to do a lot of pre-learning via online courses we produce at the university. They can then come in and do collaborative learning and problem solving in groups because to survive in the twenty-first century, students and graduates have to be much more creative. It's not enough to be able to repeat knowledge that others have given you because it goes out of date so quickly. I think one of the biggest challenges for universities is to see whether the way they teach students also makes them creative students. And we are transitioning because we think the old ways of teaching students don't make them as creative and able to work in multidisciplinary ways. I hope I've given you some insight into how we think about the future.

Interviewer: You mentioned about research, and also having comprehensive disciplines and make them very good in terms of research, in terms of disciplines. You also mentioned students and student success. That's also one of your priorities as president. Well, internationalization might be another, so I guess there are other aspects, like attracting the best teachers, best professors, and also governance reforms. I mean there are many things. How do you make a decision about what is the priority? Because I think maybe different presidents, they have different priorities. Is there a particular mechanism that helps you to make decisions, for example, because of your background as a scientist or because of your background as chief executive officer of the Australian Research Council?

Vice Chancellor: You always have to have a vision for what you want to do and then you have to unpack how you get to that mission by formulating some strong component strategies and ways to execute those. Many universities have vision and mission statements, and if people can't remember them, they're not effective. In our new strategic plan, we decided to have a very short vision and that is "knowledge leadership for a better world." That's very easy to remember. What does that mean? Well, there are at least two components to that. One is to create the requisite new knowledge and do so at the leading edge – that's the research excellence piece. Second, you need to develop a pool of people who can act on that new knowledge and make it work in society, and that's the graduate cohorts. I don't think any university could ever think that they could only do one and not the other thing, except if it is a university funded for special purposes. But if you have students, this should be how you see your greatest contribution to society – through the hundreds of thousands of graduates you educate over the institution's life.

And for a university in our type of society, acknowledging that we live in different systems, and they are differently funded, we are pretty clear that going forward, an aging population will cost so much to look after that governments will find it difficult to find all the money necessary to run top universities. We, therefore, need to move to a situation where our graduates become so successful that they will one day say to our university, "You did really well by me, I have done very well, I would now like to help the university stay successful and to help fund the university through philanthropy." So things go full circle. You look after the students and develop them to express their full potential. When they become successful, many will become influential and recognize the value of a university education. They will therefore assist universities directly and indirectly. That's the lifecycle I'm trying to illustrate. There will of course be many universities which are not big enough to be fully comprehensive. They will have to make choices about what to do and do so informed by their own broad economic, environmental, and political circumstances. For example, I was born in Scandinavia where it's very cold, and the sun doesn't shine as much as in Queensland. In Queensland, one of the most sunny places in the world with a large incidence of skin cancer, we would work on skin cancers, and maybe in Norway and Sweden, they would become leaders in the treatment of frostbite. Even though you can do excellent research in both areas, your choices should be relevant to your country and your community. That should always be at the back of a president's mind. What are the big issues for our community? And then you have to make choices all the way.

One thing you can never ever stop thinking about is whether we're doing an excellent job. You should always set meaningful goals and measure how well you do to meet those goals. If there are areas in which you're not doing well enough, you need to understand whether you can change it by having a conversation with people or whether, if that does not work, you have to attract new talent. Similarly, if somebody does really well, it's very important to celebrate that they're doing well because then others will look at the people you celebrate and say, "What is it that they did which the university likes so much?" Furthermore, as the president of a university, indeed for any leader of a group of people, the most important thing is not what you say but what you demonstrably do. In my experience, people do not so much listen to what you say, but they certainly observe what you do! What you do is always what you believe in, and that's what people should look at. So make sure that you do the right things, and then of course it should fit with what you said. It doesn't help to say that we should go north, and then you proceed to go south. Then people get confused. When people are confused about the direction of the university, it will not perform optimally.

Interviewer: And I actually think that's also the motto of Tsinghua University: Action speaks louder than words. You just mentioned the fundamental goal. That's also very important. How do you define a fundamental goal?

Vice Chancellor: In our institution, we do comprehensively check and update our strategic plan every three years. We start by doing what we call environmental scan. An environmental scan is really to try to understand as much about the world around us as we can. Then we can say, this is what has changed since we developed our last plan. From that, we put up some suggestions for how we should change because the environment has changed. Then we go out and engage very deeply with all our staff and other stakeholders. All our staff have an opportunity to say, "We think we should do this; we think we should do that." It doesn't mean that they determine what we do. We determine that, but we are informed about their views, and it invariably improves our planning because good universities have many incredibly smart people with the skills to predict and shape the future. You have to understand that there are things that you didn't see but they saw, and you should be very respectful of that new knowledge they give you and reflect on that.

Sometimes you get more ideas than you have the capacity to pursue, and you have to prioritize what is in and what is out. That is often difficult. Under those circumstances, you have to look at society's needs and what is covered by other institutions. For example, if everybody decides we should do something about, say, climate change, but no one has chosen to do anything about an aging population and dementia, you have to say this can't be right. So if two other very good institutions hopefully work on the extremely important matter of climate change, but no one works on what we call healthy living and aging, that's what we should do because society needs all of it. You can't just say that this is what my institution wants to do without looking at what else is needed in society and, indeed, what everybody else is doing. You could imagine if you wanted to build a car, and everybody said we want to build wheels, but no one wants to build an engine. You're not going to get very far. It is quite complex to tell you how exactly you set directions, but these are the thought processes that you have to go through.

Interviewer: Do you have a group of people that you talk to a lot?

Vice Chancellor: Yes, we call it the University Senior Management Group.

Interviewer: Ok, so they're from different faculties?

Vice Chancellor: In my university, I'm the president and I have five vice presidents reporting directly to me, including the provost. We meet as a group and individually weekly. We have six large faculties, each led by an executive dean, and four large research institutes led by a director. Those ten people report to the provost. Additionally, my vice presidents each have one or two senior people reporting to them. So we have group of about twenty-five people who contribute to the University Senior Management Group. That group meets every month for at least half a day to discuss the big issues, and then we individually communicate with staff across the university. It's a layered approach, but we always find that if you don't share information, then the right things don't happen. The other thing we are learning is that it's not enough to just tell your direct report what you want to happen because sometimes maybe they misunderstand you, and they tell the ones below them something different. So regularly we actually go two layers down or three layers down, and then once a year we'll have a meeting where we talk to all staff. Also, internal communication is very important to get your organization to a line behind the goal. This is something we can get better at.

Interviewer: It seems that as the president, you have to do a lot of communication

Vice Chancellor: Yes, and to be honest with you, it's still one of the things that I think we need to do better. I think we actually can use technology better as well to spread the message through the organization but also to receive input from below without feeling threatened. Sometimes it's uncomfortable when somebody says, I think you're doing the wrong thing, but it's better than never being told that you're about to crash the plane. It's better that somebody says, oh, I think we're running out of fuel and should land now to refuel rather than running out of it before we reach the final destination. So that's a culture we try to have. Everybody understands that the president has the last word, but it's important that the president understands that it's good to get as much input as possible before you have the last words, that way decisions get better, and more people work enthusiastically to succeed. That requires a lot of communication. Of course, sometimes when universities are very busy places, you have to balance what you have to do and what would be nice to do. Many decisions need to be made quickly.

Interviewer: So probably to be a scientist helps, as you have the academic background or talent to deal with it?

Vice Chancellor: I do not think disciplinary background is the determinant of whether you will be a good president. What is important is whether you have shown yourself to be a world-class scholar and been able to successfully lead a large number of people in a complex environment with both internal and external stakeholders. At UQ, we had a very good president who was an English literature professor but who had shown he could lead a younger and smaller university successfully first. The University of Melbourne had a very good social scientist who, like me, also had shown he could lead a younger and smaller university successfully first. I think, in the end, critical and systematic thinking is what is required. However, scientists have one very big advantage because the research they do often is in very large groups. So you might have a group of one hundred people you have to manage and secure funding for from external sources. Scientists and engineers have had the advantage of always having to manage people and substantial budgets on their way up the system. I think that's possibly one reason why you see more scientists running universities. And of course, then there are also differences between countries. Many of your universities are more science based than an old European university, so you might well find that in China because more people are educated in science, you will get more presidents with a science or engineering background. However, as I said, I have seen some top presidents who come from the non-sciences.

Interviewer: And you also mentioned research, that you have to be best in research, and you also focus on looking after your students. Most of the time we feel that doing both best research and best teaching is very difficult; there is conflict between them. How do you support your professors to manage both demands?

Vice Chancellor: Let me just say that the first month I came to UQ, I gathered more than one hundred senior people. I told them that you're rightly very proud of what you're doing in research, but we are not doing enough for the students. For the last seven years, I've been trying to change that. It is indeed very difficult to change. You can only do it in the way that you reward people. There's an old saying I believe a lot in: "Tell me how you reward people, and I will tell you how they behave." It comes back to what I said before. It's no good the president saying we should be much better at teaching and have much better student satisfaction if you don't reward people when that happens. We have managed to do that, and our staff surveys show that people now agree that teaching at UQ is more valued.

Interviewer: So rewarding you mean?

Vice Chancellor: Promotions. When you get promoted, you get financially rewarded, and you get recognized by your peers because your title changes (for example, from associate professor to professor). We decided to raise the importance of teaching quality and innovation in our promotions criteria to be more equivalent to that of research performance – now you really have to be good at both to get promoted in most circumstances. I'm very proud to say that of all eight research-intensive universities in Australia (we call it the G8 or Group of Eight), UQ easily has the highest student satisfaction. In that sense, I say we are a most comprehensive university because we are good at both teaching and research across virtually all disciplines.

I've just completed a staff survey. Every three years, we have a confidential survey in which we ask staff about one hundred and fifty questions. This year, six thousand five hundred staff answered. One specific question asked whether teaching and learning is rewarded at UQ. Compared to three years ago, the number of staff saying "yes" had gone up significantly and the vast majority agree. When you do something, you also have to measure whether what you're doing is working. In this case, it is. But I think for us, increased student satisfaction will be the saviour of the university in ten, twenty, thirty years' time. Because in ten, twenty, thirty years' time, our graduates will be some of society's successful leaders, and they will make decisions knowing our university taught them well and was part of their success.

Interviewer: Well, that's very interesting, but you make it clear that to balance research and teaching is the most difficult thing.

Vice Chancellor: It comes back to one of the things I said to you. You can always predict what people will do by how you reward them. One of the reasons I think universities are in danger of losing the focus on developing the best graduates is that all the ranking systems have a very strong focus on research. And one of the reasons why that is so is that research is much easier to measure than student achievement. Student achievement is something that you can only see ten years, twenty years ahead. There's an old saying, I don't know who said it but it's one I like: don't make important what is easy to measure, learn how to measure what is important. I think as research universities, we absolutely all believe research is super important. It is what has created the society we have now. You know, we have longevity, life expectancy is much longer, health care is much better, the proportion of people living in abject poverty is much reduced, and many more people have an education. So all that is based on really important research and the innovation that flows from it. However, without well-taught and educated people to implement those research and innovation outcomes, those advances would not have been made. That is why both top research and top teaching must be rewarded. I'm just saying we have to remember that focusing on giving talented students the best opportunity in life by maximizing their potential is equally important to doing great research, and in the last twenty years, we were in danger of forgetting that.

Interviewer: I am so pleased to hear you saying that. It's also a kind of challenge to our university in which, you know, we are trying very hard to improve our teaching as well.

Vice Chancellor: You can't say it once. You have to say it all the time.

Interviewer: Yes, you have to behave in this way, to reward. I just read a piece of news yesterday about the Ramsay course. So what's the Ramsay course? Is that kind of Western civilization?

Vice Chancellor: The Ramsay course is a course that tries to understand the strengths and the weaknesses of Western civilization, to try to understand how we got to where we are. What are the strengths? For instance, the period of the Enlightenment, the period where people started to believe in medicine instead of putting leeches on you to suck your blood. There are many very good things that research and innovation have done in Western civilization, and they have been of benefit to the globe. But there are other things that have been done in the name of Western civilization which have been appalling and people have to understand that as well because if you don't understand what goes wrong, you will make the same mistake again. This is not meant to be an uncritical celebration of Western civilization. However, it is meant to preserve a deep understanding of how we managed to make so many advances over the past centuries and to learn how to do that even better going forward. It's been quite controversial in Australia, but I believe it should not have been. It's about how you teach. You don't celebrate, you analyze. You don't tell students what to think, you tell students how you think independently to arrive at a conclusion that you believe to be objective.

Interviewer: Is that kind of general education or something?

Vice Chancellor: No, not for all. You have to choose to do it. It's what we call a major, sitting inside something called a bachelor of advanced humanities or bachelor of laws/advanced humanities.

Interviewer: Ok, I see. Here comes probably the last question. It's about Tsinghua or China's higher education in a general sense. What do you think are the prospects, and also the challenges, for Tsinghua?

Vice Chancellor: Let me first talk about my first exposure in detail to Chinese universities in 2006. There was a celebration of the 20th Anniversary of the formation of the National Chinese Science Foundation. I was invited to be the speaker from Australia. At that time, it was clear that things were happening in China with respect to its strength in academic research and university capacity building. But what I have seen since then, the explosion in Chinese university capability and capacity, is astoundingly impressive. The Chinese research and innovation system as a whole has become an absolute powerhouse in the global context. You see how much people collaborate with China; they do that because they know that there's so much strength to collaborate with. For the reasons I talked about before, talented people find talented people, and of course inside that exploding capability building in China, Tsinghua sits as a leading institution with few peers. It is easily in the top fifty of the world's more than ten thousand universities and still moving up the rankings at great speed. Of course, you have the hugely impressive Chinese Academy of Sciences, and you have other very impressive C9 universities, but this is a stunningly strong university which is going to get stronger. I think you realize that everybody wants to come and visit Tsinghua because so many want to become a closer partner because they know that the quality, quantity, capacity of what happens here and that it is going to grow because you have very strong people. I think that's a given and clear. I think universities such as Tsinghua will be part of realizing the ambitions that China has for herself and her people, and I hope that this will be done in collaboration with top institutions across the globe so we indeed can progress "knowledge leadership for a better world."

It is important to look at what you have got now and decide what you need to supplement that with to go from being unbelievably good to extraordinarily strong. For example, I think we all have to think about the greater intersect between various disciplines. I'll give you the example of one of the key pieces of work that we started at UQ but which now involves Tsinghua University, the Indian Institute of Technology in Delhi, and Princeton University. It is what we call the "rapid switch" project. People are saying we really should transfer much, much faster from carbon-based fuels to renewable, or at least non-polluting, sources but this is not only a technology play. For example, I know that China is building lots of nuclear power plants, but one of the bottlenecks to just doing that more widely globally is that we simply don't have enough nuclear engineers, we don't have enough nuclear manufacturers. That's a bottleneck. If you wanted to change, let's just say for example, totally away from coal, in many countries, the railways survive because they transport coal. If you suddenly take coal out, the railways may no longer be viable. Then people lose their transportation. So people could say, we don't want to switch away from coal. It's not because they don't believe in climate change. It's because they're losing their means of transportation. These very big changes require multiple insights. Why don't people want to do something? Well, maybe they invested in a very expensive new coal-fired power plant five years ago, and you have to understand the economics of stranding assets when you move to something new. I think that's an example of how research ideas have to be formulated from a more broad societal perspective and need and solved with all this in mind because society is complex with many moving and intersecting parts.

We have people who now don't want their children vaccinated anymore, at least in many Western countries, because they have forgotten how terrible it was before vaccinations were available. Then children didn't get vaccinated, and you can say that's very silly, but it's something we have to deal with because when people don't want to vaccinate their children then they could spread diseases that shouldn't be spreadable. I don't know enough about how Tsinghua is working, but generally for universities, I think they have to start to think in a more societal, systems-based approach. That change should be reflected in how we formulate and execute our research and, very importantly, how we educate our students.

7

PROFESSOR NANCY ROTHWELL, PRESIDENT AND VICE CHANCELLOR OF THE UNIVERSITY OF MANCHESTER, UNITED KINGDOM

Interview background

President Nancy Rothwell, president and vice chancellor of the University of Manchester, visited Tsinghua University in September 2019. She exchanged views with President Qiu Yong on furthering future cooperation between the two universities. On 18 September 2019, Professor Hamish Coates of the Institute of Education at Tsinghua University interviewed President Rothwell.

Nancy Rothwell, female, British, born in 1955, neuroscientist, PhD, graduated from King's College London. In 1994, she was appointed dean of the Department of Physiology for the University of Manchester and served as the research chair of the Medical Research Council from 1998 to 2010. She was appointed as a member of the Royal Society and was made a knight of the British Empire for her contributions to medical research. In addition, she served as the president of the British Neuroscience Association, the founding president of the Biological Society (now the Royal Society of Biology), and co-chair of the British Prime Minister's Science and Technology Committee. In 2003, she won the prestigious Pfizer Research Prize. Rothwell has served as president and vice chancellor of the University of Manchester since 2010. She is the first female president and vice chancellor in the university's history.

The University of Manchester is a world-renowned, comprehensive research university located in Manchester, the second-largest city in the United Kingdom. It is also one of the founding members of the Russell Group in the United Kingdom. The University of Manchester ranks in the forefront of the major global university rankings every year for its excellent teaching and research quality and is ranked 27th in the world in the 2021 QS World University Rankings. As one of the world's top research and teaching institutions, the school has twenty-five Nobel Prize winners. The University of Manchester has established a school-level

DOI: 10.4324/9781003248286-9

FIGURE 7.1   President Nancy Rothwell and Professor Hamish Coates

cooperative relationship with Tsinghua University and has carried out strategic cooperation in many fields.

The interview covered the president and her personal background, leadership team, the president's university, Tsinghua University, Chinese higher education, and global higher education. President Rothwell talked about how she distributed her time between internal management and external liaison, the need to be personally engaged with the institution and in community affairs, the importance of good dynamics and balance within the senior leadership team, and the role of the top leader in internal and broader social change (Figure 7.1).

The interview

Interviewer: First of all, just a sense of where you invest your energy, or maybe your time, as a leader? How do you see that investment, if on a weekly basis or monthly?

President: Very varied. No two days are the same. Rarely is a day as you expected it to be. Obviously, I would say the majority of my time is in Manchester, but I also spend a lot of time on national committees with politicians, with funders. A lot of time with visitors to the university. Obviously, international. I was in Hong Kong yesterday, Beijing today, Singapore next week, US November, so quite mixed. I do also spend quite a lot of time, when I can, in open meetings with staff and students. I've started to have open meetings where they can come and ask anything.

And we're just starting a new, informal chat, where twenty people at a time can sign up and just come and see me and say, "I don't like this," or "I think we should change that." So it's very mixed.

Interviewer: And what sort of value do they add beyond formal feedback? What sort of issues come up?

President: Oh, everything. Sometimes very local issues: "Why have the windows not been fixed in our building?" Big national issues: "What's the funding like for the university?" You know, "What direction of travel are we going on?" There's no agenda. There's no question off the agenda. You can ask what you like. Sometimes people are very forthright, you know, and they tell me what they don't like about the university. It's very rare they will tell me something I don't know, but that's not the point. They've been able to tell me. I give them an answer, and it's come straight from me.

Interviewer: And those meetings have been going long enough now that you're able to trace a connection between them and institutional improvement?

President: Yes, I think so. Well, we do a staff survey every two years, and there's quite a strong staff engagement, and I think it's become an expectation. The deans also do open meetings. I quite like the fact they're mixed, so they might be junior faculty, senior faculty, technicians may come. I do meetings also for the building attendants, the gardeners who have a different set of questions. I write a weekly message to all staff. This week I'll be writing about my travels, but sometimes I write about issues with funding, or pay, or student recruitment.

Interviewer: What are the big ways in which you invest your time specifically? How would you carve up the average week?

President: I would say probably forty per cent would be on senior management issues: everything from how is student recruitment going, where are we up to with the next international strategy, what's the budget looking like for this month, what's the government going to do for universities? That will be forty to fifty per cent of the time, I would say. Then I would say, probably of the rest about a third would be internal communications and engagement. About a third regional, working with regional government, local companies, partners. About a third, wider, bigger picture. I've been meeting with ministers in government or travelling. This is roughly, but of course, it varies a lot. During semester time, more time visiting students and so on, and I meet with the leaders of the students' union very frequently. For example, half a day a week is senior management meetings where we all come together.

Interviewer: Would you say that most of your focus is within the institution, or within the region, within the country, or international or global? Whatever all of those things mean.

President: It is all of those. Probably the slight majority is within the institution, but sometimes it's hard to separate. Is it institutional or is it international when we have a visiting president or a visit such as the Chinese minister for science and technology whom I spent the day with? That's both international and internal, so I don't think there's a compartment. They merge in.

Interviewer: Okay. How do you think your disciplinary background affects the way you lead the university?

President: As my discipline, I'm a scientist, a neuroscientist. I think it makes me quite analytical. I nearly went into maths as a subject when I went to university, so I'm quite interested in finance, financial projections, and so on. I'm quite unusual because at school my last subjects were maths, physics, chemistry, and art, which is most unusual, so I went to art college. I have a strong empathy with the humanities and the fact that they're not quite as different as they might tell you they are, but they are different to the sciences without doubt. I would say I like to see evidence. I like to see what the facts are and analyze the numbers. I think that probably influences me. Also, I come from a very much a team science background. In biology, you work in big teams. I've always felt that universities are about collaboration and partnership and teamwork.

Interviewer: I'm not aware of the discipline background of the university vice chancellors or presidents in the UK, but do you think that makes a difference in terms of how they, in general, would lead a university?

President: There's quite a strong proportion of medical doctors, actually. I think that might help because they're very used to interacting with people. I guess, for me, whereas I'm not a medical doctor, I'm a science doctor, I have throughout my career done a lot of media, public engagement, public speaking, talking to schools. I think those things help because whereas once university presidents were distant figures that sat in a grand room that nobody ever saw, I think they're now becoming much more engaged with the wider university, with the wider community around. I go to local community meetings around the university. I think that is shaping it. In the UK, nearly all members of the Russell Group, the top twenty-four, are fairly strong academics. One or two of the university leaders have got different backgrounds, but most of the research-intensive universities have got strong academic leaders.

Interviewer: Just maybe a final question about you and your role as the president of the university. What particular experiences, if you like training or informal accidents, do you think really shaped your work as a leader? Can you pinpoint a few things?

President: Throughout my career, I've sat on quite a number of committees, and chaired a lot of committees. I've been on the councils of charities, of government funding. I was on the main board of AstraZeneca for nine years as a non-executive director. I got a feel for the governance and the management of quite big organizations. The fact that you have to worry about things like health and safety, audit and accountability, and public views of you. I think those things helped me a lot.

Interviewer: Experience administering organizations.

President: Yes. Administering and leading, and watching other leaders.

Interviewer: Could you have guessed when you were a child that you would be doing this job?

President: Never. I couldn't have guessed even ten years ago I would've been doing this job, and I've been doing it for nine years. No. It was never in my plan. Never. My plan was always to be a scientist.

Interviewer: Do you think it's possible to curate or cultivate people for leadership, or do you think it somewhat just happens?

President: A bit of both, I think. There is a certain amount of natural leadership. I never aspired to be a leader at all, and when I was appointed, and it was obviously an international search, and I told my mother, she said, "I'm not surprised." I said, "Why not?" She said, "Because you were always so bossy as a child. You always tried to organize everybody!" Maybe there was something innate, but I was very much cultivated as a leader, particularly by my predecessor who was an Australian, Alan Gilbert.

Interviewer: Just shifting a little bit more broadly to your leadership team, how do you balance the different capabilities between performance people, operations people, and innovation/creative people?

President: Okay. It's quite a small senior team, actually. It's ten people, of which seven are academic leaders. There are three vice presidents who are deans of the three faculties. There are three vice presidents who are policy leaders for each of our three goals, and my deputy. They're all leading academics. They are very much driving academic mission. Three, more operational, are the registrar, who is effectively the chief operating officer, the director of finance, and director of HR. It's quite a balanced team. It's a smaller team than many university leadership teams. We're quite close.

Interviewer: You don't have any international vice president?

President: The deputy president takes the lead on international, so being my deputy, he has a key role in international.

Interviewer: Do you find that those people manifest their roles or have grown into their roles? Or does the registrar think in creative, externally focused ways? Or is it very much an operations, internal focus?

President: No. He's joined us fairly recently. He's run another university. I think one of the things that we insist on is that they have a core role, but when they're on the senior team, everybody's equal, and they need to have a view or express an opinion about something even outside their area. I don't expect the dean of science and engineering to only focus on science and engineering, or the dean of biology, medicine, and health only – they need to be part of the running of the university. Whether it's the financial or the international, it is quite a shared leadership.

Interviewer: Is there consensus-based decision-making?

President: Absolutely. We fight like hell and then when we leave the room, we all agree – that is an absolute requirement. I say, within that room, we can argue as much as you like. You are free to express your opinions. Once we come to a view, we stick to it.

Interviewer: How do you keep the balance between internal focus and external focus, control, innovation? What time horizon do you put around thinking through how you – well, how do you, yourself, manage that on a daily basis?

President: Yes, I suppose quite a lot of time on longer term, for me. Five to ten years. We're actually going through a period of refreshing our five-year vision at the moment, so we've done a big consultation. The senior team has worked through it. We have focus groups. I would, in particular, but others would as well, be thinking as I've just come back from China, what have I learned from China? What direction is China going in? I see particularly my role as pulling together big, external things. Other senior colleagues do also, but they have big internal jobs to do. I would more frequently meet with government ministers or leaders of industry. I've just been to Tsinghua Science Park and met the chairman and the CEO, so I would go back and say, "Come on. We need to be thinking about this differently." I think that's quite a big part of my role.

Interviewer: The ideas can come up, for sure, but you see your role as innovating the ideas within that leadership team, in creating new directions?

President: I would certainly. They do as well, but I would certainly see a key role I play of not only innovating but challenging actually. Sometimes saying, "Hang on. We're all agreeing on this, but there is another point of view. Let's have a look at it." Or saying, "Have we thought about doing this differently?" Sometimes we have a debate and everybody says, "No. That's a silly thing to do. We're not going to do it." Sometimes it does shift thinking quite significantly, so I'm quite keen on it. I worry that universities can get into internal bubbles and group thinking. I'm quite keen on bringing in people who will challenge. I brought in a speaker last week who believes that universities are partly to blame for the divide in society. I didn't agree with him entirely, but he had some valid points to make, and I thought it was right that we got somebody in who would challenge us.

Interviewer: Can you somehow register the leadership work that you and your senior management team do, and maybe others in the organization, with concrete institutional changes? After nine years, I suppose, you've actually seen some decisions.

President: Yes.

Interviewer: Not just structural things but more dynamic cultural factors or the like.

President: Yes, we've undergone a very significant restructuring of the university. We've taken a much bigger international focus. We've initiated several quite significant new areas of research. One of the big changes we made a few years ago was that we identified five of the biggest areas of research for the university: research beacons. That was very difficult indeed because we started off with about fifty. Everybody wanted their area. They all went away and thought about it and came back with eighty. We got it down to five. It was quite a challenge. We brought in some quite significant changes for student experience, to give students an experience well beyond their academic discipline, to stretch them outside their boundaries. There have been quite big changes, some instigated internally, some in response to external funding, or a challenge, or trends. Much more commercialization than we used to do in terms of business engagement, start-up, spinouts, have all been changes within probably the last ten years, I would say.

Interviewer: How much of that do you think is explained by your internal work, and how much is reactive? How much have the students had the capacity to play a leadership role in shaping their environment?

President: It's difficult to say. As a rough guess, I would say seventy per cent was our decision as opposed to external factors, although these very much shape our decisions. It's looking for trends.

Interviewer: Seventy per cent of the changes.

President: Yes, it's very much shaped by looking for trends. What are students wanting to study? What are big government schemes? What's industry doing? While it might be an internal decision, it's taken in the round, after looking at what's happening, and sometimes looking at what might be a great thing to do. But sometimes we agree that we're doing too many things at the moment. We don't need a new thing to do, and if we do, we've got to stop doing something. Because that's one of the problems of most organizations. We always want to start things, but you never stop anything, so you just get busier and busier.

Interviewer: Since we've drifted to talking about your university more broadly than you or your leadership team, what kinds of challenges – you've mentioned a few in general – but specific challenges you think have been really meaningful for the organization during your time as a president?

President: One external and one internal. The external one is the UK higher education system is facing a massive challenge over the pensions for staff because it's a very expensive scheme. There have been national strikes. That was very difficult for all universities. It was very difficult. We may be going through it again with another strike ballot. That meant a change in the way we engaged and discussed with staff. It certainly caused a lot of anxiety. Then another example that we determined internally, we moved from four faculties to three faculties.

Interviewer: When you merged?

President: This was about four years ago. Quite a major structural change. I think the big issue about that was selling the vision for why we're doing it. In other words, this isn't just a managerial thing that would cut a bit of cost, but there are real academic benefits from it.

Interviewer: What were they?

President: The fact that we had a faculty of life sciences and a faculty of medical sciences, but there wasn't enough translation between the two or back from medical to life sciences. As long as they were two separate faculties, with teaching and research separate, even though you work across faculties, it was still a structural thing there that hindered it. There was quite a lot of opposition to it, particularly from the life sciences, which was the smaller one.

Interviewer: It was hard factors like funding and buildings, or more cultural factors and traditions?

President: More cultural factors. More seeing opportunities. More forcing discussions and collaborations. There was a feeling by the life scientists, of which I am one, that they would be gobbled up by the big medical faculty. Actually, funny thing is it's been the other way. I think probably life sciences has benefited probably a little bit more, but it was quite a big cultural shift. Then we've just undergone a major change in the faculty of science and engineering. We had nine different schools – schools are like big departments – and we've gone to two. We have a School of Natural Science and a School of Engineering, and they're all together now. That was quite a big project.

Interviewer: Has it reduced the cost and increased the outcomes?

President: It has reduced the cost somewhat.

Interviewer: For the research, I guess.

President: Yes. It has reduced the cost. Not dramatically. Some reductions. For science and engineering, it's too early to say. It's three months old. For what is now biology, medicine, and health, I think it has improved research outcomes. I think it has improved research funding, particularly in cross-disciplinary areas.

Interviewer: That was driven by an internal consideration, not by external policy or regulation.

President: I was looking at the strengths and weaknesses and where there were opportunities that we might be missing or things that we weren't good as we could be at. Uncomplicated things like the faculty of medicine was paying the faculty of life sciences to teach their students, and they always begrudged that, so they wanted to teach it themselves. So there were operational things that drove it, as well as a vision from our collaboration.

Interviewer: What other challenges, or risks if you like?

President: Always risks. Well, the biggest one without a doubt is Brexit. That is the biggest risk we face at the moment. It's partly a risk because of the uncertainty. I'm asked by staff what's going to happen, and I have no idea. Nobody has any idea in the United Kingdom. We don't know how it will affect European funding of universities, European students, European staff. That's the biggest risk, certainly, I face during my tenure, and outside of my control, which is even more frustrating.

Interviewer: Moving beyond the challenges a little bit, what initiatives do you have in store? I think the current strategic plan runs through to 2020.

President: Yes, the new strategic plan will be launched in February. Within that, we've maintained our three core goals, which are research and discovery, teaching and learning, and unusually perhaps, a third one: social responsibility, which is very strong for us.

Interviewer: Why such an emphasis on that? And furthermore, why do you think it's so unique within universities to have that as a distinctive goal?

President: I think others are developing it now. I think we brought it in just as I took over. I think the distinction is that it stands there with the others. To me, it breaks down to the core question of the purpose of universities. You can talk about research and innovation and teaching. But to me, as a publicly funded organization, the ultimate goal of a university is societal benefit. Therefore, the things we do beyond research and teaching. Because an awful lot of social responsibility is within the other two goals, whether it's research into poverty or climate change or new medicines. But actually, there are quite a lot of other things we do. Somebody asked me seven or eight years ago how would we know when we've succeeded? I said, well there are lots of things. Actually, a new league table came out on the Sustainable Development Goals in which we were ranked third in the world. Two things I want to see. I want to see an increasing number of students saying, "I chose Manchester because of the social responsibility." And I want to see our local communities, very deprived communities, talking about "our" university, as being part of it. That's still a key part of the strategic plan. The three themes we've added, that cut across, are innovation, civic engagement (which is about being part of Manchester), and global impact (which is about our international role). International is much stronger in the future strategy. Business engagement and commercialization are much stronger. The broader education of students is much stronger. We're developing a big innovation district, which is probably about a one-and-a-half-billion-pound development. It will be very big. Part of our future campus plan. A lot more cross-disciplinary research and teaching than there was before.

Interviewer: How do you see student experience in ten years' time? What buildings or infrastructure need to be produced?

President: I'm not very good at crystal ball gazing because ten years ago, I said we'll have far fewer students on campus and far more doing distance learning.

Actually, it hasn't shifted that much. I still think that is likely, but the change has been slower than we predicted. We thought many, many more students would be doing flexible or distance learning. We offer, for example, a global MBA. Then it's taught in China, as well as other places, where people in work can come and do three months, or three weeks, of study, or whatever. I still see, really, more higher education going in that direction. But most universities are still absolutely traditional campus-based universities with three-, four-, five-year degrees. It hasn't changed as quickly as I would've expected. I think it will move in that direction, but we built lots of lecture theatres and labs and everything, and they're still full of students. I thought they would be less so, but that hasn't been the case.

Interviewer: So more of the same?

President: Yes. I think it will change. We are doing much more online and blended learning than we were, but it hasn't stepped up as quickly as I'd expected it to.

Interviewer: Ok. The three big new initiatives. Can I just ask you to unpack international a little bit more? That means a lot of new things for the UK potentially. It cuts across all of the university's work.

President: It does. We have quite a lot of international students. We have twelve thousand. We don't plan to increase that very much. We're thirty per cent international now. I think we could probably go to thirty-three per cent. I think more strategic partnerships but not lots and lots of MoUs. A small number of strategic partnerships. We have three at the moment: Melbourne, Toronto, and Chinese University of Hong Kong. Perhaps doubling that number. We have offices in Shanghai, Hong Kong, Singapore, Dubai. We may extend that. Possibly India, Central and South America. I think it's also a more international outlook for our students. More UK students now are wanting to have additional courses. A very popular one is learning Mandarin, not surprisingly. We've got something called University College for Interdisciplinary Learning, which is where students learn something outside their subject. For example, a physicist could learn about Chinese culture. A historian could learn coding or how the universe began. It's trying to stretch students. They do programs in leadership. They do volunteering. They do peer-assisted learning. They do something every year. In fact, it was yesterday where all first-year students come together and spend a whole day on environmental sustainability. In their second year, they all come together and have a whole day on inequalities in society. It's been stretching, such that a student graduates with specialist knowledge in physicist or history or biology, but also with a broader education.

Interviewer: If I turn now to looking towards Tsinghua, China, and then finally we'll look at the rest of the world. What do you find most interesting about Tsinghua?

President: It is an outstanding university. Top-ranked university in China. We share very common interests. I'm told you have sixty faculty who are Manchester graduates. We have quite a number of Tsinghua graduates who are at Manchester. We obviously have a shared agreement already in life sciences. I think Tsinghua has been quite innovative. I've just been at Tuspark, and that is really quite an inspiring development. It came out of the university, but it's now a global brand. They talk to us about potential partnership. Obviously, it has huge academic standing in terms of its academic mission. We would be delighted to expand collaborations. I'm sure Tsinghua has that potential with many, many universities. We like working with universities that are not just academically excellent, although that is important, but there's a sense of a shared vision. One of the reasons we went with Melbourne and Toronto was because we had a similar outlook of wanting to be both local but also global. Both have quite a strong program in what I might call wider engagement and social responsibility. The presidents of both universities were in Manchester last week for a global engagement summit, as well as the president of the Chinese University of Hong Kong. A sense of league tables and academic achievements matter, but other things matter as well to universities. You can't just be driven by how many Nobel Prize winners you've notched up, or what position you are in the Shanghai Jiao Tong, though of course, I look at it avidly. The universities are about more than that. They're about agents of change for communities. Universities, I think, can span politics. I think that's really important with all the geopolitical change going on at the moment, that academic-to-academic interactions often put aside political differences between their countries. I care about what they're going to do together. I think that's a really important role of universities.

Interviewer: What particular challenges do you think could shape Tsinghua's future?

President: I think political relations between China and the USA is an obvious one. I think that's a concern. There are Chinese students applying to Manchester – a forty per cent increase this year. It may be partly because they're not going to the USA.

Interviewer: Have you expanded your student numbers?

President: A little bit, but not that much. We'll be nearly six thousand Chinese students this year. It was about five thousand six hundred last year. I haven't seen the final numbers for this year. It'll be up a bit, but not dramatically, partly because Chinese students make up the biggest number. We are now doing much more two plus two degrees with other universities. For Tsinghua, I think like all of us, global competition is a challenge. How many things can you be really good at? None of us can be really good at everything. Picking how many areas we're going to really invest in. Having said that, the Chinese government is investing so much in university systems. I think it's in a very strong position.

Interviewer: How do you think Tsinghua could best contribute, maybe taking the proceeding remarks into account? Or completely differently, how do you think Tsinghua could best contribute to higher education? Or can I go beyond the sector to the global community?

President: Yes. I think demonstrating those key partnerships and that they are about more than just exchanging students and some money. It's very interesting. Ten or twenty years ago, the UK looked on China as a place that you would work with because it had a lot of money. That's completely changed now. We want to collaborate with China because they have outstanding universities. I think Tsinghua's leading the way on that. Our Manchester China Institute (the lead of it is here today) is talking to your academics and looking at mutual understanding between UK and China. I think Tsinghua can lead on that. There is a lot of suspicion about China in some parts of the world, not so much in the UK. I think a university like Tsinghua can lead and say, "Look. We want to be open. We are global. We want partnerships. This is about global success, not just about Chinese success." I think they could take, and do take, political leadership on their own, as universities should do everywhere.

Interviewer: If I could turn even more broadly to Chinese higher education. What are your main impressions? You've said something already about the growth of the system, but I don't know how long you've been coming to China?

President: Twenty-odd years. I think it has shifted from being – well, let me just put it from a different perspective. From the Chinese students who come to us, we used to have difficulty in getting them to understand the concept that being at university is about challenging accepted dogma. Chinese students didn't like to accept that. They are changing very much in that they're becoming much more accepting that because it's in a textbook, it doesn't necessarily mean it's right, and that there isn't an answer to everything: you come from school, and you're told that's the answer. Actually, then you then go on to university and say, well, we don't always know what the answer is. That's up to you to tell us what you think the answer is. I think that's developed a great deal. Obviously, technology and investment in places like Tsinghua are massively improved. I also think the global outlook has changed dramatically from first coming here probably twenty-five years ago when Chinese universities felt quite inward-looking. I think they're all now looking to hiring international staff, to recruiting international students. That's changed very much in the last twenty, twenty-five years.

Interviewer: What big challenges do you think are facing Chinese higher education? You've said something about the growth and the new ways, but what do you think the challenges are?

President: I think being seen to be open to the rest of the world. I think the Chinese universities like Tsinghua are more open than some imagine. Tsinghua is developing partnerships with those areas that may not be doing that well now, but they will be in the future, like Africa. These are very populous areas. They're growing, and in terms of their education, so there's been a traditional China-USA, China-UK. For us, it's been obviously USA and China. We're now looking at Central, South America, India, Africa, these emerging countries. I'm sure Tsinghua is thinking about wider engagement, different ways of learning, which must surely change in the future, dealing with a huge population of young people. But I guess for Chinese universities, there will be a demographic dip. We've had it over the last few years in the UK. China will see it much more of course, for China as a country, and I spoke on this on a visit with the prime minister. Aging society will be a challenge. I think you're going to have to be looking at seventy and eighty-year-olds learning or relearning and wanting to be employed. These are global issues.

Interviewer: On to the global factors. You've said quite a bit already in terms of geopolitics and research contributions but maybe just to bottle up those ideas or add some new ones. What are the main contributions you think major research universities should be making over the next twenty, thirty years?

President: The obvious one that would come first for us would be environment and sustainability. Climate change demands both behavioural change and new technologies. Then I think two others. One would be societal inequalities because you actually look at some of the political flashpoints: they are very much about inequalities. I've just come from Hong Kong where some say that the protests are really about inequalities in Hong Kong. Then I think, as I mentioned earlier, about being a political bridge because universities, I think, can bridge political divides and reach out to areas that our countries may have difficulties with. Universities can often collaborate. For example, academics in Israel collaborate with academics in Palestine because to them the partnership matters more than the politics.

Interviewer: A few more operational-type questions if I can. What reforms would you imagine would enhance the productivity of education and research, if you could do anything you would like? If you closed the university for a year, make the changes, and reopen it, what would you change to? Not necessarily Manchester. What would you do to make it much better?

President: I think the first thing I would do is less accountability; sometimes it seems for accountability's sake. We seem to spend a lot of time counting things and sending forms into various different organizations and being accountable. Vast amounts of data go to governments, and they don't do anything with them. I worry that we've partly lost the academic mission, academic freedom, because of rules and regulations. Okay, some of those are very, very important (for example, health and safety), but equally, they can be constraining.

Another thing is continual global rankings, which I don't think are particularly helpful. They're there, and you can't ignore them. But when you're worrying about every academic: have they published a highly cited paper? Actually, wouldn't they be better if you left them for three years to tackle a really important problem? I feel we've become a measurement-oriented set of organizations, and we've lost a little bit of that freedom. One of our members of staff who won the Nobel Prize in 2010, Andre Geim, is a very creative individual, and he likes to just be left to think about what he's going to do next. We try and do that as much as we can, but that's quite hard in universities now because we are judged on how much have you published. Did you do your teaching? I think trying to liberate from that and go back to universities as places of creativity.

Interviewer: How is that possible to achieve? Partly, you mentioned the role of government, but could universities just opt out?

President: Yes. They could go private. There are risks in that, of course. We've discussed whether that will be an option so you're free of the constraints of government accountability because although we are independent, we're very much regulated by government. There are also many downsides to it though. Government funding means that it's probably too big a risk. I think the US does have an advantage. Their top universities are private universities. They have a level of autonomy that I guess British and Chinese universities are not likely to have. We have far more constraints, I think, than Harvard, MIT, and Stanford. I think if we could lose some of those constraints, we could do better. Persuading government that when they give us money, it is sensible just to leave us alone. But persuasion doesn't necessarily work. Governments like to know exactly what they're getting for their money.

Interviewer: How about doctoral education? What specific reforms would you make to ensure that the faculty we have in the future – maybe for the next thirty, forty, fifty years – are well-equipped for their roles?

President: I would focus on doctoral, not the PhD. I would focus on post-doctoral because disciplines are changing so much that academics well into their careers can feel left behind. I still do research in neuroscience, but I feel like a child in terms of AI and some of the stuff that my younger colleagues are doing now, and I just feel that every two or three years I need a month's update. As disciplines are emerging, and merging, I think we need more continuous development of our staff.

Interviewer: Actually just leave the PhD or the doctorate as it is?

President: No some change to PhD or the doctorate but making education and training much more of a lifelong thing, which I think is going to be true everywhere in society.

Interviewer: How would you do that?

President: You could impose it, but it would be better if people recognized the opportunity and just voluntarily said, "We will give staff a month off every year." Of course, it's not without its problems because of the cost, but to be able to give them some free time. Staff say now about the sabbatical, which was very highly prized, "I haven't got time to go on sabbatical. I'm too busy." That freedom to say, "I'm going to take a little bit of time to go and do something different, to go and experience a different university, another part of the world" – that can be enormously empowering.

8

PROFESSOR ULRICH RÜDIGER, RECTOR OF AACHEN UNIVERSITY OF TECHNOLOGY, GERMANY

Interview background

Ulrich Rüdiger, rector of RWTH Aachen University, visited Tsinghua University in September 2019. He exchanged views with Chen Xu, secretary of the Party Committee of Tsinghua University, on further deepening and expanding cooperation between RWTH Aachen University and Tsinghua University. They signed a joint letter of intent committing the two universities to cooperate through programs at the Tsinghua Shenzhen International Graduate School. On 20 September 2019, Xie Zheping, an Associate Researcher of the Institute of Education at Tsinghua University, interviewed President Ulrich.

Ulrich Rüdiger, male, German, born in 1955, physicist, graduated from Aachen University of Technology. Since 2018, he has served as the rector of RWTH Aachen University. From 2009 to 2018, he served as president of the University of Konstanz. During his tenure, the University of Konstanz obtained funding from Germany's Universities of Excellence Initiative. Previously, he served as a professor and chair of experimental physics at the University of Konstanz, a member of the Conference of German Rectors, and a member of the Conference of Rectors. He has received honours such as the French Order of Academic Palms.

RWTH Aachen University was founded in 1870 and is located in Aachen, North Rhine-Westphalia, Germany. As a top technical university in Germany and the world, RWTH Aachen University is a member of TU9 (German Universities of Technology), and from 2019 to 2026, it was one of eleven elite universities in the Universities of Excellence Initiative. RWTH Aachen University has more than 40,000 students and 6,000 teachers. The school ranks 145th in the 2021 QS World University Rankings, and its high-performing disciplines include mechanical manufacturing, computers, electrical engineering, electronic communications, and economic management. RWTH Aachen University has developed extensive

DOI: 10.4324/9781003248286-10

FIGURE 8.1 Rector Ulrich Rüdiger and Associate Researcher Xie Zheping

cooperation with Tsinghua University. The master's and dual degree programs jointly developed by the two universities are exemplary programs for Sino-German education cooperation.

The interview touched on the rector and his personal background, leadership team, the rector's university, Tsinghua University, Chinese higher education, and global higher education. Rector Rüdiger discussed focusing on the future and creating the future, balancing engineering and humanities, recruiting and retaining top experts and professors, and teaching students basic and applied competencies (Figure 8.1).

The interview

Interviewer: The first question is what interests you most about Tsinghua?

Rector: Well, I learned a lot earlier today. I recognize the self-perceptions of Tsinghua, and I'm absolutely surprised. If you changed the names – take out Tsinghua and substitute RWTH Aachen University – they are more or less the same. Tsinghua's general approach to internationalization, to enabling top research, and also transfer to society and industry – all these ingredients we have also at RWTH Aachen University.

Interviewer: So, we share pretty much similar values?

Rector: Right. I'm just entering, re-entering, RWTH Aachen University, and now visiting our long-standing cooperation partners. It's so impressive! Double degree programs for almost twenty years, and all kinds of cooperation over almost four decades. Tsinghua is one of our three strategic partners worldwide, and we have really a long history together. It impressed me how many people – students, professors, staff – are involved in this cooperation.

Interviewer: Thank you very much. And how can Tsinghua University best contribute to global higher education in your understanding? I'm interested in your response because our universities share a lot of common ideas.

Rector: Well, being present, being open-minded. When students go to other locations to study, they get completely different experiences. We need open exchange of ideas, of personalities – internationalization in other words. I have read Tsinghua has a new internationalization strategy.

Interviewer: Since 2016.

Rector: Well, we have pushed internationalization in the past at the RWTH. So at the moment, we are almost hitting twenty-five per cent of our student body being international students. So that's top of the universities in Germany.

Interviewer: Yes. Students from one hundred twenty-five countries. I have the numbers here.

Rector: Number one is China, by the way, with five per cent of our international students coming from China.

Interviewer: Okay. That's very good. The coming questions are about Chinese higher education. What is your impression of Chinese higher education since you were here five years ago?

Rector: I learned today that the age group, almost fifty per cent of the age group, are going to the university.

Interviewer: Yes.

Rector: So this impresses me. We have more or less the same proportion in Germany, but Germany is much smaller, so it's much easier to organize this.

Interviewer: Yes, we're used to organizing big population exams. We have done so for seventy years. So, what do you think are the big challenges facing the Chinese higher education?

Rector: Well, educating people, being able to tackle the grand technical challenges. We both have the same grand challenges: climate change, energy provision, health, and so on. And I think this is the task number one for the universities: educate young people who are responsible, who feel responsible, for their society and for their environment.

Interviewer: So that common human challenge shapes our future?

Rector: Exactly.

Interviewer: Okay. Actually, we did some homework for this interview. Some articles, papers about Aachen University, and it is pretty interesting since you just mentioned we share some common values. I noticed Aachen University's motto is Thinking for Future. Could you please elaborate a little bit on this motto?

Rector: Thinking the future is taken to mean both thinking about the future and creating the future.

Interviewer: When was this motto adopted?

Rector: So when RWTH was founded, we started as a polytechnic school. We started in 1870, and people from Aachen, from companies, society in Aachen, were afraid that we did not have the skills needed by the employers, Aachen did not have the right people available for industrial companies, because nearby regions were booming and people started moving away from Aachen. The solution was, "Well, we need highly educated young people." This was 150 years ago and the decisions made shaped the industrial future in Aachen. We translated this vision in a new manner in 2006–2007 at the beginning of Germany's Universities of Excellence Initiative.

Interviewer: Yes, that's very ambitious.

Rector: The federal and state governments started the Initiative in 2006, and RWTH entered this competition in 2007.

Interviewer: Now the Initiative is the second term?

Rector: Third term. We just received the good news that we are still one of the select eleven universities in the Initiative. And Thinking the Future was a motto embedded in this excellence proposal in 2007. Thinking the Future was translated from, well, the self-understanding that has grown about why Aachen has had a technical university since 1870.

Interviewer: Oh, right, okay. It's a long history. The second question I'm interested in is about your engineering focus since Tsinghua is also very famous as an engineering focused university. We notice that Aachen is very demanding about student quality. That means undergraduates have very low examination pass rates. Is that still the case?

Rector: Indeed, but we really care about that situation. The success rate of undergraduates, from my point of view, should be on the level of seventy per cent, plus or minus. And we implemented a lot of measures, a broad variety of different measures, to support students when they enter the university system. We provide extra courses in math, and so on and so forth.

Interviewer: But the pass rate, the successful pass rate, is still forty per cent?

Rector: No, we increased it – for example, in mechanical engineering to seventy per cent and above.

We really invested money and time and effort to improve that.

Interviewer: Yes, to get…to lower the failure rate?

Rector: Failure rate is about fifty per cent. This is not a clever way to continue.

Interviewer: What does the university's main governance body think about your intention to improve the pass rate?

Rector: We're making the system more efficient. After you finish school and you start your study program, you are full of motivation, ideas. You have creative ideas. You would like to enter your undergraduate studies with a very positive mind that this new, well, this is the start of your professional life. If you start with problems and you have to stop your study program, you have to change, this is a very negative start. And so we have taken considerable care that students are really sure they are entering the right program.

We have a lot of coaching and advice. Is this right the right course they are doing? We provide extra courses in math.

Interviewer: You don't want to disappoint the students too much.

Rector: Exactly.

Interviewer: Yes, we have also the same question at Tsinghua. We have engineers, and we also have social sciences, natural sciences, humanities. You know, the humanities students can get a higher pass rate more easily, so the engineering students, they say it's unfair because we work so hard and do not have time to enjoy life. But humanities students, they enjoy life that this is unfair. The university still wants engineering students to come to Tsinghua, but this situation is sometimes, you know, very difficult for the university to have policies that distinguish between the academic performance expectations of engineering and social science students? Does Aachen also have social sciences and humanities?

Rector: We have social sciences, and we have just appointed five new professors.

Interviewer: Is that in social sciences?

Rector: Yes, professorships in social sciences. And this group of professors is concerned with the relationship between technology and people. Because we really have to care not only about innovations but also about how innovations, individuals, and society impact one on the other. How do technological innovations affect society and individual behaviour? Now we are implementing such research questions across our university programs so that we think about innovation and society simultaneously. I think it is not a very clever strategy having no social sciences at a technical university. You cannot separate them completely.

Interviewer: All right. You can't make the best engineer without humanities.

Rector: Exactly.

Interviewer: Okay, thank you very much. Another question is about Germany's higher education system, particularly your engineering education system. In China, we think Germany has the best engineering education. What do you think about current approaches to engineering education? For instance, industry changes due to new technologies, such as artificial intelligence. What are the new challenges, the biggest challenges, for engineering education in Germany?

Rector: The biggest challenge occurs around, let's say, hot topics like artificial intelligence, and it is recruiting the best professors available. There is international competition, and we are not recruiting from other universities.

Interviewer: From industry?

Rector: We are recruiting from industry and, for example, when we talk about artificial intelligence, we have to recruit from Google and Facebook. The salary level for these colleagues in industry is so high compared to what we can pay as a professor's salary. So I think this is really a challenge for us, not always being behind what industry is doing.

Interviewer: Could you please tell us about important new developments in German engineering education models, paradigms?

Rector: A new development is that we expect our students to study revised programs in which we teach basic knowledge and then take a very applied approach. More or less all professors in mechanical engineering are recruited from industry, so they are well informed about both sides: university and industry.

Interviewer: So students have to take jobs? Simultaneously with their studies?

Rector: This will be the next step.

Interviewer: Next step?

Rector: Yes, that is the next step, which comes also with something new on the point I addressed earlier, that it is really hard to recruit professors from industries in artificial intelligence and so on. So I think we should develop further in a way that there's no need to decide, "I'm a professor at this university" or "an employee in that company." I would like to see a system where you can switch back and forth, or you work part time in both systems so that you are close to industry, closer to innovation, actively part of transferring knowledge to industrial applications.

At present in the German system, you are a civil servant as professor, which means you are one hundred per cent committed to the university. And here, I think, we really need new models, new approaches? That it's not strictly being on one side or on the other. And I think education, the teaching programs, will profit if we open the system in such a way.

Interviewer: Right, so that means you're making reform of the education programs and also reforms about professors' backgrounds so that faculties are required to take more expertise from industry.

Rector: I would like to see, in future, colleagues embedded in both systems – at the university, and at companies – and I would like to implement in engineering faculties a tenure-track system, so the tenure track towards a full professorship. This is new for us in Germany.

Interviewer: Oh, so you are starting the tenure track?

Rector: Right now I was able to submit a successful proposal for twenty tenure-track professorships.

Interviewer: Twenty?

Rector: Additional tenure-track professorships, especially in engineering and life sciences and data sciences, in artificial intelligence, and so on. And what I would like to see also is earlier independence for young researchers.

Interviewer: So where did you hand this proposal to? To the Ministry of Education?

Rector: This is a federal program, and we submitted our proposal to the federal Ministry of Science and Technology.

Interviewer: So in China, normally we notice changes in the German higher education system. It is still very much a model for us.

Rector: A major problem in the past, and it still is, as a PhD student, you have to think about your future career – your scientific career or industrial career. Once you decide that your focus will not only be in engineering but also in neighbouring disciplines, you are deciding for the scientific career. Then you work for somebody else at an institute for ten years maybe. And then at the end of the day, you get a professorship, or not. It's a disaster. You wasted ten years of work and set aside all other jobs. Now you are too old, right? And here I really would like to change the system and add a tenure-track parallel path to a permanent professorship. But at the beginning, there's a serious exam to determine If you are the right person to go on such a tenure track, and if you fulfill the criteria, after six years you get tenure, otherwise not. But the bottleneck should be earlier than we have it today.

Interviewer: What do you think about fundamental research? Because nowadays we are much more concerned about innovation. Technology, innovation, AI, and so on. What about fundamental research?

Rector: First, a very simple answer. Without fundamental research, there are no innovations in future. You have to nurture both fundamental research and applied research. And the time constraint is different. When you invest money today in fundamental research, you invest in future, but you do not know exactly what will come out. Applied research is a little bit different. So embedded in our excellence strategy, we have measures to strengthen data sciences, life sciences, and natural sciences as a bridge between engineering and medicine. We have a medical department. This is quite unusual for a technical university.

And we have a huge hospital, and I would like to see the interpretation of medicine at RWTH as a more technical interpretation. So, tailored medicine, personalized diagnostic, and therapy. Tailored pharmaceuticals as well. And so we need much more data science and life science as basic sciences for medicine and mechanical engineering.

Interviewer: More interdisciplinary research?

Rector: Yes, that's the title of our proposal: "Interdisciplinary University of Science and Technology". The subtitle is "Knowledge Impact Networks." We create knowledge which generates impact for the society and impact for the economy, and we know that we are able to do so only if we work in our networks.

Interviewer: This proposal is submitted to whom?

Rector: For this round of the Universities of Excellence Initiative.

Interviewer: Ok, that's what? Networks?

Rector: Networks.

Interviewer: So you think the future for engineering education is actually highly influenced by advances in technology.

Rector: Exactly.

9

PROFESSOR LAURIE LESHIN, PRESIDENT OF WORCESTER POLYTECHNIC INSTITUTE, UNITED STATES

Interview background

Laurie Leshin, president of Worcester Polytechnic Institute, visited Tsinghua University in September 2019 and attended the Tsinghua-Worcester Polytechnic Institute Joint Research Center for Global Public Security Annual Academic Conference and exchanged views with Chen Xu, Tsinghua University's party secretary, on further promoting cooperation. On 23 September 2019, Xie Zheping, an associate researcher at the Institute of Education at Tsinghua University, and Liu Lu, a postdoctoral fellow, interviewed President Laurie Leshin.

Laurie Leshin, female, American, born in 1966, geologist, PhD, graduated from California Institute of Technology. She became the principal of Worcester Polytechnic Institute in 2014. Leshin is an outstanding academic and university leader, as well as a geologist and space scientist, and has conducted space research work at the National Aeronautics and Space Administration (NASA). She received the Neal Award from the American Meteorological Society in 1999, and the NASA Outstanding Public Service Medal in 2004. The International Astronomical Union named the asteroid 4922 "Leshin" in recognition of her contribution to planetary science. Since 2015, President Leshin has visited Tsinghua University four times.

Worcester Polytechnic Institute, founded in 1865, is a world-renowned private research university located in Worcester, Massachusetts, United States, with nearly 7,000 students and more than 400 teachers. Worcester Polytechnic Institute's talent training model that combines theory and practice enjoys a high reputation in the field of American science and technology education, ranking sixty-sixth in the 2021 *U.S. News & World Report* American university rankings. The well-known Chinese educator, Mei Yiqi, graduated from the Institute in 1914 with a major in electrical engineering. At present, the Institute has established an inter-school

DOI: 10.4324/9781003248286-11

FIGURE 9.1 President Laurie Leshin and Associate Researcher Xie Zheping

cooperation memorandum with Tsinghua University, and the Global Public Safety Research Center was jointly established by the two universities in 2017.

The interview covered the president and her personal background, leadership team, the president's university, Tsinghua University, Chinese higher education, and global higher education. The interview touched on the need to keep a focus on the core mission of educational institutions to help people and students improve themselves and to contribute to the development of partners and communities. This means distributing education between formal learning and external settings. Achieving lofty goals requires bringing together people with different backgrounds and experiences and focusing them on addressing grand challenges. The president stresses the need for key leaders to maintain balances within the institution and between the institution and external engagements (Figure 9.1).

The interview

Interviewer: What interested you most about Tsinghua?

President: I love visiting Tsinghua. I think it's my fourth or fifth time to visit the campus as president of Worcester Polytechnic Institute (WPI) in Worcester, Massachusetts. And WPI, as we call it, and Tsinghua have a long historic connection. A former president of Tsinghua University, President Mei Yiqi, is a graduate of WPI. He came to the United States over one hundred years ago, studied electrical engineering, and he eventually came back to China. He was an innovator in education at that time and became president of Tsinghua University. Our interest is in keeping this shared history of collaboration and innovation going. And so today, we are working together with Tsinghua on a Joint Center for Global Public Safety to carry on the tradition of collaboration between our two universities.

Interviewer: Yes, that's good. We have a long history of collaboration. There are many relationships between us. How can Tsinghua University best contribute to global higher education, from your perspective?

President: There are so many opportunities for Tsinghua to contribute with basic research – the fundamental research that Tsinghua is doing incredibly well and is known for. In our collaboration with Tsinghua, we appreciate a strong connection to industry and to communities to help make people's lives better. I think this is the mission of all educational institutions: to help people and our students improve themselves and also to help our partners and our communities get better. I hope that the focus of our collaboration will continue to be that.

Interviewer: What challenges could shape Tsinghua's future?

President: I don't claim to be an expert in the higher education challenges in China, but there are many in the US, and I imagine some of them are similar. I'm not sure of the specific challenges that Tsinghua is facing, but today, we are thinking so much about the world our students are emerging into and how dynamic that world is. The world of work is changing so much. The need for education is higher than it has ever been, and so educational institutions like WPI and Tsinghua are critical to helping to ensure the future prosperity of the people of our countries. Making sure that we are doing the very best we can to provide the best education possible for our students is a challenge, but it's also a huge opportunity for our campuses.

Interviewer: Yes, it is. We are really interested in leadership. Where do you invest your energy as president?

President: It's a highly dynamic and varied job. Every day is different. It's one of the things I love about it. It's never boring. For me, it's a mix of internal operations, sort of running the university and making sure that we're managing our resources and our risks very effectively. That is combined with external events, like the one I'm here at Tsinghua for today, to participate in a meeting of our joint centre. I meet with alumni and with partners, and constantly try to bridge those two things: the internally focused and the externally focused piece of the role. I think part of the job of the president is to help the university see the future. As we say, "Look around the corner and see what is coming." That's something I spend my time on too, making sure that I am part of organizations and conversations that are future-looking so that I can bring that knowledge back to our campus.

Interviewer: Let's talk about your background. We're interested in your discipline background. How does your discipline background shape your leadership, especially the leadership style?

President: My disciplinary background is that I am a space scientist, so I'm a geologist who studies rocks from Mars, and meteorites, and the moon, and things like this. It's kind of an odd background, but space exploration by its nature is very team-based and very interdisciplinary. I think of my experience – I worked at NASA before I was a college president – and I know that if you have really big goals, if your goal is to send people to Mars, no one person can accomplish that goal. You have to bring people together with many different backgrounds and many different experiences to be able to achieve big things. I think that is how my own background tends to play into this work in that I am very comfortable trying to bring teams of people together to address grander challenges.

Interviewer: So, in your daily life, you have a professional leadership team to assist you to deal with different issues?

President: Yes. I do.

Interviewer: So in your leadership team, what kind of balance do you think is most important to find between people interested in performance, operations, people, and innovations?

President: That's a great question. I do think there are so many parts to this role, and most leadership roles I've had have to do with finding the right balance between things. Balancing people who want change and innovate, with people who really know how to get things done, is very important. I think sometimes in higher education, we are better at the vision than at the execution. We pay attention to trying to make sure that we have that balance on the team.

Interviewer: To what extent does the work of the leadership team focus on internal and external matters?

President: It's both. Our vice presidents of finance and administration are focused more on the operations of the university. Our vice president of advancement is focused on fundraising and external relations. Our academic leadership, again, is balanced between the internal operations of academics and making sure that we are keeping up with those external trends. We talk about it a lot – this need to balance between near term and long term, and internal and external. It's something a leader does to hold those balances, to be checking, "Are we balanced correctly? Are we too far one way or the other?"

Interviewer: I think your university is quite similar to Tsinghua because we probably have the same focus.

President: Yes, technical focus.

Interviewer: What specific cultures and traditions are important to your university?

President: WPI is a technological university: STEM (science, technology, engineering, math) and also business, and we also have strong programs in the humanities and arts and social sciences but really with a focus on how we use technology to advance humanity, to make peoples' lives better. We have a very interesting approach to that mission at WPI. It's unique and project-based, so we value hands-on experiences in the real world for our students. Yes, they spend some time in the classroom, but almost all their classes are project work that the students themselves are doing. Much less of the professor giving a lecture and much more of the students doing hands-on work. As part of our curriculum, our students all complete multiple major projects, some in their field of study, some that are crossing disciplines. Increasingly, they do that not on our campus but out in the world. Last year, we sent over one thousand students to thirty-one countries, to over fifty communities in those countries, to work on real problems from sponsors in those local communities. It's a way to take what they're learning in the classroom and apply it in the real world in order to make change. Project-based learning is our big focus at WPI.

Interviewer: What about social science? Is it pretty much the same or is it different?

President: Absolutely. All students at WPI complete these projects, whether they're in engineering or science or social science majors. It's great because it does give them that opportunity to learn how to apply their knowledge to solve real-world problems. And we want them, once they graduate, to go out in the world and make a big difference, a positive difference. You can't just say that's a good thing to do. You have to teach people how to do it, and so that's the goal of the projects: to help students struggle with the challenge of an open-ended problem. I don't know if this is the way textbooks work in China, but in the US, there are many homework problems where you can flip to the back of the book and the answer is there. There's no answer in the back of the book for the projects, right? The students have to go and figure it out. It's messy and difficult, and sometimes it doesn't work out. And this is the way life is, and so it's important to give them that real-world experience.

Interviewer: Yes, it's a very good, effective way to help students develop critical thinking. We all know that every university has its strategic plans for the future. What distinguished initiatives do you plan for future development?

President: We are just coming to the end of the strategic plan that we put into place when I started as the president of WPI five years ago. In that plan, we scaled up the global projects, where our students are traveling to other countries to do their project work. Now our goal is to have ninety per cent of our students do one of their projects off campus. We have given scholarships to every student to help pay for the cost of them to go to China. This past summer, two dozen students completed projects in Beijing, for example. On this trip, I will also go visit Japan and visit our current students who are working in Kyoto on their projects. We've made it possible for any student to be able to afford to do that, so money is not a barrier, and we've scaled up the number of offerings that we had. We are focused on purpose-driven research in our strategic plan, so we get funding, much like what happens here: we get grants from the government to perform our research. We want to see that grow. We grew by sixty per cent in the last three years under the strategic plan.

Lastly, we are working on the visibility of things we care about at WPI, enhancing our reputation around project-based learning, so we started something called the Center for Project-Based Learning at WPI where we invite other universities to come and learn from us. After fifty years of working on projects, we really know how to incorporate this into a higher education curriculum. In the past five years, we have served 130 other universities which have sent teams to participate with us in the centre, and collectively, they serve 1.3 million students a year. It's a way to have an impact on a lot of students in higher education with what we are passionate about – project-based learning.

Interviewer: What about new technology? Are you using online courses? Or are you planning to integrate more online courses within the university?

President: We have about seven thousand students total, about one thousand of them are online students, mostly at the graduate level, master's programs. That's something we're looking to scale up in the next few years. In the next strategic plan, we will be looking at scaling up those online programs. So many universities are doing this, I think, especially in STEM areas. In engineering and in technology, the world is changing so quickly that we need to be thinking about models where we can make sure professionals in those fields can gain the skills they need very quickly and at a moment's notice. To me, the interesting opportunity is less about perhaps the traditional master's degrees and more about just-in-time short segments of learning, which maybe you can add up eventually to get a certification or a degree. But there's a lot of opportunity for innovation in the way we think about certifications and credentialing and the delivery of that information. We're thinking about all of those things.

Interviewer: Cool. From your perspective, what kind of institutional challenges are you facing?

President: So higher education in the United States right now is in the news a lot, and not always in a positive way. There's a lot of discussion among our population about the value of higher education because the cost of higher education to families is high. I think for us it's all about making sure that the value is really there for the cost that families are paying. And for us, all our students all get amazing jobs and all earn a good living and are able to make a great contribution to society. We need to make sure we continue to tell the story of this value and make sure we work to keep the costs down.

Interviewer: What is your biggest challenge?

President: I think the biggest challenge is just balancing the everyday operations with making sure that we continue to move toward the future. You know, balancing the near term and the long term, and always making sure that we have our eyes on the risks. Making sure our students are safe for us. At any given moment, we have hundreds and hundreds of students who are studying all over the world. There are always risks to understand and make sure we are taking care of everyone.

While we are doing that, and doing it well, we also have to be looking at innovations for the future. I think balancing those two things is the challenge.

Interviewer: Any special difference for you compared to male presidents?

President: For me as a woman? I'm the first woman president in the 150-year history of WPI. I don't know if there are any special challenges. I would have to ask the guys. But I think there are special opportunities for sure because I know that women students, women faculty, the mothers of our students, look up to the fact that there is a woman president. We have used that to increase the percentage of women at WPI. The percentage of women in colleges overall in the US, it's about equal women and men. But for technological universities, not so.

Interviewer: Pretty limited.

President: More like one-third women, two-thirds men. That's what it was at WPI when I arrived. But now, we have three years in a row where there are over forty per cent women in the incoming class. We're working very hard to increase the numbers, and it's working, so that's exciting to see.

Interviewer: What's your main impression of the Chinese higher education system?

President: My main impression is that I'm so impressed with the growth. Tsinghua has been around for a long time, but the investment that the nation is making in the higher education system in China is extraordinary. To see how fast the system has grown, the capacity of the system, and the quality of the system, is amazing. I think it's absolutely the right thing to do for Chinese citizens to make sure that higher education is available to everyone. It's so critical to the future of prosperity of the economy and of the individuals. I think my other impression is that there's still opportunity for some innovation in the delivery and the curriculum. We at WPI are big believers in project-based work and experiential learning, and I think there's more opportunities through collaboration to continue to advance those kinds of innovations.

Interviewer: In your mind, what is the biggest challenge for Chinese higher education?

President: I'm not sure I'm informed enough to know that, honestly. I imagine that such rapid growth presents challenges in making sure that the quality is there across the board and that students are receiving the education they need that is relevant to the way the world is changing so quickly. Right? I think this, to me, is one of the biggest challenges in higher ed overall: the work that our students are doing is changing. When they graduate, the work they're doing now is so different than it was even ten or fifteen years ago. How do we keep making sure that the education we're providing is preparing them for the world they are entering?

Interviewer: Is there any special education reform regarding engineering?

President: We are always adding more degree programs, more opportunities, new things, whether that's in data science or robotics engineering, which is one that we added about ten years ago and that's continued to grow. It's the third-largest major at WPI – after mechanical engineering and computer science, now its robotics engineering, which is truly interdisciplinary between mechanical, electrical, and computer engineering. That is becoming more and more common.

Interviewer: More and more common?

President: Yes. Things that cross-cut traditional departmental boundaries, what we think of as the traditional engineering disciplines.

Interviewer: All right. The differences mainly concerning the disciplines?

President: Yes, exactly. The curriculum and the disciplines.

Interviewer: What do you think about internationalization of WPI now? At Tsinghua, we have a global strategy.

President: It's very important for who we are in a couple of ways. One is we invite students from around the world to attend WPI, and we have many. That's a very important part of who we are. But another is we send our students out into the world to complete projects. Last year, we sent over one thousand students to thirty-one countries. They worked in local communities with local organizations on their local challenges. In that sense, we are truly all over the world. We are a global university. This year, we will launch what we're calling the Global School, based on this project work and building upon it to continue to offer opportunities for us to engage in new ways around the world.

Interviewer: So the Global School will be inside the School of Engineering?

President: It's called the Global School at WPI.

Interviewer: Do you have any overseas offices to support it?

President: We do not have physical infrastructure in other countries. We have many, many relationships, and our faculty travel with our students when they go to these other countries. That's the infrastructure we have – our relationships. As a college president, I like this because I don't want so much physical infrastructure right now. To me, more technology infrastructure and relationships are the important piece of it. But we're very excited about where the Global School can take us because right now, we might have a student team in three or four different countries working on something about transportation or health care or sustainability. We can start to bring together those individual experiences and do something more collectively.

Interviewer: But will that school be an independent school?

President: It is underneath the umbrella of WPI, and it will be one of our academic schools. Like our School of Engineering. We will have a big event to launch the Global School in 2020.

10

PROFESSOR DAVID TURPIN, PRESIDENT AND VICE CHANCELLOR OF THE UNIVERSITY OF ALBERTA, CANADA

Interview background

The former president and vice chancellor of the University of Alberta, David Turpin, visited Tsinghua University in October 2019. He exchanged views with the vice president of Tsinghua University on further strengthening the cooperation between the two universities and renewed the school-level cooperation agreement between the two universities. On 9 October 2019, Professor Hamish Coates of the Institute of Education at Tsinghua University interviewed President Turpin.

David Turpin, male, Canadian, born in 1956, marine scientist and botanist, PhD, graduated from the University of British Columbia. President Turpin served as the 13th president of the University of Alberta from 2015 to 2020. Before serving as the president of the school, he served as the president of the University of Victoria, vice president of Queen's University, dean of the faculty of arts and sciences at Queen's University, and professor and head of the Department of Plants at the University of British Columbia. In addition, he has served on the Board of Trustees and Advisory Committees of Canadian universities. He is a member of the Order of Canada and the Royal Society of Canada and has won the Queen's Diamond Jubilee and Golden Jubilee Medals.

The University of Alberta is located in Edmonton, the capital city of Alberta, Canada. Established in 1908, it is the oldest university in Alberta and is one of the five largest comprehensive research universities in Canada. It has more than 40,000 students and more than 3,000 teachers. Reflecting Alberta's abundant oil and natural gas resources, the school has outstanding advantages in energy-related fields. It also has recognized expertise in nanotechnology. In the 2021 QS University Rankings, the University of Alberta ranked 119th in the world. In April 2017, Tsinghua University and the University of Alberta signed an agreement to jointly build the Tsinghua–Alberta Future Energy and Environment Joint Research Center.

DOI: 10.4324/9781003248286-12

FIGURE 10.1 President David Turpin and Professor Hamish Coates

The interview touched on the president and his personal background, leadership team, the president's university, Tsinghua University, Chinese higher education, and global higher education. President Turpin discussed strategic direction-setting, communicating with stakeholders within and outside the university, keeping close contact with students and meeting regularly to understand their ideas and concerns, and building trusted and cooperative research arrangements to tackle big problems Figure 10.1).

The interview

Interviewer: Can you tell us a little bit about how you invest your energy as a leader?

President: Well, when asked that, I jokingly say that about seventy per cent of my time is spent internally, and the other seventy per cent is spent externally. I think that sums it up. These jobs require a huge commitment of time and effort. There is a very important role for the president, internally, setting the strategic direction of the institution and communicating the key messages of the institution internally, right down through the organization, from the vice presidents to the deans. Four times a year, I meet with all new faculty and staff when they first join the university and talk about the university, what our goals are, and how they can help us get there. There's that whole internal leadership and internal administrative side.

Then there's the external role. Part of the way I look at that is that the role of the president is to help modify the external environment to benefit the mission of the institution so that there's a receptor capacity out there so that as the environment changes, it changes to help facilitate us and the accomplishment of our mission. That involves meeting with government officials – locally, provincially, nationally, and internationally. It involves meeting with members of the broader community, whether that is the business community, people in industrial sectors. Again, local and national and international. Whether it's alumni. Whether it's members of not-for-profit groups and any of the other stakeholder groups that are out there. Part of that is to bring them up to date on what our university – what universities generally – is doing in particular and enlisting their support for that mission. Really, that is how I see the roles and responsibilities of the president in the internal and external environments.

Interviewer: In terms of the internal activities, how much is you thinking about strategy and development? How much is working with senior colleagues? Working with students? Working with faculty?

President: Well, it varies dramatically. On a week like this, it's one hundred per cent international. However, in the car on the way here, there are emails going back and forth. Internally, a large portion of it would be focused on interactions with the senior leadership team. That would be, I think, the largest single component. Another major component is the governance of the institution. That would be the board and the senate in most institutions. Our system is a little bit different in that we have the academic body known as the General Faculties Council. Then there is a senate, which is a separate organization that has somewhat different responsibilities. We actually have three legislated bodies that have a governance role. The Board of Governors is the governing body responsible for the finances and operation of the university.

Interviewer: External appointments and the like?

President: A lot of external appointments. Some internal appointments.

Interviewer: How many people?

President: Twenty-one people altogether. They do budget, property, that type of thing. Then there's the General Faculties Council, which deals with all academic matters. I chair that as president. The vice presidents and the deans are on it, but it's populated predominantly by faculty and students. All of the issues around academic programming, academic standards, admissions, and those types of things are dealt with by that body. Then the senate is a separate body that is dominated by external appointments and about a third internal. They appoint the chancellor, who is the titular head of the university, nominate people for honorary degrees, and also serve as a conduit for university-community relations. They don't make decisions in that area, but they provide advice.

Interviewer: For business as well? Or just the broader local community?

President: Well both. Some of them would provide perspectives from business. Some from the broader community, but it's a way to get that. Many universities will set up advisory boards. This is one way to look at that. You end up with about sixty people from across the province who provide reflections and advice. Four times a year, they get together for a two-day meeting.

Those are the bodies. Each of those would have a series of committees that would either recommend to the governing bodies the decisions they should take. Or, in some cases, they would have delegated authority to make decisions. There's a fair bit of time involved in managing, leading, motivating those groups. In terms of time allocation, you've got a good portion, forty to fifty per cent of the time, focused on the management side of it and the leadership of the university. You've got another very significant portion of time, probably about thirty or more per cent, focused on governance. Then you've got meetings with the different stake-holders, students on campus, the staff associations, the faculty associations. Then a very significant ceremonial role. I don't know how many hundreds of remarks I give a year at different events. They are actually important. Sometimes you think, well, is it really worth my time showing up and giving this little speech? Well, the fact is, it is. People want to have an appreciation for who their leaders are and what they're saying, and to have the opportunity to meet them and to hear them share some thoughts. I think initially, one of the challenges many presidents have when they come into the role is they don't appreciate the importance of ceremony and the importance of being at events. I think we often don't appreciate how truly significant it can be.

Interviewer: Can I ask, will the students see you around the campus informally? I'm just going to completely the other end of the spectrum there.

President: Well, you'd have to ask them. All our student leaders have my cell phone. I meet with them regularly. My vice presidents meet with them regularly. They know. I tell each of them, when they're given my cell phone number, that they're one of a very, very few people who have it. If they need it in an emergency, they can use it. Otherwise, "If you want to set up a meeting, here's how to do it." I have discovered over my career that it's never been abused. That if there is an emergency, and we do have to connect, they will. It helps build a level of trust. Right now, we're very fortunate. We have both our Graduate Student Association and our Undergraduate Students Union with incredible leadership. They are very intelligent, very motivated people. I can say the quality of interaction we have with them is better than at any time during my twenty-five years as a senior leader at Canadian universities. It's truly extraordinary. It's going to serve us well because we've got a new government in place that is going to impose some major funding reductions.

Interviewer: Provincially?

President: Yes.

Interviewer: When you say, "major funding reductions," what do you mean?

President: Oh, we've got a new budget. They were just elected. They ran on a mandate to balance the provincial budget in four years without raising revenues. No increase in taxes. That is, it's all going to be cuts. We don't know what's going to happen. Having a group of student leaders in place that we have a very strong relationship with is, I think, going to serve us very well.

Our budget year starts beginning of April. The budget that will come down at the end of October is for the current budget year. We're over halfway into that budget year now. We don't have a letter, a funding agreement with the government. We came up with assumptions last March. Our board approved a budget. We have an approved budget. All the assumptions may be invalid. We'll have to manage that very, very quickly. Then, in February, there will be another provincial budget, which will be for the 20/21 budget year. That's the one where we'll probably have the more significant reductions.

Interviewer: How much of your budget is the provincial grant?

President: Ok. Our budget is about two billion dollars a year. One billion of that, roughly, is what we call our operating budget. That's where we run the university out of the faculty salaries. Teaching, et cetera, et cetera. The other billion dollars is research, which is about half a billion. Then ancillary enterprises. Our residents. Our parking. All our business ventures. Of that billion, about two-thirds is from a government grant and about one-third from tuition. On average, in Canada's other institutions, the split between government grant and tuition, and the operating fund, is about fifty-fifty. We expect deregulation of tuition to some extent. The new government put out a report about a month ago that outlined the financial path for the province and for post-secondary education. It was very clear. We're going to move to more of the national average on the allocation of monies to the operating grant. That is, reduce the amount the province puts in, and increase the relative amount that students put in. What does that mean? Is this a relative reallocation? The total funding stays the same? In which case, the students are bearing one hundred per cent of the burden. Or is it a combination of a reduction in grant and total funding, with some compensatory increase in tuition as a partial offset? Then other unknown factors enter into this, including what our enrolment expectations will be.

Interviewer: Could I ask you the magical question of all higher education funding? What's the relationship between your revenue cuts and your disbursements around the university? Would you necessarily pass on a cut in tuition and raising tuition for others? Or is it more complicated in terms of your degrees of freedom to act and cross-subsidize?

President: Well, there's an easy answer to that and it's wrong. You've asked a very, very complicated question. As you've just indicated, you're aware nothing is hard-wired, shall we say. But the students cannot be expected to bear the full brunt of this transition.

Interviewer: This is a public conversation at this point?

President: Yes. As a result, I committed that a significant portion of increased revenues, as a result of increases in tuition rates, would be targeted to needs-based student financial assistance. There's a big issue there. What's going to happen to tuition? What are we going to do to student financial assistance to protect those who are most vulnerable to price shocks? Another question is, once you end up with an operating fund, regardless of where it comes from, how do you disburse it? How do you allocate it? Over the last number of years, we've been working very hard to build a budget model that will help us make those decisions. Historically, our university's budgeting process has simply been an incremental budget-allocation process with no indication as to what the key drivers are. What we've tried to do is make it a little bit more transparent.

Interviewer: In relation to cost?

President: Of revenues, or allocation of revenues. Clearly, cost would have something to do with it if it costs you more to teach a student in "X" than "Y." The chances are it will give you more, but there was no transparent way for a dean to have any idea. If I increased my enrolment by twenty per cent, what are the revenue implications for me? There was nothing to help deans see how that might work. It would be, basically, a one-off deal with the provost. What we've done is moved to a model that ties revenues to the faculty: to activities and success.

Interviewer: Activities-based costing?

President: Different students would carry different weights based on the cost of their programs. A dean could now sit down and plan enrolment. It allows that degree of transparency. There's also a portion of the funding that's allocated on the basis of research productivity and success.

Interviewer: From central sources?

President: No, in terms of rewarding the unit's capacity to bring in external money. If you have two identical units, two identical teaching-cost structures, and one unit is outperforming the other significantly on research, there will be a benefit to that unit in terms of operating funding.

Interviewer: In terms of rewarding success?

President: Exactly. What that does is, hopefully, incentivize the deans and the faculty.

Interviewer: This is just on the research side?

President: It isn't simply to deal with student need and programming need for undergraduate students. It recognizes that as a contemporary university, one of our key missions is research and creative activity. We're building the tools to help incentivize the deans to optimize enrolment, to manage resources effectively, and to realize the implications for their budgets of the decisions they make.

Interviewer: Could I just go now to your disciplinary background and how you think that might shape your work as a leader?

President: Interesting. I started off as a biological oceanographer. I got interested in photosynthesis and the ocean. I then became more interested in photosynthesis and basically ended up as a biochemical physiologist.

Interviewer: Plankton, is it?

President: Yeah. I started with plankton. Then my model system was single-celled algae, planktonic microorganisms. Used them to study photosynthesis. I'm inter-disciplinary in nature. As a biologist, I span the biological sciences. Then with the oceanographic background, I interacted with physicists, chemists, mathematicians. Everything we did in our research required collaborations. I collaborated with people around the world. If we had a problem, I'd find out who the best in the world was. I would contact them. I'd offer to send a post-doc or a graduate student to be with them and to learn some techniques or bring somebody from their lab to mine. That, for me, that focus on collaboration is what informed my leadership. Basically, I realized I don't know any of the answers. I'm lucky if I know some of the good questions. I simply worked to surround myself with really bright people to solve some of the bigger challenges we face. That would be, I think, the major influence of my disciplinary background on my leadership style.

Interviewer: Excellent. Thank you. Let's turn to those people in the structure of your leadership team, in terms of the balance of roles, perspectives, risk managers, creative people, inwardly looking people, outwardly looking people. How do you construct that balance, and maintain the balance, in terms of not just hiring people but monitoring and mentoring?

President: I often think of a stock portfolio or an investment portfolio. You need some of everything. Right? If you have all your eggs in one basket, you could, in the short term, succeed spectacularly, or fail unbelievably. In the long term, that's a terrible, terrible strategy. You need to have a diversified portfolio of people with talents and skills. The key thing is they work together and get along. You hope they don't always agree. When I look around our vice presidents' table, we've got people that have a real academic inclination. We've got those who are very business oriented. We've got those who are very numbers oriented. Those who are focused on other forms of communication and engagement. The most important attribute, I think, is that they connect as individuals and team members. They all have egos, but their ego is suppressed. They actually are willing to put the institution and its objectives before any of their personal goals and objectives. The alchemy of coming up with that mix is always a struggle because you want people to push and chal-lenge, but you also need that team to have incredible cohesion. I'm very fortunate. I think the team that I've got right now is one of the best I've ever worked with. I'm extraordinarily proud of them. Putting those teams together, I think, is the big-gest challenge any leader faces.

Interviewer: The initial recruitment and really assessing what person to recruit for – that is the key to that?

President: Yeah, the biggest challenge. Then once they're in it, there's the big role of mentoring and helping them fit with the team. And at the same time hearing from them how my leadership is doing and what I need to do to better serve as the leader of that team.

Interviewer: On to your university. What specific initiatives or contributions do you have in mind for the next three to five years? Distinctive contributions of Alberta?

President: Our strategic plan is broken down into five sections. I'm one of these people. I'm a big believer in planning, but I love that saying, "plans never work, but planning does." The plan that we've built at the University of Alberta is built around five verbs. It's a very different one than we've been and done before. The verbs are build, experience, excel, engage, and sustain. Build is about how do you build a great university? It's about bringing in great people, students, faculty, and staff. All of the initiatives there are about recruitment and retention. How do we get those faculty in? How do we diversify our student base? We had huge success in attracting the best from Alberta, and the best from around the world. We weren't known in the rest of Canada, so we built a national recruitment strategy. Just this one example; I'll just give one example from each of the five areas.

Experience is about, in large measure, experiential learning opportunities for students. Moving them out so that they have an opportunity to take what they're learning into the community, to learn and to bring back to campus some of the challenges the community faces. Whether that's in co-op education and engineering or community service learning and the faculty of arts, we're really building those initiatives.

Interviewer: Every student has an opportunity?

President: The idea is that every student will have that opportunity. We're not there yet. We've got more to do. We are in great shape. One of the things that I'm extraordinarily proud of: just a month or so ago, the global rankings QS rankings on employability had us at number two in Canada, and in employability, we were only out of first place by two per cent. It's just huge accomplishments there.

The next verb is excel. There are really two components there. There's building that broad base of global excellence. Ok. That's the base. Then, on that, establishing signature areas of where we are truly national and international leaders. We've gone ahead with that. We've launched four areas. We've probably got, maybe, another two that'll come.

Interviewer: Okay. Can you just give us an idea of what these areas are?

President: Sure. I'll tell you a little bit about the development process first. We didn't impose them. We struck what we call a signature area development panel.

Brilliant academics. Then some academic leadership on it, co-chaired by the provost and the VP of research and called for proposals. About eighty, ninety came in. Then the panel looked at them and said, "Well, there are a bunch here that are related." They got that group together and said, "Ok. Here are all your proposals. Go away and come back with something that brings you together into a true signature." Out of that came four areas. There are probably a couple more that are coming. Among the four that have been approved, energy and the environment, ok, which is one of the key global challenges. Every faculty has people working on that. We have hundreds of people. That's one of the areas of big interaction with Tsinghua.

One that actually surprised me when I first heard about it, but now it doesn't actually, is titled "Research at the Intersections of Gender." It's a little more complicated than that. I prefer to think of it as human identity. Every single social problem we're facing today is affected by the way in which individuals experience and express their identity. What's their gender? What's their race? There is no one community that you and I are a part of. We're white men, but you've had a totally different life than that. Other than that, we may come from different socio-economic backgrounds. We come from opposite corners of the planet. We have a different lived experience. If you think of the big problems that we're facing in a society today – human migration, dislocation, social inequality, income disparity, racism, sexism. It just goes on. Wow. All of this deals with the constructions of human identity. That is something we've got hundreds of people working on now.

Interviewer: In the humanities? Or across different areas?

President: Across all disciplines. That is important. I think we've got some challenges in terms of how we position it and market it, and the language we use around it to make it more accessible. Boy, is that critical. A third is precision health: the revolution in technology from the genome to managing big data. It's all connected. The capacity to bring those new tools together to deal with issues from public health to treating your rare diseases are huge. We have, again, hundreds of people working on elements of that, and we're bringing them together from all of the faculties. The final one that we've approved is around indigenous peoples and First Nations. As in Australia, huge issues. The echoes of colonialization on our society. And our indigenous population is the fastest-growing population in Canada. That community has the lowest educational attainment, the poorest health outcomes, et cetera, et cetera. Unless we deal with issues around reconciliation and the terrible legacy that was left behind, as a nation, we're not gonna be able to survive. We've got to deal with that. Again, we have hundreds of people across campus who are dealing with that in different areas. Whether it's public health – people are out there are looking, trying to get clean water on aboriginal reserves in Northern Canada – or fundamental constitutional challenges that affect the nation's ability to mobilize natural resources.

Interviewer: Each of these signature initiatives track some kind of community, but there's funding or outcomes are polled? Or?

President: There's a little bit of funding.

Interviewer: To get people together?

President: To get people together.

Interviewer: Not to fund the core research?

President: Not to fund the research. The idea is this allows us to point to those areas that we can celebrate as national and international areas of strength. It helps inform the deans in terms of how to allocate scarce resources. It allows us to bring people together from across campus who have never met. There are people who are going, "I never knew that was happening over in faculty of health sciences." We had people who had suggested certain things for signature areas that weren't supported, that had been connected. For example, we had, I think it was, three or four different proposals on micro-sensors. You had one from science. You had something from engineering. You had something from medicine. They didn't know each other.

Interviewer: They didn't talk, yeah?

President: One of the things we've done is there are some areas that we have said, "Okay, well, you're definitely not a signature area now. However, ten years from now, you may be." Keep encouraging those in the background. The idea is that these build experience and excel.

Interviewer: They're not there to stay? They might come up for three years and then?

President: The idea is that these are not going to be here forever. That was "excel." That broad base of excellences. Those pinnacles of global strength, built on those bases of excellence. Build, experience, excel, and engage. That's about community engagement. I mentioned that in my comments about the "role of the president." How do you build a truly engaged university? The title of our strategic plan is *For the Public Good*. Using that lens to view what we do, whether it's teaching, whether it's research, whether it's engagement in the community, everything we do has got to be for the betterment of our communities. That section of the plan really articulates that.

Interviewer: Can I just ask you about that? How do you, if you like, measure the outcomes or the traction that you're getting in the area?

President: Good question. The big challenge there is what level of engagement is important to reward? I think everybody that works at a university, every professor, should be an engaged citizen. I think they should contribute to the United Way. I think they should volunteer in the community. That isn't what we're talking about. That's what being a good member of society is about. This is more than that. This about taking our intellectual capital into the community, learning what the challenges are, and working together to help solve those challenges. Community could be the local residents' association that is struggling with understanding how do we position ourselves for future land use planning development in this area? A global community may be looking at refugees, resettlement, given what's happening in Syria. How do we build those partnerships and relationships so that we're learning what the challenges are, and at the same time using our capacity to help solve those problems and providing connections for our students to engage in that? That's what I mean.

Interviewer: I'm sorry I don't know, but how long have you been coming to China, professionally or personally? What are your main impressions of Chinese higher education?

President: Yeah, I've been coming for, at least, twenty-five years. The transformation has been staggering. I was mentioning to the Tsinghua president that when I first got here, you could walk through Beijing Airport in five minutes. It's different now. It takes you an hour to get from one end to the other. The transformation in China has been staggering. Its role in the world has changed fundamentally. With a quarter of the world's population, this is an extraordinarily important place in the world.

Interviewer: The last question is about global higher education. What do you think of the main roles of large research universities in terms of global higher education? Perhaps, more broadly than that, you've said something about that: now maybe look to the future? How should universities change to become more contributing?

President: Sure. I think building those global partnerships is critical because we all share that goal of making the world a better place through our education and through our research. That is such a huge challenge that no one can do it on their own. No one. Just as I am building leadership teams, bringing people together with complementary skills, bringing institutions with similar interests, but complementary strengths, that is the way in which we're going to solve some of these great global challenges. I think that one of the roles of a contemporary university president is to build those relationships and to talk about how important it is that those relationships transcend the political challenges of the day. Right now, China and Canada are having some political challenges. I'm clear everywhere I go that the relationship between universities and individual scholars, between Canada and China, will transcend those short-term political challenges. We are here. Our relationships will endure. As a community of scholars around the world, if we share those ideals, I think we'll make the world a better place.

11

PROFESSOR WIM DE VILLIERS, RECTOR AND VICE CHANCELLOR OF STELLENBOSCH UNIVERSITY, SOUTH AFRICA

Interview background

Wim de Villiers, rector and vice chancellor of Stellenbosch University, visited Tsinghua University in October 2019 to discuss cooperation between the two universities in the fields of education and research in terms of the World University Climate Change Alliance. Following discussions with Qiu Yong, president of Tsinghua University, President de Villiers was interviewed on 14 October 2019 by Professor Hamish Coates of the Institute of Education at Tsinghua University.

Wim de Villiers, male, South African, born in 1959, medical scientist, PhD, graduated from Oxford University. As a medical researcher, he has published nearly one hundred academic journal articles and received nearly 5,800 citations. Since 2014, he has served as the president of Stellenbosch University. Prior to this role, he served as dean of the School of Health Sciences at the University of Cape Town and held a number of senior positions at the University of Kentucky, including head of gastroenterology and administrative head of the Samaritan Hospital. In 2016, he was appointed a member of the advisory board of the international journal *Gastroenterology*. In 2008, he became an honorary fellow of the South African Society of Gastroenterology.

Stellenbosch University was founded in 1918 and is located in the Western Cape Province of South Africa. Stellenbosch University is a top public research university in South Africa. Over the years, the university has achieved fruitful results in scientific research and education. Among South Africa's universities, Stellenbosch University has the highest weighted research output for full-time academic staff. Stellenbosch University is recognized internationally as a university of excellence. In the 2020 Times World University Rankings, it ranked among the top 300 in the world, and among the top twenty universities in the BRICS (Brazil, Russia, India, China, and South Africa) countries. Stellenbosch University attaches great

DOI: 10.4324/9781003248286-13

FIGURE 11.1 Rector Wim de Villiers and Professor Hamish Coates

importance to cooperation with China and established the China Studies Center in 2005 to focus on China-Africa relations.

The interview covered the rector and his personal background, leadership team, the rector's university, Tsinghua University, Chinese higher education, and global higher education. Key points included adopting a stance to set strategic direction for the institution, delegating and trusting people and partnerships, fundraising and engagement, seeding value-creating partnerships, and ensuring sustainability (Figure 11.1).

The interview

Interviewer: Can you tell us how you invest your time as a leader?

Rector: Yes, so to start, I'm definitely not a micromanager. That's not the best way to spend my time. So it's really to shape the framework within which our university and the people function. I paint the broad canvas. I set the parameters for where we need to be. So it's strategic items. It's vision. It's providing direction. And then you've got to give people the opportunity to get on with the work and trust them with what they do.

Interviewer: In terms of a specific week, how would you divide your time between, say, meetings, or government relations, or meeting with students, or key faculty?

Rector: I would say in terms of strategic direction, it's probably about forty per cent. And a quarter of the time would be meeting with other stakeholders such as government. Students about ten per cent or so. But a sizable chunk in there, I think that's very common to university leaders nowadays, is philanthropy. It's fundraising.

Interviewer: And what does that involve? Bringing people to the university, or moving around the world, or around South Africa, or Africa?

Rector: Yes, all of the above. So it'd be meeting with people in Stellenbosch, in my office, but at their place, places of work. Fundraising in itself is a different matter we can discuss a lot, but it's the balance between friend raising and fundraising. And I always call it the three T's. When we engage with an alumni, it's time, talent, and treasure. It's about transitioning from the time and the talent that alumni spend – because they love their alma mater, and the talent that they invest in, helping young people and whole networks, et cetera – but how to transition that to treasure. That's the challenge. So, it's fundraising for alumni, high-network individuals, foundations, and so yes, it would entail quite a bit of travel, internationally, nationally, continentally, and also to China. I don't know whether I'll raise any funds here, but this is more about the friend raising and international collaboration.

Interviewer: How much of the university's budget is, I don't know how you would frame it, but foundational, from maybe just philanthropic sources? And so why is that a particular focus for growth?

Rector: Stellenbosch University is a public institution. We have twenty-six public higher education institutions in South Africa. Stellenbosch is one of the relatively few research-intensive universities. There are probably four or five out of the twenty-six. Stellenbosch University, University of Cape Town, Witwatersrand, Pretoria, would probably be the main ones. So traditionally they received most of their budget from the state, but that has really diminished significantly. At present, we generate more than fifty per cent of our budget from alternative sources other than the state. We talk about different revenue streams. The first revenue stream is a subsidy from the government. The second is student fees. And then the third would be research contracts: at present that's more than fifty per cent of our budget. The fourth revenue stream would be philanthropy. And then the fifth is what we call commercialization of our assets, so it would be intellectual property, spin-out companies, rental properties, et cetera.

The philanthropy part of it has traditionally been at a fairly low base, but my goal has been to get that to about ten per cent of our total budget, and that's been a significant focus of mine ever since I started as vice chancellor on the first of April 2015: is to get it to that ten per cent. We're at about eight per cent now, between seven to eight per cent. I think that's been a significant increase starting from a relatively low base of about four to five per cent. That is still quite low if you compare it to American universities, but it's more in line with your traditional British university where they also want to get it to around about the ten per cent mark. If you look at our European counterparts – Dutch, German universities – philanthropy is virtually non-existent there. So that's been a significant development for us.

Interviewer: Is there a tradition of philanthropy towards universities in South Africa?

Rector: Nascent. So that's what we're trying to develop.

Interviewer: Sorry. With regard to universities or giving generally in the community?

Rector: I think giving generally in the community is fairly common, but that would be traditionally, predominantly, to say your church, or it would be a school or some other types of other charities – the SPCA, for example, animal cruelty or wildlife preservation or something like that. But universities not so much because universities have been seen as being funded sufficiently by the state. But we have managed it. So that is how a big focus of mine has been to broaden that donor space. So if you look at a university like Harvard – or if everybody uses Harvard – then if you look at more like a liberal arts college in the United States which is quite a well-known small liberal arts college, they have about ninety-two per cent of their alumni giving. Harvard's probably about sixty per cent or so. If you actually look at the mean for US universities, it is about eight per cent. So where are we at the moment? We're at about three per cent. What I want is to really expand that base of our alumni. We have about 120,000 or 140,000 alumni nationally and worldwide, so it's not only focusing on the high-net-worth individuals, whom we all know and they're in our databases, and they get a lot of traffic and asks. But it's really to get to the broader base, smaller gifts, and also as I said, to make that transition between time and talent and, eventually, treasure.

Interviewer: And specifically from alumni or broader philanthropic sources?

Rector: So yes, you would start with alumni but then definitely with broader philanthropy and foundations as well. For example, some of the larger American foundations, whether it's the Mellon Foundation that funds humanities predominantly, or if it's the Ford Foundation, or Bill and Melinda Gates, or Michael and Susan Dell Foundation. They have specific areas that they focus on. Is that philanthropy? Yes and no because it's focused on a specific project that they're interested in. For example, the Dell Foundation would be interested in providing access to undergraduate students and then also ensuring student success. The Gates Foundation goes more recently for agriculture, for research in specific areas in medicine or. So for example, we're very big in TB research, HIV research, and malaria research. Those are all, I mean, The Gates Foundation's goal is they would like to eradicate malaria, and they would like to develop a vaccine against tuberculosis, and we're recently part of that.

Interviewer: Just moving forward to look at your background a little bit more. How do you think your disciplinary background as a medical doctor affects your work as a university rector?

Rector: Yeah, I think that's a very interesting question. I've reflected on that. In some way, as you may know, the higher education situation in South Africa has been very complex, very challenging recently, for a number of reasons. Predominantly funding reasons, and student protests, and around fees, and some political instability, and perhaps disillusionment with post-1994 developments. And we're a relatively young democracy. I always say it's a young democracy. It's sort of an adolescent democracy. So adolescent democracy comes with all the temper tantrums and the hormonal swings that go with that, so in that sense, we've had some challenges. So, I reflected on how my disciplinary background would help me to deal with some of these issues. I'm a physician, a medical doctor. I'm a gastroenterologist, specifically. And I think if you actually look around the world there are quite a number of examples of physicians that lead universities. I think we're sort of hardwired, without realizing, as part of our training to listen, to diagnose, to treat, but also to try and prevent. So we're pretty good at listening, getting the information, distilling it, formulating a differential diagnosis if you want to. Doing certain tests and interventions and then re-evaluating and going from there. The other point that I think helps as a physician to deal with very complex issues is, one shouldn't personalize any criticism. It helps one to compartmentalize which is a very, I think, important thing to do. So for example, you're scheduled as a patient in my doctor's office; it's a ten- or fifteen-minute consultation. You've got some relatively trivial problem. I deal with it. The very next patient may have a potentially lethal diagnosis with a very bad prognosis, and I need to deal with that for twenty, thirty minutes or so. The very next patient may have another type of diagnosis that's not nearly as serious, but each of these encounters you have to give one hundred per cent of your attention to. And then immediately move over to the next thing. So it's the issue of compartmentalization, and I think without really being aware of it, physicians are hardwired into that sort of thinking and dealing. I think it helps one to deal with complex issues.

Interviewer: Just looking a bit more broadly, your personal work is related to your work with your leadership team. How do you engineer the balance of that team in terms of risk takers, creative people, financial managers, inwardly looking people, outwardly looking people? In terms of specific roles, or how you run meetings, or how you hire people or reward people? What is the balance of that team, and how do you keep it working smoothly and objectively?

Rector: So just in terms of a helicopter view again, I'm not a micromanager. I give the broad general direction, and then I trust people to get on with the job. I'm very fortunate to have very capable people doing that. The specific system within which I function is not like the American presidential system, that when I come in, I bring my own team. You inherit a certain number of people and they have defined terms.

Interviewer: Can I ask you to say more about that? They're not appointed directly by you?

Rector: They're not appointed directly by me.

Interviewer: So they're appointed by other people, or?

Rector: Yes, so they would be appointed through the university structures. So by the senate and by the council.

Interviewer: So the CFO, or whatever the title may be, you don't have direct line control over that?

Rector: I do have direct line control of them, but I may not necessarily have appointed them. I may have been chair of the selection committee. I'll give you an example. In our leadership structure, we have, say, a deputy vice chancellor for teaching and learning, so a senior position. It's a person who's appointed for five years, and it's renewable for another five years. But that person was actually appointed before I started, so they would continue with that role, including a second term. What I mean is that in a sense, you inherit part of your team. There's an evolution of people that, yes, are appointed during my tenure, but not necessarily so. If I can concretize that: we have a deputy vice chancellor for teaching and learning. We have a deputy vice chancellor for research innovation and post-graduate studies. There's a position that I actually created, which is a deputy vice chancellor for strategy and internationalization. I created that position because of a very strong emphasis that I put on internationalization. And then we also have a deputy vice chancellor for social impact, transformation, and human resources. That person was also appointed during my tenure.

Interviewer: Can I ask you to say a little bit more about that role? I noticed compassion is one of your strategic objectives.

Rector: Yes. Absolutely. That's one of our core values. Again, our core values as a university – I'm a physician so it's pretty easy to remember the acronym that goes with our core values. It's ECARE. So it is excellence, compassion, accountability, respect, and equity. In terms of social impact, you have the traditional pillars. You have teaching and learning, and you have research, but we're also focused on social impact as a core contribution to society. So, given our history as a university, and as a country – a complex history – in how we really impact what we do as a university, my line would be that the research and what we do should be locally relevant, regionally impactful, but globally competitive. When I say locally relevant, we deal with some very complex issues and challenges, the wicked challenges, the wicked problems, or these multidisciplinary complex issues. My other line is I quote the four horsemen of the apocalypse: unemployment, poverty, inequality, and corruption. Those are four very difficult societal issues within which social impact all play a very important role. In this respect, the deputy vice chancellor for social impact, transformation and human resources has a very important portfolio. They are responsible for integrating and coordinating all the different products, projects we're involved with, so that both our students and our academics focus on how we impact society, and how society interacts with us. Stellenbosch University is an example of a university town. It's a relatively small town by global standards, about one hundred and fifty thousand or two hundred thousand. And our university is about thirty-two thousand or thirty-four thousand students. We're one-third postgraduate, so very strong research-intensive university. But it's a university town. It's an example of a university that's almost part of a town-gown network. There's a very close link between the town and the gown. We had our centenary in 2018, and we invited a number of other examples of town-gown universities for example, St. Andrew's, Princeton, KU Leuven in Belgium. Those types of examples. There are not many of them, so we want to form a network, an international network of university town-gown networks because there are specific issues in how you relate with your local environment. At the same time, we have a very continental look. We're in and part of Africa, and that's certainly where we see our primary focus. But I commissioned an economic impact study of the university and the local community, the municipality, whatever. What is the impact of the university? It was a very good study. It was actually very conservative, as they should be. It was difficult to know what to do with that information because it became very clear the university is the gorilla in the room. The university is so big in the local economy that you've got to be very careful about how you influence this balance. And that's what I think this town-gown network will help us to take forward.

Stellenbosch is in the Cape Winelands, which is a beautiful and picturesque area about fifty kilometres from Cape Town. It is a university town where we also have these other societal problems. That's important because Stellenbosch is actually an ideal living laboratory. It's a microcosm of all these different problems. So you can, through social impact and various community projects, really address a multitude of these different problems. Our DVC for social impact, transformation, and human resources has developed, I think, something that's quite novel. It's a social impact knowledge platform. How do we actually measure the impact? You know, we're all about numbers, we're all about data. That's pretty easy. How many PhDs? How many post-grads? How many master's students? But how do you actually measure social impact? The social impact knowledge platform is a good example of the progress we've made.

Interviewer: Is that an institutional management platform, or is it public?

Rector: It's an institutional management platform. The other very important part of my management team is the chief operating officer; the others are more academic positions.

Interviewer: So there is teaching and learning, research, social impact…

Rector: And internationalization. Those are the DVCs. And then there's a COO. It's the commercial side, so that's a very large portfolio with much more of a business outlook.

Interviewer: Human resources as well?

Rector: Human resources is actually under the DVC for social impact, transformation and HR. But in many universities, HR would be under the COO. So that's something one could look at. Here in this current environment in higher education, one comes in for a lot of criticisms about the corporatization of higher education. But my tagline there is, "Look. We actually need to be business-like, not business light." We just do not have it in our environment; you've got to work carefully with sustainability and your resources for optimum use of resources.

Interviewer: The COO, you were saying...

Rector: Yeah, their job is to run that part of the university.

Interviewer: Who does the liaison with government around policy and finance and the like?

Rector: It's me. In the end, the buck stops with me as chief executive officer. When government wants to speak to the university, they speak to me.

Interviewer: Can I just ask you a little bit more about your university's ambitions? What are the specific, if I can say, three- to five-year operational challenges around some of your ambitions? What are the major risks?

Rector: Thank you very much. Some would say I'm a sucker for punishment, but it's actually very enjoyable. So what would I say my priorities would be for the second term? There are a number of them. The major challenges specifically in South Africa, and for Stellenbosch University as a research-intensive university, are the financial challenges. It's financial sustainability against the background of an economy in South Africa puttering along – it's about one per cent, one-and-a-half per cent growth rate. It needs to be at least three to four per cent. That in itself then puts a burden how the government can fund the university. So as I described earlier, I'm trying to wean ourselves from government more and more, with more emphasis on public-private partnership initiatives. That would be a very important priority.

Another challenge is how we provide access to previously disadvantaged, or disadvantaged, students who struggle both academically and financially to make that transition to higher education? So, the sustainable nature of that funding to help them. It's not enough to provide access but to ensure success. And to ensure success, the term more and more that we use in South Africa is "wraparound support." So it's not enough to just get them to university. They need accommodation that would enable them to be academically successful. And also to make that transition to writing, reading. Those are academically crucial for success because it's a challenging environment.

Interviewer: The demography of your university's quite different to the demography of the country, and I'm not sure of the demography of the broader Cape Town region. But that's not an issue with admissions. That's clearly an issue with the schooling system and broader social factors. Can the university play a role in reaching down and changing the pipeline of students, or is that a matter of time? Or is it a matter of the schooling system? What sort of initiatives would help?

Rector: Yes, I think it's a complex question. It's not just admissions. Let me explain it this way. The university system is about a million students at the moment in South Africa in the twenty-six public higher education institutions. But the pyramid is inverted. The base should be the TVET system, the technical and vocational educational training system. That should be the broad base of a pyramid going up. Universities are elitist by nature. It's a different type of education. In the case of South Africa, there are too many students in the university system as opposed to the TVET system. We need to transition to much more significant support of the TVET system because the workforce of the future is from technical and vocational education and training. That's definitely a challenge. To come back to your question, we certainly recruit far and wide. Our demographic at this point overall is more than forty per cent black, coloured, Indian, Asian, to use that terminology. But in post-graduate it's significantly more than fifty per cent.

Interviewer: Post-graduates come straight through from undergraduate, or they…?

Rector: They come from across the country. It's a combination. If you're looking at what Stellenbosch University as a research-intensive university is producing, this past year, we had a record number of PhDs – three hundred and eight. We're about eighteen hundred master's students. But if you compare it to the system as a whole, Stellenbosch University on its own produced more PhDs and master's students than nineteen of the other twenty-six South African universities combined. When I talk about what I see as our mission, our duty, our contribution as a national asset, it is developing this academic pipeline and developing professional, quality people.

There's another reason why universities are sought after in South Africa, why you have this bypassing of the TVET system. It is we've got a very high level of unemployment in the country: about twenty-seven or twenty-eight per cent, and even higher than that among eighteen- to thirty-five-year-olds. But if you're a graduate of Stellenbosch University, your unemployment rate is four per cent – four per cent versus twenty-eight per cent. So it is seen as one way out of poverty.

Some of the other priorities that I see – it's certainly finances. That's probably the more boring part of a university leader's job, but extremely important. As would be looking at internationalization because we are part of a global world in terms of both students and staff. But what I'm extremely interested in is three initiatives we're looking at. One is that we recently founded a school for data science and computational thinking, which was quite a feat. It's a school that's alongside faculties on an equal footing, but it's multidisciplinary. It's inter-faculty. It's aimed at both under and post-grad courses students. Faculty are very enthusiastic about it, and we've received significant buy-in. So bioinformatics will feature. A lot of the economics and management sciences. And also where, I'm gratified, humanities will play a significant role, so linguistics, geography, information science, law, ethics, cybersecurity. We're getting buy-in from a lot of people on that.

The second initiative, and why I'm very pleased to be here at Tsinghua, is that we were invited to join the Global Alliance of Universities on Climate. We've got a number of research centres and centres of excellence involving academics in climate research – water, renewable energy, biodiversity, food security, all these. We've got a very strong faculty of agricultural science, so we are extremely involved in issues of agriculture economics, land reform issues. So that's the initiative on climate.

And then thirdly is if we look at the future world of work, including data science. You get the school for data science and computational thinking, and so you get computational thinking that is part of data science. And then you get the applications of data science. I'm not saying that everybody needs to do programming when you're at university. Yes, we have boot camps in programming, but it's not necessarily so that you need to know programming to work with big data sets, but increasingly the question is being asked.

As I said, Stellenbosch is a century old. Universities are institutions for change and for the ages. Some of the initiatives I'm involved now with – you know, we're developing new campuses or new buildings, for example – we may only see the benefits, or the mistakes, fifty years from now. That's an important insight to have.

But what are universities facing? Are we still relevant? We get those questions a lot.

Interviewer: While in Asia there will be a slight decline over the next twenty years in traditional university students, Africa is expected to see quite a large increase. Does that play into your thinking?

Rector: Yes.

Interviewer: How, how are you going to serve that market?

Rector: We see a very large increase because there is the large group of people below twenty-five or so – well, fifteen actually, so there's a bulge there. We see a very large increase, about a billion population, in Africa. Do I see that at our university we can physically have more students on campus? We're capped at about thirty-two thousand to thirty-five thousand I would say.

Interviewer: By government or by space?

Rector: Space. We'll either have to have different satellite campuses or do it in a different way. A strategic decision and our decision is to look at a hybrid learning strategy: it will be partly digital, partly online, and with some contact time.

Interviewer: In Stellenbosch? Or it could be anywhere?

Rector: It could be anywhere, but some contact time. What our research has shown is that it's extremely important to have these contact time periods for networking and other opportunities. That's when you can utilize university facilities during so-called dead time. Everybody said massive open online courses are going to mean the end of university. But, you know, it's the same as when Marconi invented radio. They thought, "Oh. That's the end of university." Or when Baird invented television. They said, "That's the end of the university." Or when the internet came along. "That's the end of university." No. Universities are institutions for the ages, but we have to adapt. Hybrid learning is in our strategy. It's the same courses you would get when you're a residential student, but they're stackable so you can do them in different modules.

Interviewer: How do you enrol in them? Separately?

Rector: You can enrol in them any time.

Interviewer: And at a certain point, you would just build them up into assessed units.

Rector: Yes. They're assessed.

Interviewer: I could be here in Beijing.

Rector: Correct. That's our model, and over the next five years, I would really like to put a lot of emphasis on that.

Interviewer: Some broader questions about Tsinghua specifically. What interests you most about Tsinghua? You've said a little bit, but just to go into some more detail, what are the factors about Tsinghua that most interest you? I'm not sure how long you've been coming here or your experience with China or Tsinghua.

Rector: Limited experience with China. I've been here once before. It was my pre-vice chancellor days. It was as a physician. But Tsinghua, of course, is very highly regarded internationally. It's the number one university in China. It's a comprehensive university of repute. We're very pleased to be here as part of our international strategy, and as part of this Global Alliance of Universities on Climate, to really expand this collaboration. We have our focus on internationalization; about fifteen per cent of our students are international. That's twice the national average.

Interviewer: From other African countries or from anywhere?

Rector: That is from anywhere, but most of them, sixty per cent of them, are actually from Africa. I would like to expand our number of international students because I believe that the diversity of cultures and experiences really enrich what we do. And especially because I believe universities are uniquely situated to really address the very complex societal issues we face. We will do it better if we're part of a group; for example, climate – all the different issues we need to look at in addressing climate challenges. I'm very excited to hear more from Tsinghua. It certainly plays a leading role in the Global Alliance of Universities on Climate. In addition, I do have a bias towards medicine and allied health sciences, and in research in that area, and Tsinghua has an outstanding reputation.

Interviewer: What challenges do you think might shape the future of a university such as this one?

Rector: Well, I think the sky's the limit for a university such as this one. It seems to be financially in a very favourable position. It's investing a lot of resources into research. I'm not exactly sure what percentage of its budget, but it looks very good. Can the global economic downturn affect its growth trajectory? Certainly. In a more global, political sense, there are perceptions of threats to academic freedom. That may be an issue, or a trade war with the United States.

Interviewer: Big global factors.

Rector: Yes, but that's uncertain to see. Another point I think for university leaders is, there's a lot of uncertainty in the world, and we can only control what we can control. So work within your locus of control and try and effect a positive change there.

Interviewer: What are your main impressions of China's higher education?

Rector: I think very favourable. Certainly, there is massive funding. There is a lot of planning that went into this. There's been very deliberative intervention to raise the profile and to increase access, and it's paying off. In my experience in the United States, where I was a supervisor for a number of Chinese PhDs and also post-docs, I think it was interesting. I was there for about eighteen years and towards the end of my time, more and more of them were actually returning to China. I thought that was a very interesting switch that they certainly saw their future, their academic future, their research futures, as being very favourable here. If you look at descriptions of universities, they're often thought of as very hierarchical, or there's a lot of centralized planning. But the best universities are distributed organizations. Or at least that's been my impression, or my experience: distributed organizations. I think in the Chinese setting, that centralized planning has had a very important role in the success of universities. But to ensure future success, there also has to be institutional freedom. I think that's going to be an interesting transition, where you have a highly centralized plan and the evolution to a more distributed organization. Twenty years from now when people like industrial psychologists of the world look back, I think they'll find China's universities a very interesting system to study.

Interviewer: Could you say a little bit about what should be the major contributions of universities, obviously there's a context that you bring being in Africa and working globally, in terms of your research and education contributions. What should universities be doing in this, in this sort of way to contribute this in the current global environment?

Rector: I've said quite a bit on that already. I think the important thing is really, I made mention of some of the wicked problems, some of the very complex societal problems. I think universities are best suited, from a multidisciplinary input, to address these issues in ways that are, you know, locally relevant, regionally impactful, and globally competitive. If you look at our new vision and our strategic plan, and I'm using this an as example of how we can be impactful, we want to be Africa's leading research-intensive university, globally recognized as excellent, inclusive, and innovative. We also want to advance knowledge in the service of society, and that's a very important kicker. Universities can't be ivory towers. They have to have an impact in service of society. We've chosen a number of strategic areas we'll prosecute to help with that. We've got five we're looking at, and they are really aligned to the Sustainable Development Goals: one, the natural environment; two, health and human security; three, social justice and development, and I think a very important one in South Africa at this time, four, human creativity and social innovation; and lastly, systems and technologies for the future.

The important part, if we think of a contribution to society and the future world of work, is increasingly when employers tell me they want fit-for-purpose graduates. That's not what I want to do at all. I don't want to deliver fit-for-purpose graduates. I want to deliver graduates who have all-around attributes that enable them to really adapt to the future world of work. I'm not doing what I was exactly trained for in the beginning, so there's been an evolution every five years or so. That's what we want for our graduates: to have an inquiring mind, to be an engaged citizen, to be well-rounded individuals. That's what they need to succeed.

Interviewer: Do you think – if I can focus a little bit more on doctoral education – do you think that PhD programs are training people well enough for the faculty jobs of the future? Does every PhD student at Stellenbosch learn about hybrid learning and teaching? You know, should we be doing more and different things in the PhD?

Rector: I'll answer in two ways. When we look at our undergraduate program, also post-graduate to some extent, we've got a curriculum. All right. There's a curriculum that gets on their transcripts. You passed courses A, B, and C. We've also developed a co-curricular model. And the co-curricular model is focused on imparting soft skills. How to have difficult conversations. How to mediate complex problems, et cetera.

Interviewer: Management skills.

Rector: Management skills. Softer skills. We have a number of places in the university where these courses are offered, at present mostly on a voluntary basis. But this is the important thing: when they finish these co-curricular courses, they also get put on their transcripts. I've found increasing interest from employers who look at these co-curricular activities as well. So that's number one.

Number two, you asked about the PhD program. We've got a very exciting initiative at Stellenbosch. It's called the African Doctoral Academy. It really speaks to our being rooted in Africa. For the African Doctoral Academy, over the last ten years, we have had four thousand five hundred participants from all over Africa who attend for a two-week period or so – summer, winter, and now also autumn schools. It can either be prospective PhD students, current PhD students, or young, relatively junior staff. They engage with some of our academics and with academics from Europe, Canada, North America, et cetera, who teach research methodology (both quantitative and qualitative), how to write a proposal, academic skills, et cetera, and the very important soft skill of networking. How do you develop a resilient research network that would enable you to go back to your home country to continue your work? It's when you become part of a larger academic community that you can really, in a meaningful way, look at complex problems. We've got very strong links with Malawi, Rwanda, Uganda, Tanzania, Ethiopia, Nigeria, apart from the countries in southern Africa.

Interviewer: Not just the technical skills, also the broader management skills.

Rector: Exactly.

12

PROFESSOR LAKSHMAN DISSANAYAKE, VICE CHANCELLOR OF THE UNIVERSITY OF COLOMBO, SRI LANKA

Interview background

Lakshman Dissanayake, the former vice chancellor of the University of Colombo, visited Tsinghua University in October 2019. He discussed exchanges and cooperation between the two universities and the Asian University Alliance. On 21 October 2019, Professor Hamish Coates of the Institute of Education at Tsinghua University conducted an interview with President Dissanayake.

Lakshman Dissanayake, male, Sri Lankan, born in 1955, demographer, PhD, graduated from the University of Adelaide, Australia. He is mainly engaged in research in the fields of demography, regional development planning, health demography, and post-disaster reconstruction. He has published many professional books and many academic papers in international journals. From 2015 to 2019, he served as the vice chancellor of the University of Colombo and founded the Colombo University Community Centre to promote the development of the university system in community service work. Before serving as president, he served as a member of the Executive Committee of the University of Colombo Alumni Association and vice president of the University of Colombo. He is also a fellow of the Royal Society of Arts, has won the Sri Lanka National Award (Vidya Nidhi), the University of Colombo Excellent Research Award, and awards from the university's chancellor and board of directors.

The University of Colombo was founded in 1921 and is located in Colombo, Sri Lanka. It is one of the top ten universities in South Asia. It leads particularly in the fields of mathematics, computer science, and law. The school has a multiethnic and multicultural group of teachers and students and is committed to promoting social harmony, cultural diversity, equality of opportunity, and unity. The University of Colombo is a member of the Asian Universities Alliance and has established extensive contacts and cooperation with many universities around

DOI: 10.4324/9781003248286-14

FIGURE 12.1 Vice Chancellor Lakshman Dissanayake and Professor Hamish Coates

the world, including Durham University, Moscow State University, National University of Singapore, Tsinghua University, and Peking University.

The interview focused on the vice chancellor and his personal background, leadership team, the vice chancellor's university, Tsinghua University, Chinese higher education, and global higher education. The interview emphasized quality as a top priority, being selected as a vice chancellor, international connections, and sustaining national conversations amongst leaders and government (Figure 12.1).

The interview

Interviewer: Could you tell us a little bit about how you invest your time as a leader, how you spend the average week?

Vice Chancellor: Ok, now in fact, I'm very much interested in the quality of university education. That's number one priority for me because I recognize a university is a student-centred institution, so they are at the centre. So, I really want to improve the quality and also the relevance. Quality is number one priority. We think, ok the quality is all right at Colombo University, the best university in Sri Lanka, and we can compete with anybody. We have the best students. I have about forty-plus years' experience in the university as a teacher and a researcher, so I know exactly what quality means. It's not just because I've been teaching. We all have to eventually change our teaching, right – materials, everything. We have to update our knowledge. In that context, the academics, teachers, and the researchers, they have to actually improve their knowledge in order to deliver the best knowledge that you can think of in that particular discipline.

Also, whether you like it or not – because I know that so many people argue that, ok, university is for education, not for anything else, and so we should not be actually linking with other parties and so on. But my position is different. I really want to go along with the world, where the world is heading, right? So, during my tenure as the vice chancellor, I tried my best to look at the relevance of the University of Colombo's education to the country, as well as in global terms. That's where in fact, I put a lot of energy into that because I really wanted to improve the quality. That is why we have a quality assurance unit.

Interviewer: But you meant quality in terms of the global standing and recognition, not just the internal quality? So in terms of the average month, how would you have gone about executing that agenda?

Vice Chancellor: Yes. You see, all the universities in Sri Lanka are public universities. There are fifteen public or state universities. There are private university colleges affiliated to international universities, but they are not recognized as universities. So there is an umbrella organization, the University Grants Commission (UGC), and it has a Quality Assurance and Accreditation Centre. We have set up internal quality assurance units in all the universities, so Colombo University also has one. During the past four years, I have never missed one single meeting. I actually chaired the meetings. If I am not there, it will surely postpone until I return because I really wanted to show my colleagues' quality is the number one priority because whether we like it or not, there will be some private university colleges very soon, right? It is inevitable. We need to prepare for that. There is huge competition, but we don't have competition in terms of undergraduate education because our undergraduates are given to us by the UGC, right? So, Colombo University gets the cream, right, but that won't be there for many more years, right?

Market could change, but the post-graduate students are very much stable. I was the dean of the faculty of graduate studies some years back, so I tried my best to improve post-graduate education at Colombo, and I still try my best. I am a believer that unless you improve the quality of post-graduate education, you will not be able to improve the quality of undergraduate education because the research, the teaching that you do at post-graduate level, will have greater impact on what we do at undergraduate level. There is a strong link between the two.

Interviewer: Would you say there was quality assurance? Did you get strongly attracted to the quality agenda because there was a problem with the quality, or because you just saw that it was innate to specifically move ahead with that?

Vice Chancellor: Because, you see, as academics sometimes it is taken for granted: ok, we do well in all our disciplines. But we don't do well, right, because I have seen problems in many areas, even though we assume that we are doing really well. And also, we do a lot of tracer studies also with our undergraduates to see if they've got proper employment and so on.

Interviewer: You were doing that or the government? UGC or you did that?

Vice Chancellor: We do that. Yes. Because we start actually with the graduation ceremony. Then thereafter, we do studies, tracer studies, so that will give us some feedback whether we are doing right or not because they have to be employable. I mean when it comes to their soft skills – because you see now, there are jobs in public sector organizations, but private sector is moving in Sri Lanka. So I mean that is where the most employment opportunities are generated and, therefore, we need to prepare students for that.

Interviewer: Did you spend much time speaking with employers?

Vice Chancellor: Yes.

Interviewer: How did they influence or react with the UGC? I mean, does UGC consult with employers or that's your job as well?

Vice Chancellor: No. We can actually because we are bit autonomous, so I wanted to be autonomous. We get a hundred per cent funding from UGC, but that is not enough if we really want to be innovative and dynamic and take things forward.

Interviewer: They control the funding support, if you like.

Vice Chancellor: If you are a powerful vice chancellor, you can still negotiate, and you can, in fact, get the funding that you want. That is what I did because I'm senior enough to do that. It's something to do with your personal network, in our part of the world especially, because the UGC chairman and I stayed at the same hostel, right, during undergraduate days. And also the other people like the minister of higher education, he was one of our students. He did his LLM in Colombo, and the secretary to the treasury. So I have actually worked with him, examined PhD thesis, and so on.

Interviewer: So the stars lined up for you to effect some change?

Vice Chancellor: Yes. For me. That cannot be seen as a common thing, so it's a special case. That is why you need that maturity when you reach the vice chancellor's position and you occupy that seat. You should have that network ready for you, then it gives a big advantage to the university.

Interviewer: So did you manage, through your leadership, to change some of the protocols around how the UGC would support the further growth of the university? What are key changes?

Vice Chancellor: Now, because we have a Vice Chancellor's Committee, all fifteen vice chancellors get together every month across the country. And then once every three months, we meet the UGC, so UGC with the vice chancellors. We put forward our proposals to them and then we discuss. So the UGC is very much interested in increasing the number of students, but even sometimes without thinking of funding. But, ok, if you really want to increase the number of students, we need to improve the environment in the university to accommodate them.

It's not the number, but we have to think of so many other things when it comes to the number. For example, an area that I have in fact put effort into and changed the UGC's mind is the disabled students. We have about fifty blind students and some other disabled students with a lot of walking difficulties. So we have started in fact preparing our buildings because we didn't have elevators, we didn't have ramps. We have blind students who couldn't find our rooms, offices, which has been fixed, right? They have access now. They can come to my office by touching the signboard that is outside. And also, we have set up an information centre in the library where other students read some books and make recordings. And also gender aspects of our student population. I'm a demographer, so I'm very much interested in that, and we in fact do a lot of work related to gender issues, and I was one of the people who prepared the women's policy for Sri Lanka also.

Interviewer: Women's policy.

Vice Chancellor: Policy on women, yes. That is on several aspects because women are the majority: fifty-one per cent.

Interviewer: In the country or the university?

Vice Chancellor: In the country. At the university, in some faculties, we have eighty per cent girls and twenty per cent boys. So we have adapted a policy even at the university to give women an inducement to study higher education.

Interviewer: I'm starting to get the sense that a lot of your time is invested in working with the other universities and UGC, and with government, to try and advance the broader standing of the university, as opposed to running internal processes.

Vice Chancellor: Yes, we are the oldest university, and we have great traditions. We are about one hundred and fifty years old – we are celebrating that milestone next year. So the mechanism for running internal processes is set, right? We have the heads, the deans, and the senate and all that, so I ran all these meetings and the Deans' Committee.

Interviewer: They're fairly well oiled.

Vice Chancellor: Yes, they're well organized, and then we have the registrar, the bursars, and others. They're ok, but you need to be, you need to be hundred per cent sure that they are really well because you need to be very thorough about meeting the requirements of the University Act. That is what the university's run by. We have internal circulars. We have UGC circulars; they bombard us with many circulars from time to time, but we post also. We have tried our best not to actually.

Interviewer: A circular is a slight policy revision or amendment or something?

Vice Chancellor: Yes, for example, recruitment procedures. UGC will say, ok, you have to have two years for lecturers. The schemes of recruitment and so on are governed by the UGC.

Interviewer: Can I just go through a little bit more your background as a demographer and how that would've shaped your work as a leader?

Vice Chancellor: Yes. A demographer is a social scientist, right? So because of my discipline, I had to do a lot of research at grassroots level and also you need to look at the social behaviour of people. You need to understand, you have to connect with, people. That's very important, right? So I did a lot of research, I still do research, and that helped me to do a lot of good things as vice chancellor because being analytical, you can actually – when there is an issue you try to logically argue, ok, what would be the best solution for that? Also, being a social scientist, you can connect with people. When the student unions come and see me, I know how to connect with them because I was also a student activist during my younger undergraduate days. I know exactly what they wanted from the administration. I tried my best, even as a demographer, to take the university beyond its physical boundaries because when we are undergraduates, we just were there and in isolation. In the university, we didn't have much contact with the outside world. So I tried my best to take the staff out, bring in experts from the private sector, industry, and so on. We set up spin-off companies which worked with private sector, and we have gone for innovation, product development, and so on.

Interviewer: So, understanding people and their perspectives?

Vice Chancellor: Yes, I'm interested in their characteristics. For example, I'm interested in the gender policy because I have been thinking of that for many years. So when a man, actually the boss, talks about gender issues and all that, I mean, it's very important not to take that for granted, and for the women at the university to come forward and work on the issues that affect them. We have set up a gender centre in the university, and if there are any views or anything like that which are inappropriate, they can go and complain, and we do incur inquiries.

Interviewer: Can I return to your leadership team? We've said a little bit about these people already. What was your capacity to design or recruit those roles or manage them? How did you get the right balance between people who were doing innovative, externally facing things, or progressing internal change, and people who were running the business, running academic affairs? Just a little bit about those.

Vice Chancellor: Yes, so the university is structured, the vice chancellor is there and then, you know, the governing body. In our system, we have the council, that's the governing body, which includes outside people plus the deans and the directors. The vice chancellor chairs the council meetings. The deans are usually elected by the faculty, so the dean has to be a leader. If you want to be a dean, you have to be a head of a department because you need to have that maturity with some experience. From the heads, one person will be elected. Most of the time it's unanimous because we don't want conflicts created at faculty level. But outside council members, usually the ministry and the UGC, send them to us. But if you are powerful enough, you can…

Interviewer: You can actually talk to the minister and the UGC chairman and say, "I want this guy. I want a lawyer. I want an accountant." So in fact, the council's appointed and the deans are elected, so your capacity to appoint people around is fairly limited?

Vice Chancellor: Yes.

Interviewer: Compared with, say, the American or the Australian cases where people build their own executive teams. It's quite different.

Vice Chancellor: It's a very prestigious position to be a member of the Council of the University of Colombo. Members come, and we make some payment for sitting. But our council has the people, right, like we have accountants, we have lawyers, we have private-sector business guys for the IT sector and other places of industry. So, it's really good.

Interviewer: The council or the leadership team, the people directly reporting to you?

Vice Chancellor: No. That is the deans. Deans are the senior management team, together with the registrar and the bursar.

Interviewer: So who manages, for example, international relations or research?

Vice Chancellor: International relations, we have an international office. There is a director.

Interviewer: They're not in the senior leadership group?

Vice Chancellor: They're coming under me. No, we don't actually invite them to the leadership meetings.

Interviewer: So, it's quite a traditional academic or collegial leadership structure.

Vice Chancellor: Yes, we inherited that from the British.

Interviewer: Yes, within the deans, you're going to have people who are more entrepreneurial or people who are more educationally focused?

Vice Chancellor: Yes, but usually to become a dean, you have to be smart enough because otherwise, people won't recognize you. So therefore we usually get a better person as the dean, but if the vice chancellor is smart enough, he should be able to actually convince someone to another way of thinking, and this is what I have done. In fact, together with my deans, we created two new faculties during my short span of time as vice chancellor. We didn't have a faculty of technology: now we have one. We also now have faculty of nursing. We actually had programs in two other universities, but I thought it would be better that we have a faculty of nursing.

Interviewer: How about some of the big challenges and opportunities for, and distinctive characteristics of, Colombo as a university? You can think as big as you want. I mean, it's the national flagship, so there's a global challenge; there's a regional challenge.

Vice Chancellor: Yes, we have those challenges. As an undergraduate and then an academic, I spent a nearly half-century, forty-six years, in the University of Colombo. I have seen a lot of changes, a lot of changes in the higher education sector, locally as well as globally, because I was able to go overseas for my postgraduate studies. I travelled for workshops, conferences, and all that. I have seen the changes taking place. With all that experience, I have been trying my best to educate my fellow vice chancellors in the system, not just thinking about Colombo but also the whole higher education system.

Interviewer: Who appoints the vice chancellors in Sri Lanka? Are they appointed by UGC, or are they elected?

Vice Chancellor: It is elected. It is usually advertised in the media, then we apply, right? We apply, and then there will be a screening process to look at our credentials; there will be an evaluation committee, and a group of council members do that. Then you need to go and make a presentation before the council. Then the council elects three people, and they send those three names to the UGC, which recommends those three according to the priority. It's like a post office, just stamping. And then it goes to the president of the country.

Interviewer: For all universities or just Colombo?

Vice Chancellor: All universities, yes, president of the country. So I was in another vice chancellor position before this one.

Interviewer: Oh, you reapplied?

Vice Chancellor: No. I applied in 2007, and I was elected, but I was apolitical. I am not a political guy, so I was not elected. It's a bit political. It's not just your background.

Interviewer: The UGC supported you, but the prime minister…?

Vice Chancellor: No. In those days, the UGC was different, highly politicized. It's different now; not the same people. So, therefore, I could not actually get supported the first or the second time. The second time when I was denied, there was, there was a huge protest from the university committee that gave that decision, the whole system, because they thought, ok, we should have the autonomy to elect our own vice chancellor because that applies to any university. So the third time, then it was a very new government, so they just gave me the chance, and realized, ok, it's better that we give the university autonomy to elect the chancellor.

Interviewer: So the universities get more autonomy?

Vice Chancellor: Yes, autonomy because I have shown the difference, shown how we can improve, how we can run a university in a better way, being impartial and being non-political.

Interviewer: That's one quite substantial development or initiative that you've succeeded inadvertently in changing.

Vice Chancellor: Yes.

Interviewer: Are there distinctive other actions where Colombo fits in terms of regional, global engagements? I mean, you're here visiting Tsinghua. Have you sought to internationalize the university?

Vice Chancellor: Internationalization, in fact, I promoted it very much. I had two things in my mind in the last two years of my tenure as the VC. One is we need to do more on internationalizing our education, our university. You can't just do things in isolation, and I have attended so many meetings. I mean, I've met some universities, which also has provided a huge opportunity for me to share my experience with some of the best university presidents in that network, so I took that experience with me, and I tried to internationalize. We were looking for partnerships, so partnerships matter a lot for any work that you do; it's not just the university. I do a lot of partnership work with many universities in the world over the last four years, and also improving the research profile.

Interviewer: You mean globally or regionally?

Vice Chancellor: In the region and globally because we all have some contacts with a strong base through our PhDs. If you take the University of Colombo, I think more than eighty per cent or ninety per cent of faculty had PhDs from the West or the developed countries, right? Therefore, we have very strong international faculty teams. Now I got my PhD from Adelaide, I'm a visiting professor there, so a few back, I went there to do a lecture. You see now, we still have those connections, and we send some of our junior colleagues to them for post-graduate training. Similarly, I encouraged others also to establish those relationships.

Interviewer: People-to-people links.

Vice Chancellor: People to people, like what is seen in the BRI – Belt and Road Initiative, right? That is very important because you need connections. Why not, build upon those? But Asian Universities Alliance (AUA) was something very new to us, and I was a very active member in AUA. I thought lots of good things that can happen to higher education in the region and beyond. It can make a huge influence on Asian countries.

Interviewer: What are the most interesting perspectives that you have about Tsinghua? What interests you most about Tsinghua?

Vice Chancellor: Tsinghua is actually a very high-ranked university in the world – I think twenty-seven or something around the twenties, and number one in Asia. So you would naturally take the university to a higher level and also, innovative, right? Innovation is something very important and dynamic, something like the AUA, and now Tsinghua has realized that they have lots of connections. But if you really want to make an impact on the global map, you start going beyond your physical boundaries. That is what Tsinghua has said. This is something that I really admire, and that is why I said so. The decision to go beyond your physical boundaries has to be taken by the leadership and the management of the university because nobody else is in a position to make that decision. So I really appreciate the work that the leadership has done and also the effort put into this because you see now some of the best universities in this region are together and already better things are happening, and they have produced a higher education report. We can do more, much more, right? And we can look at how we can make an impact, like looking at what I suggested some years back: accreditation of some courses, quality assurance. So if the AUA can actually take the leadership in that...

Interviewer: You mean shared AUA courses that are transferred amongst the universities?

Vice Chancellor: Yes. Start with the region. If Tsinghua can actually do that. I'm very fascinated with this Belt and Road Initiative network because you see already, we have this Maritime Silk Road, right? So there were lots of connections with China, the trade, and the civilizations, lots of connections. You don't have to invent something new. Already the BRI network is there, right? If you go along with that network, then you go beyond Asia because it goes beyond Asia, and AUA has to get that link...

Interviewer: Align AUA with BRI. There's a job for you.

Vice Chancellor: Yes. I'm just thinking. Yes, I've been in fact thinking because I've read the BRI, and I'm fascinated because you see what is lacking. Even if you look at, China, the government of the state, actually invests a lot. What I have been telling my government also, you ought to invest. You pick certain good universities and invest. Unless you invest, you will not see any innovation. If you don't see any innovation, you won't be able to establish or produce a creative economy. It's not just a knowledge-based economy. You need to have the creative economy. So there is a strong link. If China wants to do that... Now China invests a lot of funds in higher education sector, but at the same time, you have to attract best-quality students. Sometimes – because I have been trying to encourage some of my colleagues to come over here, some of my students to go to China – I have seen a different China because you see what some people don't know, right?

Interviewer: How many years have you been coming to China?

Vice Chancellor: That is the difference with some of my colleagues. My first visit was in 1986 or '87. That's a long time back. So I have seen the changes.

Interviewer: Before your PhD?

Vice Chancellor: Before my PhD, yes; immediately after my master's I had the chance to go to Honolulu. So there was a field trip, actually because I was in the East-West Institute, and the Population Research Institute, so I was there for a month, and we came here – Shanghai and Beijing – for a one-week visit here. About seventy-five of us were here, not from Sri Lanka but all over the world. So I have seen the changes, and my goodness! But I saw the symptoms of development also during that time, and I thought, ok, they are moving forward fast. If they really want to attract more students from our part of the world, they're going to actually talk to people. At the undergraduate level, ok, Chinese language is all right, but if it is post-graduate level, the people are looking at English media courses. So that is something that the universities here have to —.

Interviewer: Are you talking about the Chinese proficiency of Sri Lankan students, or the English proficiency of Chinese teachers, or a bit of both? There's a language issue?

Vice Chancellor: Yes, it is the language that truly works as a barrier. Because you are competing with the best, right? Because definitely, the US, it is Australia and New Zealand, the UK, are doing that. You see now, two hundred Sri Lankan students actually work at NASA, right? I mean, every year, our science graduates, they go to the United States. But also, if you go and see some of the laboratories, the IT faculty, and so on, they are doing very well. So that exposure is not there. So, you see now, the BRI, one of the five concepts is people-to-people connection, right? You need to actually put a lot of effort into that so that the embassies, the other institutes, can play a greater role in that aspect to educate local people. I don't think that is happening to my expectations.

Interviewer: Can I ask you the final set of questions? They are really about the contributions that these researching universities can make to the world. Forgetting what they are doing, what should they be doing? It may be with your knowledge about educational research or doctoral programs or something else.

Vice Chancellor: Yes. Doctoral programs. We have to devise evaluation procedures. Take, for example, doctoral education. You need to attract the brightest students, the brightest innovators. They will not care to come to a university that is fifteen or twenty-four hours from their home base, just to work in a tiny space. Can they come and have a working space in your department? I have been talking to my colleagues, saying we must be able to accommodate them, right? And so the working conditions have to be changed, right? I know the world is heading for AI. The social scientists are scared of that, and they are thinking, ok, the whole world, the universities, are heading for that. But social scientists have a seat at that process because they are the people who find issues, problems. Others can criticize IT people, but social scientists will find solutions to the problems that IT people unearth.

Interviewer: So, how to give energy to the social sciences?

Vice Chancellor: Yes, because you need to understand that, right, so then you are on the basis of what we find, the other people actually try and find solutions and also the consequences. We are the people who can actually find what are the consequences of those innovations, like, so they know what—has the solutions. Are they good for the society or bad? For example, Facebook and all that? So, I mean, you see the social consequences. So, we try to actually find them and disseminate that knowledge and try and find solutions, again the technical solutions, but maybe the alternate solutions.

Interviewer: Like the creative humanities, create responses in the humanities. I think that's a challenge for most countries.

Vice Chancellor: Yes, you have to create this. It's not the social science that we had long years past, but you have to be creative within your discipline and also you have to be entrepreneurial now. It's not just education for education's sake; we have to have partnerships beyond the university boundaries.

Interviewer: I think that's a big enough agenda for the next forty years.

Vice Chancellor: I really want to point out something very important. You see now the way that we improve ourselves. We will have more and more centenarians and super-centenarians. It's not just we die out around seventy or eighty years of age. You'll reach one hundred years, one hundred and ten years, and so on, right? So what happens then? You work for about thirty, thirty-five years in the labour force, workforce, and then you reach sixty or sixty-five, and then you have another forty years to do whatever, right? That's the biggest issue for governments. Universities can be very innovative if you think about lifelong learning, so there shouldn't be any age discrimination if you look at it from the demography point of view. So you need to be creative.

Interviewer: So going back to school and retrain is the answer.

Vice Chancellor: Yes, I mean that is why I always say if you really want to solve the issue of the burden of your elderly population, you will have to invest in the current labour force. You have to create more decent jobs. You have to improve their income, productivity. That will improve their saving capacity. By the time they reach sixty or their retirement age, they will have some accumulated wealth in their pocket, so they can use that money for their long lives.

Interviewer: OK, thank you for talking with us.

13

PROFESSOR GUIDO SARACCO, RECTOR OF POLITECNICO DI TORINO, ITALY

Interview background

Guido Saracco, rector of Politecnico di Torino, visited Tsinghua University in October 2019. On 24 October 2019, Professor Hamish Coates from the Institute of Education at Tsinghua University interviewed Rector Saracco.

Guido Saracco, male, Italian, born in 1965, engineering scientist, PhD, graduated from the Polytechnic di Torino. Since 2018, he has served as rector of the Politecnico di Torino. Prior to this role, he served successively as a professor of chemistry at the Politecnico di Torino, and head of the Department of Applied Science and Technology. He is a member of the Turin Academy of Sciences. An expert on the energy sector, Professor Saracco is also a member of the Steering Committee of the Advanced Materials and Processes for Energy Applications section of the European Energy Research Alliance. As a well-known engineering scientist, he has published more than 500 papers in national and international journals and is the author of eight patents.

The Politecnico di Torino was founded in 1859 and is located in Turin, Italy. It is one of Italy's oldest and largest universities of science and engineering. It ranked 47th in the 2020 QS World University Rankings of engineering and technology. Its architectural design, computer science, civil engineering, automotive engineering, mechanical engineering, and other fields enjoy a leading position in Europe and the world. The Politecnico di Torino is one of the first universities in Italy to offer English courses and has carried out extensive inter-university cooperation on a global scale. The school and Tsinghua University have in-depth cooperation in student exchange, joint scientific research, and master's dual degree programs.

The interview touched on the rector and his personal background, leadership team, the rector's university, Tsinghua University, Chinese higher education, and global higher education. Key points included the need for the school to catalyze

DOI: 10.4324/9781003248286-15

FIGURE 13.1 Rector Guido Saracco with Professor Hamish Coates

innovation within the region, forming partnerships with companies, listening to and motivating faculty, fostering young researchers, and inspiring people to be proud of the institution (Figure 13.1).

The interview

Interviewer: Can you tell us a little bit about your disciplinary background – you're an industrial chemist – and how this affects your life?

Rector: I'm a chemical engineer; this is the place where you are learning how to manipulate matter for good use and to produce goods. Chemistry is where you have the management of energy and matter together, so it's very nice engineering; it's at the bottom line of several things that happen in the real world. Also, life in a way is based on engineering and molecules, and that's nice, I have enjoyed being a researcher for a long time, in fields like environment protection and renewable energy, CO_2 removal, and conversion, giving back life to CO_2. That was my background, that bridges science and technology: it's a mix that is represented very well in my university, that is a university of technology. The technology is science-based and so I feel the centre of gravity within my discipline and my university that is a technical school, so engineers and architects basically.

Interviewer: And does this affect your work as a leader?

Rector: Well, not the discipline itself, but the career. I was first a single researcher, elbowing up to become as fast as possible associate and then full professor. Then I was going abroad and I was developing my own publication record. But when I became associate professor, I needed to establish a strong group in the department, and so I became a leader of a group. Leadership was a matter of inspiring young researchers and bringing funding opportunities to the group because it's an expensive field of research.

The next step was to become head of the Department of Material Science and Chemical Engineering. Then a further step was to promote the merger of this department with the Department of Physics, and then I became the head of the Department of Applied Sciences and Technology. That was preparing me for a next step, but for various reasons, it was not time to be a candidate for president of the university. There was a two-year gap: when I finished my period as the head of my second department mandate, I decided to get outside and lead a research centre at the Italian Institute of Technology as a director. It was dedicated to sustainable future technology, so always in my field. The Italian Institute of Technology is based in Genoa and has some eight hundred researchers, but in satellites, and one was in my town. After two years there, it was sort of, let me say, a final destination to become a candidate for rectorship. From the time I became full professor at thirty-seven years old, I liked very much to take care of people, and I think that function of a leader is essential. I was a candidate for rectorship; I had to learn better the rest of the world outside the very technical, and that was very nice because I spent some nine, ten months getting to know architects better, which is different to the world of engineers, designers, and planners, and they are quite peculiar because they have social sciences inside. I thought they're so different from engineers. That was important, and that was inspiring because I believe that social sciences that are present in those departments should be present also in the departments of engineering because now the world is so complex. If you don't have these tools to understand the diseases of the society you encounter, and the reaction of mankind to technology, then you cannot be a good designer of technology as an engineer. Creative engineers, I call them, instead of nerds. And it's funny. You become a better person, as well as you start communicating. That was a time where I really designed this program as a rector, and I was competing with one lady and one guy, so it was a strong wind. The rector by the way is elected, so when you talk about leadership, it's an election and it's a struggle; your mandate should come from the people. It's an election, and so you should not evade them. But I'm a good motivator basically, someone that likes to go beyond and give opportunities, and this my way of handling things.

And I convinced my university, and I'm now very happy with what I do. After my election, the next surprise, I would say, after being astonished by the culture that was present in other departments from mine, was that as a rector, I became an important person for the rest of the city, maybe also the rest of the country. I met a lot of people I didn't know before, and that opened my mind further, gave me more opportunities to exert my leadership role. As I am an opportunity maker with a problem-solving attitude, that is nice, really nice. It's a wonderful time for me.

Interviewer: Can you just say a little bit more about the mechanics of how you moved into the job? You were in the university, you moved out of the university for two years?

Rector: For two years. It was not necessary to go. It was just I wanted to get out of the contest for the new rectorship, and there are several reasons for that. But then I came back. You can have a sort of sabbatical year, but I had a couple of years. It's called going into a "waiting position"; something like this is the name it has in Italian.

Interviewer: Yes. It's not uncommon?

Rector: No. You still remain a professor at Politecnico, but then you move outside. I was fully paid by another body, and then I came back. It's kind of like an industry placement or a transfer. But it was also giving me...any time I move, any time something changes, you grow.

Interviewer: Say a little bit about your campaign. You have to go around the departments and meet?

Rector: Yes, it's like a politician, politics, but it's not offering things. It's learning and proposing something. I'm not a sharing politician; I'm a creating politician.

Interviewer: So you go around and basically give people a sense that you can help them create a vision for the future? Your opponents are also doing this?

Rector: No, they were more door-to-door, feeling similar to people and thereby acquiring their votes. I didn't see much vision. They tried to comfort people with, "You are similar to me, I will preserve you." But I think that we are in a crucial moment because we need to change as universities. Change the way we are teaching people, doing more applied and interdisciplinary research, and try to favour technology transfer by merging with industries in sort of colocation centres where university and industry live together. For me, this was my strategic plan. The reason is that outside the world is changing so fast due to technologies that in a university you cannot grow that fast, and you need to have someone from outside to help you teach. You need to provide those that are outside with continuous education because you are doing the research. But my motto shifted from a "manufacturing university" that produces the same quality engineer that it shaped 160 years ago, where we were funded for basic science in the first year, then technology, and so on. We need to move from this concept to a "platform university" where you are mixing with society and having professionals, managers helping you.

Interviewer: From industry?

Rector: Yes, to teach and to bring the students to some real problems, complex problems. How to solve them is not a mathematical equation. It is a way of thinking that you need to create a bigger sense, and this is difficult. We are in Italy, underfinanced by our government, and we are flooded by students, and so it's difficult to have this way of discussing things. We're looking for an alternative to transferring information from one teacher to a class of two hundred people, and first year is like that. So it's a huge task, and we need to build new spaces for this new way of educating with round tables rather than seats in a cinema.

And we need to bring companies inside – we call them challengers. So within your career – independently, whether you are a chemical engineer or a mechanical engineer, an architect or a designer– if you work together on a specific challenge, you can find solutions that are much more than when you have only one type of engineer. So, these kinds of classes or summer schools with different universities now provide the students credit that they're valuable for whatever recreation course. But this needs to be done, and involve as many students as possible, because now you need flexibilities, capability to interact with people with different expertise, and a capability to communicate things, starting from a strong background of your own. This is my great project.

Interviewer: I'm going to come back to that. Can I stick with your leadership for a little? How do you invest your time as a leader? how would you say in, maybe, a week or a month or whatever period, how do you actually go about doing your work? Walking around the campus, working with the government, working with the companies?

Rector: I have different ways to be close to the people. First of all, I have a team of vice rectors, that is numerous, much more numerous than ever before. I have twelve vice rectors and one deputy rector, and one of them by the way, Michele Bonino, is the vice rector for China. That's so important, China. I meet them every week for one half hours.

Interviewer: All twelve?

Rector: Fine-tuning, all twelve together.

Interviewer: Just bring all the problems and all the issues together?

Rector: Yes. Then I have two governmental bodies, the senate and the Board of Governors. I have three meetings in between the official sessions where they decide things because there are so many things running with my rectorate that you need to keep them updated. Every six months, maybe less than six months, I go and meet people. I divide into three-hour sessions, dividing them into areas like electronics, and telecommunications, and informatics, and mathematics. With also the technicians and the administrative people together. I talk about major issues and explain things and get their feedback. And with these things, I think this is needed, otherwise you get lost. And if you get lost, I mean if you lose the attention, the motivation and the understanding of people, I mean in and since you are elected and we are so burdened by work for the students, we have a tremendous rate, the students versus professors. It's our Achilles heel, to be honest at the moment, but it's like that in Italy in general, because of underfunding, and then so many people too. If you lose any single—any single professor is essential, so if you start losing people, it's not good, so for this reason I tried to talk with them. It's a lot of work, but part of the game as a leader is played by being inspiring, doing things that make our people proud to be part of the university. For this reason, I try to inspire people by shifting from self-referencing to a university that is producing an impact on society.

We have gained a lot in this year for our reputation. Just to mention, I proposed a concept for making a strategic plan for the city of Torino where our campus is. A plan referencing new manufacturing, outer space, merging with companies. That strategic plan with the town itself was not there one year ago. Two days ago, I was asked – by the unions, the industrial association, all the major industry of the town, the governor of the region – to present this plan to the prime minister of Italy. It was all the people; that was nice.

Interviewer: So a lot of your time's been working with people outside the university?

Rector: My role is first of all to catch opportunities outside.

Interviewer: Within Italy, or Europe, or international?

Rector: I have three vice rectors for international affairs. One is general international affairs, one is in Europe, and one is in China. In a way, when you want to have an impact as a university, you should dedicate to your territory and your country as a must. And this is the way we get out of this crisis and reset our direction: international activity is important, but we need to bring our country abroad with us. We're in China. We're discussing just a few minutes ago establishing a legal entity here in Tsinghua, which Politecnico has a good relationship with. Through this legal entity, we can bring also our architects, for instance. We have plenty of architects in Torino and not many things for them to do in China, but they could design things like health facilities. In Uzbekistan – which is in the middle of the Belt and Road Initiative – we have a school of engineering, established ten years ago: our Turin Tashkent Polytechnic University. We are producing world-class engineers with fifty of my professors that go there and teach Uzbeks.

Interviewer: Governed by your university?

Rector: No, it's a private university, funded by Uzavtosanoat, that is the car making company of Uzbekistan, formally was General Motors. My university hosts the largest General Motors reserve centre in the world outside US, and we have a good relationship. General Motors decided ten years ago to start producing cars in Uzbekistan. They needed us there, and they opened this university to produce engineers for them.

And now we have broadened the offerings to ICT and civil engineering. We are doing many things. I was this morning talking to a former Uzbekistan minister of foreign affairs, Dr Norov, who is now head of the Shanghai Cooperation Organisation that links Russia, middle Asian countries, China, and other Asian nations. This is nearly forty per cent of the world's population.

Interviewer: Shanghai Cooperation Organisation – SCO?

Rector: SCO, yes. When you have an education body so important, it's the best university in Uzbekistan at the moment, you have a leverage effect by bringing companies with you from your country. I mean we are teaching the new talents of Uzbekistan, and Uzbekistan is growing. It's a better situation than expected. I mean you can do things there. Russia has sanctions against it. I have someone taking care of the issues with Russia, but it's difficult to work with Russia, and now it's becoming difficult to work with China, but it's essential to work with China.

Interviewer: Can we move to your team? These are your reports, but there may be other people. How do you get the balance of people right between creative types, between administrators, between the international people, between the academic affairs people, government relations?

Rector: Yes, there were some criteria that I followed when selecting the people.

Interviewer: You get to select these people?

Rector: Yes, myself. I nominated them, I decided. I was elected, but then I decided all of them. First of all, a loyal team. I was not going to waste effort to gain some support from those areas that maybe were not supporting me as a rector in their vote. Because I said, well, I'm going to be a driver. I'm going to have a bunch of people; I need people who have my full confidence. And we are going to be judged; I don't want to waste time. On including someone. It was a strongly won election. I was elected with twice the votes of the second person.

Interviewer: You pick your vice presidents from the faculty?

Rector: Yes, I take all from the faculty. You may be elected as a vice rector also from outside, but it's very rare and so it's an internal process I will say.

Interviewer: How about women, in your team?

Rector: Yes, they are half and half. I selected my deputy, a lady; she's a professor of urban economics, and I have six male vice rectors. I decided to give a signal in that direction, but you know it helps. However, you know, STEM has a worldwide problem for women. But we are doing as much as we can.

Interviewer: You meet with the vice rectors for one and a half hours a week. How do you maintain the balance of the interest between growth and new developments, and dealing with problems, dealing with staff problems and student issues, dealing with money, dealing with the politics? How do you reconcile all of those competing demands?

Rector: Yes, what I feel is that this synthesis among different issues is on my shoulders a lot. There is no one else who has this sensitivity, let's say, and responsibility. And it's complex. But when you want to drive a holistic system like a university, with confidence towards objectives, everything is linked to anything else. Anyone, from a single professor to a single department to a single vice rector, only sees its part and tends to evaluate things – global things – only from his or her point of view. I feel it strongly, but I feel rather confident about this. I think this is my duty and if I don't take the right decisions, then it's worse. Maybe I can force a beat, but then when you see things globally, my duty is to find win-win conditions. The more I find, the more people feel confident and will follow me.

Interviewer: Exactly what period of time do you have?

Rector: Six years.

Interviewer: Renewable or six?

Rector: No, it was four plus four, but the legislation changed and only one so that you can really do something, have enough time to do something, but you cannot be re-elected. And the idea is that if you have a second mandate, then you're not doing much in the first mandate to be re-elected. As I told you before, I don't trust this way of thinking, because I think that I must involve people. And so I don't fear any election. I even proposed to have a check, with secret vote, after three years. And if I'm not able to bring people with me, I have no problem. But this…

Interviewer: Don't waste their time.

Rector: Yes, even if it is not foreseen by the legislation. Just going to be a poll, like that. But now we have the reshaping of our annual budgeting, that is to be done, and I'm doing very in-depth work on the spending review.

Interviewer: That you reformed, you mentioned education but also research realignments with business. Does that actually involve structural change and change of the business process?

Rector: I'm not free because as a public university I'm bound to some roles, and so on. Then I have the administration that has grown a lot in the last decades. There are twice as many administrative people than technicians, and I changed it.

Interviewer: Twice as many administrative staff than…

Rector: Yes, technicians in the laboratories.

Interviewer: Not faculty.

Rector: Personnel not doing research but helping with technical things. As a research university, it used to be the other way around: more technicians and less administrative people. But the bureaucracy is burst a lot, has grown a lot.

Interviewer: So you see your role as to adjudicating between different perspectives and trying to make the value creation that you can?

Rector: Yes. But there is one instrument I have. Some psychologists from the University of Torino – this is the other university in Torino that is quite complementary because they have social sciences. These psychologists have developed a test for the index of motivation and stress on your job, and I am applying that on all my personnel from academics to administrative people, technicians and personnel, general personnel. And I have the index of how people feel, the different departments, in the different areas, and I am going to ask the managers, the heads of department, to improve this. It is going to be an index of evaluation of their structures because I really think that motivating people is important.

Interviewer: Is it a questionnaire of some sort?

Rector: Questionnaire, yes, with professional psychologists that look through the answers.

Interviewer: All faculty do this or just the managers?

Rector: All. And by forcing this to become one of the evaluation things, I am expecting that most of the people are going to reply, so this is important for statistics. From the first application, it turned out fifteen per cent of my academics are burned out. You know what that means, burned out? Those that are feeling so bad because they are not, well…

Interviewer: Is there any that feel supported, rewarded, encouraged, inspired?

Rector: No, they feel angry because they feel a value in themselves, but they feel exploited and not taken care of by the system. I used to say when I succeed in motivating someone, this is equivalent, more or less, to hiring someone new.

Interviewer: Yes, turn them around.

Rector: It's nice. I suggest this survey is something to be done everywhere because we have agreement to administer surveys, and I'm going to have this survey as one of them.

Interviewer: Sort of staff health and well-being surveys?

Rector: Health, well-being, and motivation. It's also needing to understand the motivation and how you feel valued not just stressed. It's a bit more complex, and that's fine. I take care very much of this.

Interviewer: So far, you have given a sense of your background, and your work as a leader, and your work with your colleagues across the university. You've said already a few things about your distinguishing initiatives or challenges. Where are you pushing forward? You mentioned obviously budget. And you've talked about industry; I don't know quite the word but it seems more than "collaboration," almost a synthesis with some industry in terms of knowledge, shared knowledge creation. What are the big challenges that are around for you?

Rector: Yes, I think that education is the largest because you need…

Interviewer: What level, the PhD or the…?

Rector: Everyone, because you need to create creative engineers, which is something that someone thinks, oh no, an engineer is a sort of nerd type, and not a creative guy. First that. And I told you more or less what is needed for this. Second, you need to provide an education to managers of manpower in the industry because technologies are changing. And you are doing research, you are the closest to the new wave of technologies, and so on. And this a completely new stuff. You need to reshape the content of graduation courses fast. You step into a five- to six- to seven-year track of courses – it depends on how good you are obviously – the courses need to change. If you are trained according to the courses approved seven years before you finish your program, then you get out, and it's a completely different world and so on. It's complex, but it's the main challenge.

Interviewer: How long does it take you? If you think of a new course or program or whatever you call it, to get them approved?

Rector: Oh, it could be a year. But I cannot change alone because you have a certification every year, and so on. But it can be done, it can be done.

Interviewer: It takes a year?

Rector: Yes, takes a year to change, but the problem is that my colleagues that are professors, they tend not to change or tend to…. I have created a teaching lab where you are educating the educators.

Interviewer: Just say a bit more about this.

Rector: It's a place where they meet pedagogy experts that are telling my professors how to shape their courses, having less information and more discussion. Having an exam done to understand better whether the guy has not just a good memory but a critical sense on things that he learned or she learned. It's a nice thing. I call it the beauty farm of our teachers because they go there to refresh and become better teachers.

Interviewer: Can you just say a little bit about the professors at the university" It's a lifetime position, like tenure?

Rector: Yes.

Interviewer: So how can you…?

Rector: If you hire them then you are done. If you don't make a good choice, and especially if they become burned out, then it's for life, and then it's not acceptable. There is a colleague of mine who conceives of competition in this way, that eighty per cent of people don't add value, and twenty per cent of people in the university do anything useful, and you should reverse these proportions. But this is nonsense, I mean for me at least. I need to change things and create the win–wins.

Interviewer: How do you get people to change?

Rector: Incentives. We are giving every faculty some money for its research. Now we are asking them to invest them along the guidelines of the strategic plan. Not just freely, but if you want to improve your course, or if you want to buy an apparatus, or if you want to invest in the PhD student with this money, then you can do that. It's about money; it's about giving them a bit of freedom. When any single ant goes in the right direction you have movement in the university. You can't overrule a professor in Italy. You cannot say, "Well kick him out or kick her out." The only chance is to motivate our people. I think I'm a good leader for this. I would not be a good leader for, in times of crisis, to divide people and to say no. I'm good at heart, and I don't want to blame people too much. I would like to inspire them and get them out of the hole where possible.

Interviewer: Let's turn to look finally at Tsinghua, then China, then the world. When did you first start coming here and what are you most interested in about Tsinghua?

Rector: Last year I was involved in a very interesting conference on the topic of changing education that automatically classifies Tsinghua as a leading university. I think that as the world is changing so much, also we have to change a lot as a university, and we are changing a lot as a polytechnic. Those that change and do the right things better have a chance to become the best universities in the world. It's not really my goal to climb up the rankings. But you know, I feel we can do a good job. My impression of Tsinghua was good, very good, and I'm back here. I've just asked to create the only hub of my polytechnic, a legal entity, exactly on this Tsinghua campus because of the fact that this is the best university in China.

Interviewer: What challenges do you think Tsinghua and Chinese higher education more broadly might have?

Rector: I simply think that first of all it will be stupid not to have engagement with Tsinghua or, you know, China. There are some geopolitical issues that are tremendous at this moment and I'm facing pressures from US representatives sometimes to take care, be careful, et cetera. But I think China in some sectors, like informatics or mobility, energy conversion, is now the best in technologies; it will be simply stupid not to cooperate. That's the first thing.

Interviewer: From a scientific perspective?

Rector: Yes, but also, I hope, since there is a lot of economic growth and opportunities, that my country also can catch opportunities in China. I mean we as a country are too weak to be protectionist. Italy is facing a bad period with this. Protectionism is killing us, because when US fixes taxes on products from China, China's overproduction bursts into Europe, and we are just killed whenever protection starts, starting with taxes, and that's bad for countries that are not strong enough. So this is a very bad moment and I tend, within the limits of politics given by the politicians, to do as much as possible. For this reason, I believe that it's important to cooperate with China because now China is the leader on technologies.

Interviewer: So can I just ask you to go the final part, the role of universities, and the role of the research university, in the world? Where do you think it needs to go?

Rector: I think that technology is becoming – for any kind of profession I would say, including humanists, sociologists – there is a need to know about technology because technology is influencing our society a lot. With this in mind, a technical university such as ours' has the responsibility to convey, outside its borders, knowledge to society, and to explain things. I think that the role of universities, and of the research university in particular, is now fundamental to this very peculiar moment when we are facing economic crisis.

Interviewer: In Italy or internationally?

Rector: Yes, internationally. In Italy, we are not well off because of several intrinsic weaknesses, but globalization is…

Interviewer: What specifically do you mean? Political or economic or historical?

Rector: The weakness of Italy is fragmentation and small, medium enterprises, only a few heads of big companies. And yes, there is this weakness, but universities now can be a sort of catalyst. The research, if it does impact society, applied research and basic research is cheaper than what you could do as a company on your own. We have seen that when the General Motors centre came into our campus, and all the buildings around filled with companies that are making partnership agreements on education because they need education. In turn, they give us education and applied research. So we are creating this concept of colocation centres; it's something similar to what the European Institute of Innovation and Technology created in Europe. Knowledge and innovation communities are places that mix blood between university and public bodies, decision bodies and companies. Something similar is happening in London in White City with Imperial College, merging with companies there. In Pittsburgh in the US, something similar; so there was a crisis after the steelmaking companies failed and Pittsburgh based its rebirth on the university, and now they have a wonderful health district, for instance.

Interviewer: So building knowledge and innovation communities?

Rector: Yes.

Interviewer: And sometimes the small steps happen quickly, but is there really change of culture in terms of the university?

Rector: Yes, but in Torino, we have a nice situation: we have former industrial areas that are now empty.

Interviewer: So you have space?

Rector: And then with the remainder of the companies around, we are going there, finding the gaps and recalling new companies there, around disciplines. So there is a district of industry 4.0, the digitalization, the district of automotive, the district of aerospace.

Interviewer: Can I ask you how you envision training the faculty or the workers, if you like, for that new future? Do you think the current PhD or undergraduate program is sufficient? You've said a little bit about this.

Rector: The PhDs are disciplinary in nature because they tend to, we say in Italy, split a hair, split a body hair into four pieces, but it's also nice to see how much you are asked for by companies, by society, and so this should motivate people. Of course, it needs some leadership to my professors, but I'm succeeding in getting a lot of investments from outside to go in that direction of engaging with companies and society. Of course, I would not go in that direction based on my own resources because it would be immediately cutting into our budget for something. But if it's the strategic plan of my town, region, or country, and they invest in me to go in that direction, it helps a lot. I see that there are also companies ready to do this. So it's a matter of not taking financial or logistical resources from people working for me to do the same job better, improve it. Anything extra should be funded from outside because it's for the sake of boosting the outside. And this is working.

Interviewer: So in a way, it's new communities but also new resources?

Rector: The point is that if you split the resources into single, small projects as they used to do – not only the governmental bodies, also the bank foundations that were just doing social things by giving money here, here, here – now they're also working together to produce leverage effects. So putting resources where they can create more value, and everyone is focusing there. Now in my town, we are the driver of this process, yes, but it was not there two years ago, so it's something that is coming out of our design or vision, and it's an exciting time. But our region is six points of the gross internal product, which is less than in 2008, so we are not recovered yet. It takes time to build new industry and new economies, but then when it starts, you grow a lot. I think that we are at the right moment to do things, with critical mass, with cohesion between every possible actor. I feel optimistic, and I think that we can provide a new model for other regions, other districts.

Interviewer: What sort of benchmarks do you look for around the world for these sort of new innovation communities? I know the Dutch are doing work like this, the Chinese.

Rector: White City in London and the Manufacturing Technology Centre in Coventry. In Pittsburgh. The innovations where they work with the university. But generally, as far as research innovation is streamlined, not education, Germany is structured with big university institutes that are applying the research towards the companies around. The knowledge and innovation communities are something funded by the European Institute of Innovation and Technology, and that already has several locations on specific themes. What we plan to do in our town is to have six of these on the strong points of our town: manufacturing, industry, cars, hydrospace, circular economy, regeneration of urban sites. We are an ancient town but we have a lot of buildings from the sixties that are simply breaking to pieces because concrete is failing, and so there is a lot of work. Health is important where we have a big hospital; we can merge the medical department with bioengineering department, create a good mix to have research for companies like pharmaceuticals, robotics for surgery, and that's going to be another interesting point. As in Pittsburgh, it is something similar to Pittsburgh: they were doing steel. It has this strong health-related research.

Interviewer: Ok, thank you for your time.

14

PROFESSOR AIJI TANAKA, PRESIDENT OF WASEDA UNIVERSITY, JAPAN

Interview background

Aiji Tanaka, president of Waseda University, visited Tsinghua University in October 2019 and had an in-depth exchange with President Qiu Yong on further strengthening cooperation. On 31 October 2019, Luo Yan, an associate professor of the Institute of Education at Tsinghua University, interviewed President Aiji Tanaka.

Aiji Tanaka, male, Japanese, born in 1951, political scientist, PhD, graduated from Ohio State University. Since 2018, he has served as the president of Waseda University. Since taking office, he has upheld the university governance mission of understanding and respecting multiculturalism and emphasizing the cultivation of international talents. Before serving as the president, he served successively as Waseda University's director of academic affairs, deputy provost and senior executive director of the Academic Affairs Executive Committee, and director of the Global Education Centre. President Aiji Tanaka has long been active in international academia. He is dedicated to the study of voting behaviour and the field of public opinion and served as president of the International Political Science Association from 2014 to 2016.

Waseda University was founded in 1882 and is located in Tokyo, Japan. It is known as the "first private university in Asia." The Ministry of Education, Culture, Sports, Science, and Technology of Japan focuses on supporting universities in pursuit of "academic independence, flexible use of academics, and model citizens." Waseda University is a member of the top universities of Japan's Super International University Program, the Pacific Rim University Alliance, and the Global University Advanced Research Institute Alliance. It ranks 189th in the world in the 2021 QS World University Rankings. The school attaches great importance to international cooperation and exchange and focuses on integrating industry and academia.

DOI: 10.4324/9781003248286-16

FIGURE 14.1 President Aiji Tanaka with Associate Professor Luo Yan

Since 2009, the number of international students enrolled at Waseda has ranked first in Japan. In 2019, President Qiu Yong visited Waseda University and signed an agreement to expand the scope of academic exchanges between the two universities.

The interview focused on the president, his personal background, leadership team, the president's university, Tsinghua University, Chinese higher education, and global higher education. The president talked about investing time to improve the university, recruiting outstanding and promising young professors and managers who will surpass us in the future, focusing on scientific research, cultivating students' resilient intellect and encouraging them to dare to face novel problems, and being sensitive to people from diverse cultures and backgrounds (Figure 14.1).

The interview

Interviewer: Where do you invest your energy as a leader?

President: I'm trying to invest my energy in sharing the value of making my university better. Actually, I'm saying to my fellow professors and also my colleague administrators, "Let us think that we have to make up our minds. We should be determined to make Waseda one of the universities in the top grouping in the world" – what I'm calling "a world standard university." Waseda should be one of the top leaders, the top thirty or top forty, or it could be top fifty. If everybody in the world, I mean university professors in the world, hear the name of Waseda, then they should recognize it and say, "Oh, that's a good school." In philosophy, in literature, in mathematics, in physics or economics, or education, or political science, or in law, or whichever – in every single field. If university colleagues in the world think, "Oh, I know someone in Waseda who is doing good research, and I know that Waseda is educating good students, and their education's good, and their research is very interesting." That means Waseda is one of the top universities in the world. Tsinghua is such a university. Tsinghua is already a top university in the world. I'd like to share that kind of value with my colleagues. To achieve that goal, the most important thing is we have to employ, hire, good people – good young professors and young administrators with potential who will exceed us. Young professors will be better political scientists than I am in the future. We will employ young administrators who will be better than directors and managers among my colleagues. Waseda should be raising our students to be those who will be contributing to the world, not only to Waseda itself, not only to Japan itself but also to the world. That's the kind of value I would like to share with my colleagues. I have to spend most of my energy to share this same value with my colleagues.

Interviewer: That means the value of being excellent?

President: Yes, being excellent. Waseda should be the university which can receive international respect.

Interviewer: Yes, international respect, just like Tsinghua University wants to have this kind of reputation. I noticed you mentioned your background is political science, and you spent ten years in United States. I just wonder, how does your disciplinary background shape your leadership?

President: I studied political science, but I did not want to be politician or political leader, so actually, learning political science did not really help me to develop leadership. I don't think learning political science helped me develop leadership, but I think I learned how to make decisions. I think political science is not really governing the government, but it helped me in the broad sense of learning how people make decisions. Decision-making science is political science, I think. That kind of experience, and my experience of exposing myself to the different United States education system, probably helped me shape myself as a university leader. First, I was exposed to the Waseda educational system. I went to the United States, Georgetown University, and then went to university in Virginia, and I went to Ohio State University. I was exposed to American higher educational institutions, American universities. Also, I taught three years at a university in Japan before going back to Waseda, and so I was exposed to different universities, different educational systems, and then learned how to make decisions. Those kinds of combinations probably helped developed my leadership.

Interviewer: That means experience in higher education means a lot for your leadership?

President: Yes.

Interviewer: About your leadership teams, in your leadership team, what kind of balance do you think is important to find between those people who are interested in performance and those who feel interested in operations, in people, and in innovation? How do you balance them?

President: Actually, I am emphasizing research. Research is very important for Waseda University. All the professors should be very serious about their research. Not every single professor is devoting himself or herself entirely to research, but I think they should value research very much. Academic research is important, but at the same time, education is important too, as a university. Each professor should do good research: conduct research and then reflect research results in his or her education. Then there are administrators in the universities and then professors in our university, and I don't know which is more important, but we have to make balance between them, good balance. Also, professors know how to do research and how to teach. Administrators are not engaged in teaching or doing research, but they know how to run the university, how to administer universities. The professors and administrators should be working together in good communication and achieve the same goals, sharing the same values, making Waseda the top-notch university in the world, and then educate our students to be better than us. In that sense probably, administrators and professors should be working together. Balance-wise, it's very difficult, but probably professors should place more weight on research and education, but listen to the administrators, and administrators should listen to the professors to do better administration. I may not be directly answering your question, but that kind of balance.

Interviewer: No matter what kind of person or the group they might be, they should feel in their mind that research, the quality of research, is the focus of this university. Everybody should just say no matter what kind of road you take, the destination's Rome.

President: Right. Each person has his or her own role, and they should play their role, but they should communicate with and understand each other, I think.

Interviewer: The main mission is research.

President: Right. They're sharing the same mission, same concept of the mission.

Interviewer: The next question concerns balance between internal and external control and uncertainty. As president, you have a lot of pressures from all sides. You can control some things, resources, but sometimes you are out of control. How do you balance those things?

President: When we face some risks, like an unexpected accident or incident happens, and we have to manage that risk, we should not be panicked. We should be ready for anything that may happen. I would like to think that one thing is transparency. Whatever happens, like some uncontrollable thing or some uncertainty takes place, how we respond to that incident really should make our decision-making process more transparent so that everyone can understand what kind of decision is made. That's one thing. Also, if we keep the same vision, the same understanding of the mission, strong understanding of the mission, then we do not change our mind so quickly, not the wishy-washy bumbling. We should keep the same kind of stand. We go through the same mission, providing good education to the student based on good research, and make the decision based on what's good. Then all those people who make decisions will share the same value, the same mission. Then, from that standpoint, we will make correct judgement, I think. That's the best way to control uncertainty. Financial risks, or some accident to students, or anything could happen to the university, but we should be thinking, "For the sake of the students, what is the best for the university? What is the best for the students?" We should not change our policy, and then we should respond to each incident with that same kind of stand, a confident stand.

Interviewer: That means shared values, shared governance are keys to control. Thank you. About your university, what kind of specific cultures and traditions are important to your university? This question I feel very interested in.

President: Waseda University is the top private university in Japan. We attract good students. We are one of the best universities in Japan, but besides that most of our students and many of our alumni, graduates, are willing to serve the society, continue to serve other people, and do volunteer work. Many of the students are volunteers. Right now, every year, ten thousand students register for volunteer work. We have about fifty thousand students, and about forty thousand undergraduates. From forty thousand students, every year about ten thousand undergraduate students register for volunteer activities. One out of four people devote themselves to volunteer works. That's kind of our tradition in our school.

Interviewer: There's a kind of spirit of service, serving the society.

President: Exactly, service.

Interviewer: What distinguishing initiatives do you plan for your university?

President: Distinguishing initiatives? Ok, since I became the president last year, just last November, one year ago, I'm advocating two things. Fostering of students, or educating students, with resilient intellect. "Resilient intellect" means our students should be challenged with new problems, problems to which no one knows answers, no human beings know answers. Right now, human beings face problems to which no one really knows the correct answer: global warming, or conflict between the different divisions, or polarization within one country, and so forth. Many things we don't know the answers to, but our students should think through the new solutions as their hypothesis. Then they have to verify their hypothesis with some evidence. If the hypothesis may not work well, then he or she will start thinking from the beginning about new solutions. That's one thing, resilient intellect. The other one is flexible sensibility. This means that our students should understand people other than Japanese. How other people think and look at the world. How other people think about Japan. We should understand other people, other values, different languages, different cultures, and different religions. If our students can understand how other people with different cultures, different languages, different religions, and different genders, then their solutions would be more persuasive to people in the world. Those two things, resilient intellect and sensible flexibility.

Interviewer: Oh, that's really impressive. What big institutional changes are faced by your university? Do you think your university is now faced by some kinds of very significant changes?

President: I think globalization is the biggest change. Actually, globalization is our tradition at Waseda University. Our university was founded in 1882. Then, in 1905, only a few years after its establishment, Waseda University created the School of Chinese Students. Also, that affected not only Chinese but also Koreans and some other Asian students, but many Asian students started studying at Waseda from 1905. Then Japan went to World War Two so we had to stop it. After World War Two we had been not very international, but in the 1990s, we became much more international. We are going back to our tradition, and now Waseda University is the most globalized university in Japan. We are receiving almost eight thousand international students to study at Waseda last year. Then, we are sending out four thousand six hundred Waseda students to study abroad. We are aiming to receive ten thousand international students a year, so one out of five students will be international students, and we are aiming to send out about six thousand Waseda students to study abroad. Six thousand means excluding international students, and almost every single student who grew up in Japan should go out of Japan to study abroad, to look at Japan from outside of Japan. That's what we are facing. That is the biggest change, institutional change, and we are on the way to complete this change.

Interviewer: What do you think is the social contribution your university makes?

President: Probably teaching the people of Japan to accept diversity. Japan has been a very homogeneous country, so narrowly minded, narrowly focused. Waseda has been very accepting of diversity. Now, more than four thousand seven hundred Chinese students are studying at Waseda every year. Before World War Two, Waseda received a total accumulation of three thousand Asian students, most of them Chinese. Three thousand Asian students studied at Waseda. Now every year, we are receiving more than four thousand seven hundred Chinese students, almost eight thousand international students. That kind of thing provides understanding of diversity, which Waseda University can teach to other Japanese people: the importance of understanding diversity.

Interviewer: The next question is about Tsinghua University. What interests you most about Tsinghua?

President: I'm very interested in Tsinghua, which was established in 1911, and then according to my understanding, Tsinghua University was very good at every single field like philosophy, or history, or cultural studies. After 1949, according to the government policy, Tsinghua became very famous for natural sciences and engineering, like MIT in the East, MIT in China I learned from President Qiu, and I asked him when the shift came. Now Tsinghua, you know: almighty! Tsinghua is very strong in every field. I asked him, "When was the shifting time, change of the paradigm?" and he said, "Early 1980s." So 1980s, shift from being the MIT in the East, or MIT of China, to become a world-leading, all-around university, and in political science and public policies. That kind of change is very interesting.

Interviewer: How can Tsinghua best contribute to global higher education from your viewpoint? Do you have any recommendation or suggestion in practice or policies? Thank you.

President: Well, Tsinghua is doing so well now. Tsinghua is already contributing to global higher education. In a very short period of time, Tsinghua transformed from a natural science and engineering school to the all-around leading university in China. You achieved that. That you can show that model to the world. Tsinghua University must have had a very clear plan and a good vision, very ambitious vision and clear plan. Tsinghua would be one of the good models. Also, Tsinghua University must be very rich, I think. You are receiving good donations from all over the world. You can show a good model to other universities in the world, I think.

Interviewer: This is very interesting to us. That means you think the model of Tsinghua, with its expansion into many diverse disciplinary fields, is a good model.

President: Good model.

Interviewer: What challenges could shape Tsinghua's future? Globalization?

President: Now Tsinghua University is facing challenges by inviting very good and prominent professors from all over the world. The key issue will be if they can educate their students to be as good as these professors. The Tsinghua student is very smart, and great professors from Cambridge, MIT, or Stanford will come here to Tsinghua to teach. The idea would be for their students to exceed their American or British professors, or French, or whatever. Those Chinese students who learn from those great professors should be even better than their professors. If that would happen, then Tsinghua will be very successful. That is the key. The same thing at Waseda. Our students will be better than us, or not. Tsinghua students will be better than their professors, or not. That is the key. If you succeed in that, then Tsinghua's future will be very bright.

Interviewer: I agree with you very much. About Chinese higher education, what are your main impressions about Chinese higher education?

President: Very good, I think, because I received several Chinese students in my graduate program. They are not from Tsinghua. They are not from Fudan, but they are very bright. Not the very top schools, probably second-tier universities in China, but those students whom I taught in that graduate level were very bright. Chinese university official system is, I think, very good. Good quality. Provides good education.

Interviewer: One final question. Perhaps you could offer some remarks about the role of your university in a global higher education context?

President: Higher education institutions, Tsinghua or Waseda, whatever, have to lead young people, educate our students. Those students should contribute to the world and have a broader perspective, broader view. That's our mission. Higher education institutions in China, like Tsinghua, or in Japan, like Waseda – we share the same mission. We have to educate the young people to understand the world and then also contribute to the world in any way, in some way. That's my thinking.

15

PROFESSOR ROBERT J. ZIMMER, PRESIDENT OF THE UNIVERSITY OF CHICAGO, UNITED STATES

Interview background

Robert J. Zimmer, president of the University of Chicago, visited Tsinghua University in November 2019 and attended the inaugural meeting of the School of Public Administration's Global Academic Advisory Committee. On 2 November 2019, Xie Zheping, an associate researcher of the Institute of Education at Tsinghua University, interviewed President Zimmer.

Robert J. Zimmer, male, American, born in 1947, mathematician, PhD, graduated from Harvard University. Since 2006, he has served as president of the University of Chicago. Before serving as president, he held faculty positions at the US Naval Academy, the University of Chicago, and the University of California, Berkeley. He served as the provost of Brown University from 2002 to 2006. In addition, he has served on the National Research Council's Mathematical Sciences Committee, the President's National Medal of Science Committee, and the National Science Council. President Zimmer received honorary degrees from Tsinghua University and Colby College in 2011 and in 2017 received the Philip Merrill Prize for Outstanding Contribution to Liberal Education from the American Association of School Councils and Alumni.

The University of Chicago was founded in 1890 and is located in Chicago, Illinois, USA. The University of Chicago is one of the founding members of the American University Association. It is a world-renowned private research university. It ranks among the top ten in world university rankings such as QS, THE, and ARWU. It ranks among the world's best universities in fields as diverse as physics, law, and economics. In 2018, based on a foundation of long-term cooperation, Tsinghua University and the University of Chicago established the Tsinghua University-University of Chicago Economic and Finance Joint Research Center to jointly promote theoretical research and talent training in the economic field.

DOI: 10.4324/9781003248286-17

FIGURE 15.1 President Robert J. Zimmer with Associate Researcher Xie Zheping

The interview focused on the president and his personal background, leadership team, the president's university, Tsinghua University, Chinese higher education, and global higher education. Key points touched on by President Zimmer include focusing energy on formulating and implementing the school's strategy, appointing the right people into leadership roles, working with people and maintaining full communication to help the university cohere, paying attention to rankings, and encouraging people to explore new ideas (Figure 15.1).

The interview

Interviewer: The University of Chicago is one of the leading new universities in modern history. We're actually very much impressed by not only the history but also educational ideas contributed to the higher education, like…

President: Hutchins?

Interviewer: Hutchins, yes. Because his book, *The Higher Learning in America*, which was translated in Chinese by a very senior scholar, has a great audience of readers like me. It was published twenty years ago in China. May I ask you, what is your chief challenge as president?

President: Well, the University of Chicago, as you pointed out, has a very particular history and had a very particular and forceful set of values that it's always upheld. And, from the beginning, it was a place of great seriousness of purpose around intellectual and scholarly investigation. So, this deep commitment to rigorous inquiry, challenging assumptions, new paradigms, multiple perspectives, free expression, ongoing argument – this has been a culture that's been deeply embedded in the university. And, I think, there are two important challenges around this. First, it's a very singular and important type of perspective for an institution, and it's very important that that be preserved and enhanced. And there are a lot of forces always at play that make people not want to have that type of rigorous environment – and we're deeply committed to maintaining it.

The second thing, though, is how you realize it in new ways. So, you have a set of enduring values, enduring perspectives, but then the way that those get realized can change over time because there are new problems to think about, disciplines evolve, new disciplines emerge, problems emerge, partnerships emerge. So one needs to constantly be thinking about how you realize enduring values in new and powerful ways.

Interviewer: Some things never change, some things change.

President: And knowing which is very important.

Interviewer: I noticed you got a first degree at Brandeis, not from Chicago.

President: Right.

Interviewer: Does the University of Chicago have a tradition of selecting its leadership from among those whose academic career has been in other universities? For example, Hutchins was from Yale.

President: Yes, he was, and I would say many people who have been presidents have not been alumni of the University of Chicago. So, you know, there are advantages and disadvantages of taking people from the inside. The advantages are that you believe they know the institution, understand the institution well, recognize what's important about it and what its values are. The disadvantage can sometimes be that you don't get additional external perspectives, which are always important to get. You can't be complacent that you have everything right and everybody else doesn't. So, I think, a very important thing for the presidents of Chicago that they be selected as people who share the enduring values of the university but are willing to think about how to realize those in new ways. And I think that that's the way things have gone. I'm just trying to think back, and I think the last three presidents before me were not alumni, but the one before that was.

Interviewer: Yes. Where do you invest your most energy as a leader, normally?

President: I'd say several things. First is a type of very high-level strategy of what are the key big things that we need to get accomplished. So that included starting our first engineering school. It included the nature of the evolution of our undergraduate college and the question of what it means to have an undergraduate college in a great research university. We've been thinking about that a lot. Our whole global strategy, and so on. So, there is a set of very high-level issues that I need to think about.

Second, I spend a lot of time trying to appoint the right people who are vice presidents and deans because they have to do a huge amount of the work. And then, I have to ensure that they are working together, that there's enough communication so that we're acting as a university as a whole, not just a holding company for a bunch of separate things.

Interviewer: How do you think your disciplinary background shapes your leadership? I know you are a mathematician.

President: Yes. One of the interesting things about mathematics is that you look at different sorts of phenomena and you try to understand what lies behind them. So, how do you have a larger structure that integrates things that may not look like they're the same but actually have a lot in common? That's a common mindset for a mathematician, and I think that's been something that's been very useful for me, just as a mode of thought about the university: it looks like you have many different things happening, but how do you actually think about them in a more organized and coherent way?

Interviewer: Yeah. And in your leadership, what kind of balance do you think is important to find with people who are variously interested in performance, options, people, and innovation?

President: The interesting thing about the University of Chicago, and it's true of many universities, is that you have what I would say is this umbrella culture that's very strong, and that's what I described earlier. But then you have lots of different parts of the university that fit under that culture, and they're thinking about things in very different ways, and that's good. I mean, you want people thinking and focusing on all sorts of different things, and a part of the value of the university is, in fact, just all these different points of view, different things they assign importance to, as long as it's sort of fitting inside this bigger culture. So, what I like is seeing people explore and focus on what they want to do and where they can bring their own enthusiasm. But I also like it if they're talking to each other so that there's some kind of coherence and understanding of what everybody else is doing because that will inevitably add new things and more value.

Interviewer: If you ever know the challenge of being a president of a university, would you do it again?

President: Absolutely. You know, it's an interesting job, so if it suits your temperament and suits your personality, it's a fantastic job. But, if it doesn't, then it's not so good. So for me, I find it is challenging, interesting. There are lots of different things to think about. I learn new stuff all the time. I meet all sorts of people all the time, and I hear what they are thinking about. So I like it.

Interviewer: I notice you received your higher education in the 1960s – your bachelor's degrees. It was at a time when there were some great university presidents like Hutchins and Clark Kerr from UCLA, California University. He created a very popular term: a university by that time was not only a university but a multiversity. Do you still agree with that concept? Is there something to it?

President: I don't know. It's certainly the case that universities have gotten more complicated. Some of that stems from the fact that they have a big impact on the world, and so all sorts of people expect all sorts of things from universities, and that's fine. But I do think it's very important to keep a clarity about who you are as an institution, what your actual mission is, and how all of the demands on a university are responded to in a way that reflects a coherent view of what your fundamental mission is, what your values are, and what you're about. The minute you start thinking, "Well, I've got so many things to do, and I'm just sort of balancing them," you lose way too much. So I'm not sure. I like the term "university" because I think it indicates that there's something integral about the whole thing, which I think is an extremely important thing to keep in mind.

Interviewer: I agree. Actually, from Tsinghua's point of view, President Kerr and President Hutchins – they are heroes, something like that. They offered some very radical reforms for the university. What do you think of President Hutchins' legacy to the University of Chicago?

President: Honestly, I think Hutchins' greatest legacy, and what's important about him, is this absolute commitment to seriousness of educational purpose, and his protection of free expression as a piece of that in a very complicated environment. Hutchins had a very clear sense of values, and I think that served the university well in a complicated way. Whether he was a great administrator or not who made exactly right decisions about this or that, there's a lot of argument. But I think the clarity of his commitment to teaching people how to think and that that's what we're about, and how demanding that is, and how challenging it needs to be, I think that's what is important in a positive way about Hutchins.

Interviewer: I think in the future you will also leave a lot of ideas for researchers to study. When we are doing research about university histories, your legacy will also be in the files. Let me turn to universities today, operating as they do in a global higher education environment. Are they aware enough of their global context and of perspectives on that context like rankings?

President: The rankings. So, the rankings can be thought about in a pretty simple way which is you have to think about how they're put together. So they decide on a set of metrics, and some choose just a few metrics, some choose lots of them. The metrics, individually, are of interest. I mean, generally speaking, you want to know about them, and you pay attention to them. Not all of them, but many of them. Then comes how they are actually used in the rankings, which is they're put together by somebody by creating an arbitrary formula that combines them in some ways. So, that's how you have to think about them, which is that the data is of interest, but that every ranking is fundamentally defined by the arbitrariness of the formula. So of some value, but one needs to understand how arbitrary they really are. And the rankers have, you know, interest in how the rankings turn out. Let's put it that way.

Interviewer: Yes. For outsiders, the way the University of Chicago combines research and teaching is admired because normally, for a university, for faculty members, this combination is very difficult to balance. What is your strategy in putting forward research and teaching together?

President: Yes. I'd say two things. First, is the nature of the teaching. If the nature of teaching is just, you think you're standing up and delivering information, you know, it's a little boring to do that kind of teaching. If what you're doing instead is actually engaging in a serious kind of intellectual discourse, where you have very smart students who will be challenging to you and who you will challenge, and who will challenge each other, that's way more interesting. And, in fact, it is way closer in spirit to a research environment. I think a lot depends on how you think about teaching, how you think about the nature of challenge inside a classroom, and how important that is so it becomes something that faculty are happier doing because it's not totally separate – it's not a chore. It becomes exciting. Now, you need really good students to do that, but we have really good students, so it's okay.

The second thing we're doing, and this is sort of new, is that we're now trying to get programs connected to all of our schools teaching our undergraduates – the business school, the public policy school, the law school. Not that every single person has to teach, but that there are programs that are connected.

Interviewer: The faculty from each is associated?

President: So, this is right. This is both expanding the collection of faculty that our undergraduate students come in contact with, but a lot of the faculty from these schools actually enjoy it because our students are so strong and it's such a challenging environment. I think the main thing is to just keep the classes, and keep the courses, and keep teaching, to be of real intellectual challenge so that it's kind of gratifying for everybody.

Interviewer: The very last question: What do you think is fundamental to, or characteristic of, the spirit of University of Chicago faculty and students' research and learning? It should be challenging?

President: Yes. I mean, I think you know, this environment of mutual challenge and constant challenge is the spirit of the whole place, and the economics seminars and workshops are interesting examples because they're famous for the following feature: there are a lot of Nobel Prize winners in economics but everybody, including the Nobel Prize winners, expects to be constantly challenged. A graduate student will feel perfectly comfortable challenging a Nobel laureate, and you have to have an answer. You don't get to say, "Well, I'm a Nobel laureate. Then who are you?" That's not an answer. You need an argument, and so everybody is constantly in the environment of just this ongoing, mutual intellectual challenge.

Interviewer: So, you think they inspire each other.

President: And that's what it feels like.

Interviewer: It's great. It is fun. Do you also encounter the challenge we have here when you give a C-plus, or D-, or fail grade to students? The young generation is unlike older generations who accepted the grade they received from their university professors. The new generation is more egocentric. They say, "I'm good enough, professor. Why have you just given me a C grade instead of a B grade?" Do you come across such questions?

President: Well, we don't let anybody get away with that, you know. I mean, they're in an environment where that's not an argument. How you feel is not an argument.

Interviewer: All right. Is this the first time or second time that you have come to Tsinghua?

President: Oh, many times.

Interviewer: Okay. What interests you most about Tsinghua?

President: What interests me most is similar to what interests me most about China, which is this tremendous sense of ambition and wanting to accomplish something real and fast. It's an invigorating environment.

Interviewer: Thank you. Yes, Tsinghua is like that. Our motto describes us well: action speaks louder than words. How do you think Tsinghua can best contribute to global higher education?

President: Oh, to global higher education? Yes. Well, you know, I think it's very important for a lot more people to spend time in China and certainly important for a lot more Americans to spend time in China. I mean, the knowledge of China and understanding China in the United States is very low. And part of the reason that we've been very active in opening centres in Beijing and Hong Kong, and encouraging students to come and faculty to come, is because we think it's both important at a high level, and important for their work, to actually understand what's happening here.

Interviewer: I did a little survey about your overseas office. Your centre in Beijing is very successful.

President: It's interesting because a lot of successful American universities had questions like, "Why should we send students abroad when it's so great to be in our university?" And you know, for a time, we had some of that to be honest. But I think that's changed a lot, and I think kind of the global perspective is really one we push constantly and is now quite deeply embedded in the university. It required some work, but I think it's very important and I think it's particularly important for countries like the United States and China, where you know these are big countries with powerful internal cultures. You know, if you look at Europe, you walk five feet, and you're in another country with a different sort of culture, so in Europe, you're just very used to all sorts of things, all sorts of people, all sorts of ideas, all sorts of cultures, language, histories. In the United States and China it's too easy to think, "Well, we're the story." And so I think it's just very healthy for big countries, in particular, where you have to make a conscious effort to have people come and to send people out.

Interviewer: Very last question. What challenges could shape Tsinghua's future in your view?

President: Well, I think with China developing at such a fantastic speed – yes, speed is great, and rapid development is great, but it's always going to create some things you discover you have to fix up. That doesn't mean you shouldn't go really fast. It just means you have to be attuned to you're not going to get everything hundred per cent right when you're going really fast, and that's okay. You just have to fix them up as you go along.

Interviewer: What would be the biggest challenge, from an outside perspective?

President: It looks like it's a place that's making huge and rapid advances. My statement was really just kind of an abstract one. Sometimes we go.... I mean, at the University of Chicago, we've also been trying to go very fast in the last decade, and you know, there are things we see...well, you know, maybe we need to fix that up a bit because we didn't get it quite right the first time.

16

PROFESSOR YONG-HAK KIM, PRESIDENT OF YONSEI UNIVERSITY, KOREA

Interview background

Yonsei University's eighteenth president, Yong-Hak Kim, visited Tsinghua University in November 2019 and attended the inaugural meeting of the School of Public Administration's Global Academic Advisory Committee and "2018 Anticipating the Future: Forum on New Civilized Cities and Sustainable Development." On 2 November 2019, Xie Mengyu of Tsinghua University interviewed President Yong-Hak Kim.

Yong-Hak Kim, male, Korean, born in 1952, sociologist, graduated from the University of Chicago with a PhD. He served as the president of Yonsei University from 2016 to 2020. Before serving as president, he served successively as Yonsei University's deputy director of planning, director of admissions, dean of University College, dean of the faculty of social sciences, and dean of the Graduate School of Public Administration. He has won the Yonsei University Academic Excellence Award, the Gallup Outstanding Paper Award, and the National Academy of Sciences Outstanding Publication Award. During his tenure as president, he proposed the "Future Challenges 10 by 20" strategy, which was prepared for the school's centenary by drawing up ten policy tasks to be completed by 2020.

Yonsei University was founded in 1885, and its main campus is in Seoul, South Korea. Yonsei University is Korea's first modern university. It is a member of the Alliance of Pacific Rim Universities, the Asian Universities Alliance, and other university groups. It has played a key role in cultivating talents needed for economic development and industrialization in Korea. Yonsei University ranks second among Korea's comprehensive universities in the 2020 CWUR rankings, and 85th in the world in the 2020 QS World University Rankings. Its School of Business Administration enjoys a global reputation. Yonsei University cooperates

DOI: 10.4324/9781003248286-18

FIGURE 16.1 President Yong-Hak Kim with Researcher Xie Mengyu

extensively with many well-known international universities and has cooperative relations with more than 20 Chinese universities, such as Tsinghua University, Peking University, and Renmin University of China.

The interview touched on the president and his personal background, leadership team, the president's university, Tsinghua University, Chinese higher education, and global higher education. The interview talked about the growth of Tsinghua University; being warm-hearted, as well as knowledgeable and smart; distributing resources; and shifting the institution to encourage development (Figure 16.1).

The interview

Interviewer: Let's talk about Tsinghua University. As a university president, what interests you most about Tsinghua?

President: Well, to be frank about it, I think Tsinghua's development is the fastest in the whole world. Twenty years ago, early '90s, I came here. Of course, back then it was full of bicycles on the street. Tsinghua University was very silent, small activities. But every year, I come back and come back, and it's changing drastically. And Korea also has developed fast. You know the story. But even having experienced that speed in Korea, I am amazed by the speed of Tsinghua University's development. So for example, top scholars in certain areas, there are many in Tsinghua. Every field. Among most cited papers in certain areas, you may find one scholar at least from Tsinghua. So that's really amazing, as a president.

Interviewer: Yes. How can Tsinghua contribute to global higher education?

President: That's a good question. I think Tsinghua has many creative minds. In research, it does lots of creative research that have impact on society, for example, gene editing. That's definitely having an impact on society. In that area, I think Tsinghua will lead the world for many years to come. Another area that Tsinghua could lead, and I hope it will lead – it's something I will talk about at this afternoon's session – is creative minds and that having many different kinds of knowledge in your brain will be less important in the future. A creative mind is important: knowledge and smartness are not all that is important. I emphasize also at Yonsei University that you must become a warm-hearted person. Like a waterproof watch, an AI-proof person is needed in the future society. An AI-proof person is one with the quality that AI cannot emulate for the time being. Yesterday Jack Ma said, "Human beings have hearts, and AI doesn't." I don't know if there ever comes a day for warm-hearted AI, but until then, human beings must be very human-hearted, having love and caring for others, and helping those in need and distributing what you have with people. If Tsinghua can produce that kind of mind, what I call "shared value," then Tsinghua will become the top leader in the world.

Interviewer: Your reflections prompt me to ask if this need for warm-heartedness is also a challenge for public policy?

President: Sure. The basic goal of public policy is to solve the problem of public goods. Why do you want to solve the problem of public goods? Because they are distributed almost inclusively, to anybody – universal benefits to almost anybody. Market failure – for example, failure to provide public goods – is suboptimal for society. We cannot solve that with creative minds alone, but if you have a warm heart, then you will see something that others cannot see. You will find new areas of interest.

Interviewer: Yes. This one will be a little bit tough. What challenges do you think would shape Tsinghua, and maybe a university like Yonsei University, in the future?

President: Well, it's really tough to answer. As a president, I know I have my own experience. If Tsinghua is shown to anyone in the world, what would be the first word that would be associated, that comes to their mind? What word would that be? When you hear the term "Tsinghua," then what word association comes to your mind? What would that be? Finding that term will be a unique value to Tsinghua. At Yonsei University, when people hear the word "Yonsei," somehow people associate it with "freedom." That's probably because we have a long tradition of free culture. What do you think? I'm not saying it's good or bad, but if Tsinghua wants to be unique among world universities, then it might need a symbolically significant identity that underpins Tsinghua's existence.

Interviewer: Sure. That's really important. I know you have a strong background of social sciences so maybe you have a very different perspective from other university presidents. That's really important, and also a very important contribution to this project. As a university president, as a leader, where do you invest your energy as a leader? Which aspects?

President: In my inauguration speech, I said I will change the direction of Yonsei's development by a 0.5-degree angle for the future. My meaning is that predicting the future is hard, but I can say currently we are here and pointing this way, so I will twist the direction of development to accommodate that direction. So far, I have been constantly trying to do so. I'll give you an example you may be interested in. Just a simple example. Do you want to hear more about this?

Interviewer: A little bit, like what do you consider to be a 0.5-degree angle of change?

President: Yes. Let me ask you a question. What do you want to become in your life? If I ask the same question to my students almost all of them would say, "I want to become a lawyer, I want to become a musician, or I want to become a fund manager." They all answer with occupations. But how long will these occupations last? I mean, they are aiming at the future that would not exist. Right? "What's your dream?" "I want to become a lawyer." It's not a dream. "What kind of person do you want to become?" That should be the right question, and that should be the right answer. When I say, "What do you want to become?" I mean "What kind of person do you want to become?" They all answer in occupations; occupations will disappear, you know. AI will replace many things. But if I ask a second time, why do you want to become a lawyer? "To make money." That's a realistic answer; that's identity, what I call the legitimacy of your existence. But what's the meaning of being a lawyer, the significance? I think that's a very important thing to consider, but people hardly ever talk about it. Sometimes they do, but our education system is all about emphasizing jobs.

Let me quote one sentence from the philosopher W.E.B. Du Bois: "I insist that the object of all true education is not to make men carpenters, it is to make carpenters men." Universities so far didn't do that. I'm not saying that expert knowledge in education is not important. I'm saying that we have to add more to education by changing direction, vision, and mission. So far, we have been mistargeting. Maybe it has been good so far before the emergence of AI or the current level of technological developments.

Interviewer: Let me go broader with maybe the final one or two questions. Where would you see China in five years or ten years? Maybe not only China, maybe about Chinese higher education, Chinese public policy. These perspectives.

President: I mentioned this briefly yesterday already. Society needs trust. People should be able to trust in the government, in public institutions, and in universities. But all this trust is going down rapidly. China is a little bit of an exception so far, but in Korea, people put much trust in the government or religious institutions. The trust is dwindling rapidly, declining rapidly. But will the society disintegrate because of that? No we should not, so we should find something else. That's the role of public policy, to make something people can rely on. I tried to talk about this yesterday, but I didn't have enough time.

Interviewer: I think that's the original goal of public policy in higher education. Education is still, I think it's originally getting at, training professional bureaucrats.

President: I agree, but the enemy that we are facing is a technological enemy: internet. Internet is making our foundation very shaky because if there is one misbehaviour in the government or university, it spreads fast across the society, and people talk about it as if it is all of government. Even a fraud in a tiny fraction can make people feel as if the whole government is corrupt. Universities are facing a similar situation. Newspapers and journalists spread these rumours without checking the facts. This is what I call the "battle of stories." There are lots of different battle stories, and people only want to listen to lots of amusing stories, like a drama. For this reason, the level of trust dwindles every year, every month, every day.

Interviewer: Would you think some technology policy is necessary or some other kind of policy maybe?

President: When you read a newspaper, you will probably notice it's all full of bad things in society, but you should also keep in mind there are good things happening in society as well. Who is telling these good stories? We are losing the battle of stories to bad content.

17

SHIGEO KATSU, PRESIDENT OF NAZARBAYEV UNIVERSITY, KAZAKHSTAN

Interview background

Shigeo Katsu, president of Nazarbayev University, visited Tsinghua University in November 2019 and attended the inaugural meeting of the Global Academic Advisory Committee of the School of Public Management of Tsinghua University. On 2 November 2019, Dr Liu Lu, a postdoctoral fellow at the Institute of Education at Tsinghua University, interviewed President Shigeo Katsu.

Shigeo Katsu, male, Japanese, born in 1958, international relations scholar and economist, graduated from the University of Tokyo with a PhD. He has thirty years' experience in the World Bank and from 1999 to 2009 served as the director and vice chairman of the World Bank Europe and Central Asia. From 2011 to 2015, he was a member of the advisory team to the Asean+3 Macroeconomic Research Office. In 2010 and 2011, he served as a consultant for the Asian Development Bank and the World Bank and cooperated with governments and non-profit organizations. Since 2010, he has served as the president of Nazarbayev University, a member of the Kazakhstan National Committee for Modernization, and a consultant to international and bilateral development agencies.

Nazarbayev University was founded in 2009 and is in Nur-Sultan, Kazakhstan. It is a member of the Asian Universities Alliance. The school was founded on the personal initiative of President Nazarbayev of Kazakhstan, and it is also the first autonomous university in Kazakhstan. Nazarbayev University has engineering, science and technology, social and humanities, and medical schools. The teaching system of Nazarbayev University is drawn up in accordance with international education standards, which is intended to promote the rapid development of Kazakhstan's science and education system and its early integration with international standards. Since its establishment, Nazarbayev University has shouldered the

DOI: 10.4324/9781003248286-19

mission of setting an advanced model for reform in Kazakhstan's higher education. In September 2016, the presidents of Nazarbayev University and the president of Tsinghua University held talks hoping that the two sides will further deepen their cooperation based on the Asia University Alliance platform.

The interview concentrated on the president and his personal background, leadership team, the president's university, Tsinghua University, Chinese higher education, and global higher education. President Katsu discussed the importance of standards and integrity to prevent corruption or scandals, curriculum innovation which helps develop students and also faculty, fostering a high degree of internationalization in both academic and research aspects, and the importance of regular contact and communication (Figure 17.1).

FIGURE 17.1 President Shigeo Katsu

Source: United Nations Industrial Development Organization.

The interview

Interviewer: The first question actually is about yourself. So, where do you invest your energy as a leader at the present?

President: Ok. Nazarbayev University's only nine and a half years old. We started in 2010 when we opened our doors, and we started with the one-year Foundation Program, which was necessary because in Kazakhstan the length of schooling is K–11 years, not K–12 years. So we felt it was a little bit tough on young high school graduates, sometimes only sixteen to seventeen years old, to immediately immerse themselves full time in an English-speaking research university. So we asked University College of London to run their Foundation Program for international students in Astana, and then in 2011, we started our first under-graduate program. In 2015, we had our first graduation cohorts, and so over time, we added schools to the list, in particular graduate schools. In the first years, I would say from 2010 to 2015, in some ways, it was very much foundation years. My energy really was spent trying to make sure that, on one side, we ensured that we have a very good academic product from the very beginning, and at the same time we also had a more or less good governance system, management system, in place that we built up.

Our foremost concern was that we don't have any corruption or other scandals. Number one. Number two, we also needed to establish on the academic side with the public that in this university, nobody enters through the back door through connections, by paying under the table, and so on. You only get in by meeting our standards and on a merit basis. This was something very new for Kazakhstan, and it took us about three years to get the public to understand because until then we had lot of pressure from many people. We started to get the best high school graduates from the country. We have pretty good faculty, so in theory, when they graduate, they should be able to go on to good places. So we started to focus increasingly more on research, on innovation, on building up our medical cluster, and all the while, in parallel, we also had one obligation and that is to share our experience with the other universities in the country. Why? Because we operate under special Nazarbayev University law, so for the first time in the space, every academic freedom and institutional autonomy is legally enshrined. So we have a lot of privileges that others don't because we do not report, for instance, to the Ministry of Education and Science. We have our own governance structure and so on. It just happens that our board is very powerful.

Now, however, after nine and a half years, since sort of end of last year, start the beginning of this year, we launched a major transformation exercise that covers all aspects of our university system. You may ask why? We decided we need to sort of rededicate ourselves to the original mission and vision of the university but also to overhaul all the system's administration, finance, procurement, HR, everything because the initial systems were put into place in a haste. After nine years, they were not anymore good to help guide us to our ambitious goals for the second decade. So, administration, finance – we are in the midst of a big transformation agenda.

On the medical side, we are transforming the hospital system with the help of our strategic partner from the US.

On the academic side, we changed our curriculum with last year's fall new academic year. We basically decided to introduce a common core curriculum. So basically all our first- and second-year students for the first at least twenty months take almost three-quarters of their classes together, regardless of whether they're going to engineering or science or humanities or social sciences. They all take them together. The reason is because we want to educate and train both sides of the brain. So, our engineers and scientists have to study moral philosophy or ethics or history, and so on. Critical thinking. And so in our humanities and social sciences, we want to make sure they have a minimum understanding of quantitative methods, math, computer science, programming. Then also, in addition, we have introduced for everybody entrepreneurship courses. So that's where I'm putting most of my energy.

Interviewer: The second question is, What your disciplinary background?

President: No, my career was nothing academic. I used to do lectures at universities around the world partly, but just lectures, because my background was with the World Bank. And so for more than thirty years, I was with the World Bank. Then over time, I rose obviously through management ranks, and then I was vice president for a region – basically Europe, the former Soviet Union, that includes central Asia and the Balkans, and Turkey. And in a way, it's a very diverse international organization and full of people who think that they're very smart and intelligent. Very knowledge intensive and you have to develop a certain management style so that you make sure that they come along. I think, in a way, I treat this building of a new university in some ways in a similar manner. I try to tell also my national colleagues who use very much top-down approaches that it makes an old legacy. I say, please, stay away from this top-down. We have to give young people a chance and build it much more bottom-up.

The reason why I also do this major institutional transformation is because I want to change the whole mindset, you know. We need to develop a mindset of serving students, the professors, our clinicians, and so on. In a way, they have to be at the centre. We all have to support them, and also we have to develop this DNA – particularly in administration, finance, but everywhere – of professional excellence. So I often tell our people, be it in HR or in finance or budget, doesn't matter, in administration, I want somebody from outside to come and say, "Mr. Katsu, I have a problem in my company with budgeting. Can you help?" And I say, "Sure. Take any of our people." The whole list; I can take any of them, and they will be able to help you as a profession. I tell them, "I want you to be that type of profession because then you do not worry about a career here. You can always go somewhere else, but you will find satisfaction in trying to become adaptable in your profession." That's in many ways my management philosophy.

Interviewer: So, the next part is about your leadership team. So you would need a very professional leadership team to assist you to deal with daily issues, especially management and governance issues. In your leadership, what kind of balance do you think is most important to find between people who are interested in performance operations, those who are interested in innovation?

President: You know, leadership team in many ways is like a marriage, no? Basically, you have to recognize that you bring together totally different people, different backgrounds, and different cultural backgrounds. In our case, all the academic and research side's very international. Administration, finance, very national. And putting them together is quite the challenge, so, in a way, you have to constantly make sure that they meet often. So, we have at the minimum weekly senior management meetings. We have in addition all kinds of committee meetings where pretty much everybody's also there. We have, thank God, a new vice president: executive vice president for administration, finances. Very inclusive. He's national, but he's very inclusive. He always thinks about students. He thinks about doing things together. It's great, so we try to create an atmosphere where the national and international side as management mixes, and that's quite a challenge because, you know, the national side grew up on the old system, and our international academic and research side did not. So, that's why I say it's like a marriage. I have to pull them together.

Interviewer: Right. Thanks. So to what extent does the work of the leadership team focus on internal or external matters, or control, or uncertainty?

President: Well, it used to be control, but I tried to ban the word. You know, in Russian control – when you say even "monitoring control" something – they tend to translate it as "control," and then it has a totally different, you know, connotation. You know, top-down. So, I try to ban the word "control," you know? You supervise, but in order to learn, not in order to punish. So, in many ways the face to the outside, I have to do that, vis-à-vis government, vis-à-vis the president, and also in a way international sponsors otherwise. Our provost is fully in charge of the academic research side. Also, vis-à-vis our academic partners and our executive vice president, his time is more on the internal administration side, but we are now gradually also trying to in some ways internationalize administration because this dichotomy is not very good. It doesn't help us, this constant separation. And then obviously, we have a specialized person for medical. A vice president for medical, a vice president for innovation, as well as a vice president for student affairs.

Interviewer: Thanks. So let's talk about your university. As we know, the NU is a very young university. It is only ten years old.

President: Next year. We will be ten years in June, yes.

Interviewer: It's a very young university. So what specific cultures and tradition are important to your university?

President: From the very beginning, you know, we told everybody that, one, academic integrity is very important. So, we were very tough from the very beginning on cheating, plagiarism, and so on, and this was also something new. You know, we kicked out students for cheating and plagiarism, and they came back and protested. The parents came back and said, "But it's only cheating." And I don't think they understand, you know. And I told them, Mr. President has given us a mandate to become a world-class research university. As a world-class research university, it starts from everybody – the youngest students all the way upwards: academic integrity is number one. And so we start that and then obviously, closely linked to it is a meritocracy sort of a thing: it's merit based, and then we have obviously certain building blocks such as, you know, the decision was taken early on to do everything in English. Obviously, Kazak language we also teach mandatorily; otherwise, it cannot work in the public service and so on. We also developed strong strategic partnerships with top international universities, but there were partners for each of the schools, so early we introduced a system teaching and learning for undergraduates, teaching and research from undergraduate level onwards. We have a pretty much now well-developed quality enhancement framework, and so we try to put a lot of emphasis on quality assurance. And we are also obviously very value oriented, such as integrity, but in addition, you know, we have our graduate attributes, and I will show you a brochure. Our graduate attributes as to how we want our graduates to be known, and there we bring in elements such as inclusiveness, being considerate of others. But they're all trained to be leaders and so on.

Interviewer: So, regarding the future development of NU, do you have any specific strategic plan for the university?

President: We do have. We do have a strategy 2030 which was approved by our board ten months ago, in December last year, I mean. That's where, concomitant with our transformation, and so we have a lot of ambitious goals. We have also targets for internationalization of our student body. We have a goal, obviously in a few years, to complete all our program accreditations and so on. And we want to make sure that we respond to some of the key requests from the authorizing environment. We're going to expand our institute and develop a national platform, and so we've also been asked to contribute to the sources of future economic growth by helping government and the industry develop the foundations for future, diversify industry, meaning away – gradually moving away from just all gas and mining commodities and so. And then also, although it was always there, we've again been asked to make sure that we train future leaders, including also train senior civil servants.

And we have one particular goal right now which arises because we operate under the special Nazarbayev University law, meaning we are the only university which has academic freedom and institutional autonomy. There's the rest of the university system, and as I said, by 2025, we want to make sure that we may be a little bit more of a hub and spoke. But we really reach out and work with all the key universities, be it on research or teaching exchange, and so on, so that we can share really our experience with them and also bring them in. And by 2030, we said we would like to very much see us not just being a dominant part but more an element in the network in the chain of strong universities. Then, we can together become much stronger and engage also stronger internationally. So that's our agenda.

Interviewer: So in the development process of the universities, what are the kinds of challenges you think about, that the university will face in the next few years?

President: Well, I mean, in many ways, that's why we do this transformation. One thing is, you know – it's one of the themes of the conference yesterday and today – is science and technology and how you bring in the impact on governance, as well as on education. For instance, today but also yesterday, we had a lot of discussions on how you share China's development experience with the world, and how you make the world understand China, and other things. And the role of the School of Public Management at Tsinghua University, you know, resonated a lot with me because we also have our young graduate school in public policy, and we sometimes discuss similar things. That's why it's a good model in a way for me to look at.

And, in that context, I would say that one real challenge was and will continue to be is that we're a very international university. Our faculty professors come from fifty-six, fifty-seven countries. We are like a mini-United Nations. Three-quarters of our faculty is international. They all have the Western-style PhD, so we recruit for teaching and learning – teaching and research, sorry. But our administration is very domestic, and many of them come from government backgrounds, and they don't want to take risks. Or they don't want to be blamed and so very risk averse. It's like trying to put a round peg into a square hole. So that has always been a big challenge. It will continue, but gradually, hopefully, it will become better, and that's why also partly we do the transformation to change minds.

The other big challenge is going to be that every country is now trying to do something similar. Research universities, but also research leading to science and technology discovery, and then commercial applications is a worldwide competition. Every country tries to get there, no? And that means we will compete for brains. We have to compete for brains, but we know that our students are talented. They are also in some ways brainwashed to come to us, but we also see that increasingly, Korea, Hong Kong, sometimes China, the Europeans, they found out that our students are so good so, they say, "Let's try to recruit some high school graduates directly." So we still have to compete for our own top talent, but also, we need to compete for international good brains to continue to be faculty, postdocs. Competition is obviously very strong, and we have to make sure that we create the good conditions for international whether it be international faculty research, postdocs, whatever – that we create a good, you know, a welcoming environment, a good ecosystem, and obviously in some ways, especially technology, costs. So we have to convince our authorizing environment. I tell them, you want this? It will cost you money. But also, our politicians. We have to convince them, saying that Kazakhstan has to stay open for research, so you cannot close yourself. It will be very negative for Kazakhstan's development because unlike China with 1.4 billion people, Kazakhstan is only eighteen million. Eighteen million. It's too small to expand, so we are dependent on international brains coming in. And so that is something that is going to be a big challenge, because we are at this point not yet well known: we still need to build up our brand name and get people to understand when they come here, they get top-quality education and can do top-quality research. So, there's another big challenge.

And that is the first nine and a half years. I mean, especially those who joined and worked with me from the very beginning, you know, building a university is like a marathon, but we have been running this marathon as if it is a hundred-meter sprint. So burnout of our colleagues is a big concern for me; that's why I wanted to make sure that we need to continuously motivate them, give them new challenges, rotate them so they try new things. Put them sort of outside their comfort zone and all this. So, those are a lot of the challenges.

Interviewer: So the university is part of the society, and you should have some commitment to social engagement?

President: Sure, service is one of our keys.

Interviewer: Yeah, so what innovative social contributions does your university make to the society?

President: Actually, at our student level, we encourage first that they are not only entrepreneurial and do start-ups, commercial or profit start-ups. We also encourage social entrepreneurship, and we are very proud of that. We advertise these types of student engagement and successes. We have students that started running, and we give them space to run, cafes, so restaurants on campus where they employ and train people with disabilities. Mental disabilities. In Kazakhstan, that's also part of the Soviet legacy. People tended to be institutionalized inside, sort of locked away almost. We also bring them out and train them so that society doesn't have prejudice and stigma, for instance. Another group of students created their own school to deal with kids with autism and others. And the leader of this undertaking recruited – and she was herself an undergraduate – two hundred other students. And to start teaching, she realized she needs also some theoretical practices, so she came from humanities social science. She went to our graduate school of education, got the master's, and now she's doing her PhD at Cambridge University. Or others have adopted orphanages and do a lot of fundraising for orphanages and children, so I'm very proud of them, and I tell others, please join. And then we also run increasingly open lectures for citizens.

Interviewer: Sounds good. Let's quickly talk about Chinese higher education. So what are the main impressions for you as you think about Chinese higher education?

President: I mean, number one, I cannot say that I'm an expert on Chinese education, so it's a very impressionist view probably. And also just reading from your work through the AUA (Asian University Alliance), and of course, AUA are elite universities. But elite universities cannot exist in a vacuum. There's a whole ecosystem from early childhood through primary, secondary education, and then you have the whole ecosystem where maybe at the top you have the top research universities, but you have to have a good balance of teaching universities, and also vocational and technical streams and so. Yeah, both university, or the level of what you would call in the US community colleges where you would teach more practical skills. And in all this, you know, I see many ways in Asian societies in which parents, everybody, are very goal oriented. Engineering has always had a little bit more of a higher standing than maybe lawyers and economists, and so as a result, the humanities, social sciences education was de-emphasized a little bit at the elite universities. So that's my impression, and I think it's important, therefore, to educate both sides of the brain. Creativity and creative industries, products of digitalization, the industries that will actually grow – a lot of them involve creativity, create. And so globally, I think we see one key issue is a crisis of lack of trust, loss of trust, in institutions, and that is a problem of advanced economies as well, in the West. There is a crisis of confidence and crisis of trust, and that extends not only to politicians. And because of relentless right wing, or whatever you call it, rhetoric it also leads to a loss of trust in science. So many people, and you heard it today, maybe a professor talked about, you know, the loss of trust in science and so also a little bit the anti-vaccination people, and this is a serious threat.

So with global education, we all have to put our heads together and think about how we can re-establish trust in higher education institutions at the secondary school level. Try to teach students from a young age onwards how to think for themselves. That's why critical thinking is important so that they can actually think through and start to discern what is fact, what is fake news, and so this ability's going to be even more important.

That's one, and the other that is increasingly important is to be able to tell a story, a narrative. It's not just only, like yesterday, of how China will tell its development success story to the world. Actually, it's everybody. Students, faculty, university leaders. We all have to be able to communicate better and tell a narrative, a story, that makes sense, that the people outside understand. Communication is going to be even more important.

18

PROFESSOR LUC SELS, RECTOR OF THE UNIVERSITY OF KU LEUVEN, BELGIUM

Interview background

Luc Sels, rector of Leuven University, visited Tsinghua University in November 2019 and exchanged views with Chen Xu, secretary of the Tsinghua University's Party Committee, on furthering cooperation between the two universities. On 19 November 2019, Professor Hamish Coates of the Institute of Education at Tsinghua University conducted an interview with rector Lu Sels.

Luc Sels, male, Belgian, born in 1967, sociologist, PhD, graduated from Leuven University. Since 2017, he has served as the rector of KU Leuven University. Previously he served as an adjunct professor at the University of Rochester's Simon Business School, professor and dean of the School of Economics and Business at KU Leuven, and as an honorary professor at Cardiff University's School of Business. In addition, he serves on the Belgian High Commission for Employment as a representative of the federal minister of employment and as director of the Centre for Research on Work and Social Economic Policy.

KU Leuven was founded in 1425, and its main campus is located in Leuven, Belgium. KU Leuven is a co-founding university of the League of European Research Universities. As one of the top ten universities in Europe, and a world-renowned first-class research university, KU Leuven ranks among the top universities in the world in various world university rankings, such as *Times Higher Education* in 2021. It enjoys a world-class reputation in the fields of economics, psychology, law, and computer and electrical engineering. KU Leuven has extensive cooperation with many top universities in China. In 2007, the school signed six cooperation framework agreements with Tsinghua University, aiming to strengthen in-depth cooperation in personnel training and exchanges and scientific research cooperation.

The interview focused on the rector and his personal background, leadership team, the rector's university, Tsinghua University, Chinese higher education, and

DOI: 10.4324/9781003248286-20

FIGURE 18.1 Rector Luc Sels with Professor Hamish Coates

global higher education. Rector Sels talked about building interdisciplinary institutes, ensuring the strategic plan is activated at the academic level, and forming a balanced executive team (Figure 18.1).

The interview

Interviewer: Could you describe a little bit how you spend your time as a leader? Maybe in the average week or month, what you actually do in the job.

Rector: That's a very tough question. It's almost changing on a daily basis, but taking into account the complexity of the institution, most of my work is divided over the three main areas within the university. It's a comprehensive university: fifteen faculties. We have all disciplines in that very large house called KU Leuven, but we also have a large academic hospital, actually the largest in continental Europe. We are very well-known for technology transfer, so we have a large tech transfer office, the second in Europe actually, after Imperial College. That's why we are also – now for the fourth year – leading the Reuter's ranking for the most innovative university. The three together – the three legs of the tripod called KU Leuven – made the job extremely demanding and complex because running a hospital is a completely different type of affair compared to leading the faculties and the departments and the academic part of the institution. Dealing with complexity, making sure that the line managements can do their job adequately is, I think, the most important responsibility.

Second, you could say that in Belgium a rector is maybe best described as a combination of a president and a provost in the US system. There's the internal responsibility in terms of governors and management, but there's also the external face of the university, so the external representation is a very, very important part of my job. That includes talking to, and trying to convince, the government and government leaders in Belgium and in Europe – European Commission – on the importance of, informing them about the importance of, academic research and how it influences and impacts society. Also, fundraising is a large part of my job. All kinds of inaugurations. Let's say that management, financial responsibility, external representation, make up two-thirds of the time through many meetings, of course. Traveling is very important. Internationalization, and trying to become a truly international university, is the top priority now, so I spend at least a week a month abroad talking to other presidents, visiting other universities.

Interviewer: You mean outside of Belgium or outside of Europe?

Rector: Outside of Belgium. Outside of Europe. That's why I was now a full week in Japan. This year, I spent a full week in South Korea, Taiwan, and India, Japan twice, China now. Yeah.

Interviewer: Is the strategic plan of your creation, or was it pre-existing?

Rector: Yeah. Actually, I wrote most of it myself, so it's not only the work of the executive committee, but it's actually the plan that I had in mind. It contains five chapters. It's about becoming a truly international university. There's a chapter on future-oriented education, a third one on going digital, investment in learning analytics, and MicroMasters. We are on the platform. I think the fourth is interdisciplinarity. We are establishing a few university-wide interdisciplinary platforms. The fifth is on sustainability. Today, around ninety per cent of the strategic plan has been approved in the Academic Council and the Board of Directors, and it's now in full implementation. That's all going very well.

Interviewer: Has your work changed over the last two years? I guess initially planning might have taken up much time, but as you say, day by day new surprises or opportunities arrive.

Rector: The strange thing about becoming a president, and I heard other colleagues saying exactly the same, is that first of all, the learning curve is extremely steep, but that's good. I'm now far more efficient in the job than two years ago. At the same time, every year it takes more hours of the working week, so it's now a fully seven-day working week from early in the morning until late in the evening. That is due to the fact that your social network expands, and more and more people are demanding your time or specific efforts. Government is starting to know you better. It's using your advice and so on, so the weeks are becoming more and more intense, meeting becoming shorter, and the optimal use of time is at its maximum, I think.

Interviewer: Can I ask you, in that environment, how do you make decisions as to where you invest your time and what to say no to, what to delay, what to bring forward?

Rector: First, the real compass is the strategic plan. Second, the external political agenda. We are a private institution but funded by government, so we have a hybrid mixed system, meaning that I not only have to watch the way our strategic plan is received by the faculties and departments but also how external regulation changes and how we can impact that. Lobbying is a very important part of the job, not only lobbying in Belgium. And that's a complexity that adds to the situation in Europe, at least if you're leading a large research-intensive university. There's a European dimension, so being so close to Brussels, I do not only represent our own university at European level but also the League of European Research Universities. Their office is in Leuven. It's based at KU Leuven. I'm not answering your question, but it simply gives you an idea about – yeah, so the compass is internal and external.

Of course, I have no line responsibility in the academic hospital, but I have full line responsibility within the university, so talking to deans, heads of department, making sure that they, in their budget plans, let's say try to align with the central strategic plan is extremely important. Trying to change and prepare the internal organization structure of the university; being out there for almost six hundred years in more or less the same shape and form is a very, very high priority. You could say that is an additional dimension. If you want an example, to create what we are now building: Leuven Institutes that are transdisciplinary in nature and overlap the fifteen faculties. That is a change after so many centuries that was in the beginning not very well received by most of the faculty. Today, it is, and they now start to understand that it is a change that we need to make to prepare ourselves for the future. The strategic plan, yes, very important.

The change management part is also very high on the priority list. Talking to deans, convincing them, joining in faculty board meetings. So I'm very decentral in focus and make sure that a strategic plan becomes more than a text and starts living and is well received and implemented at the levels where academia really exists, and that it's not at the central level of the university, that it's with the researchers.

Interviewer: When you say the strategic plan wasn't initially well received, you mean by the faculty?

Rector: The plan was well received. The plan was well received except for the section on interdisciplinarity because that has a very strong impact on the organizational structure of the university. Where now at least those who are willing can have dual affiliations, so they remain a member of their faculty or department but at the same time can become a member of the university-wide institute, which receives substantial funding, so it's not without importance. That's a change because you get two types of leadership. All of a sudden you have to start talking to people from completely different disciplines. We, for example, started the KU

Leuven Brain Institute, which includes engineers working on imaging of the brain, people from medicine, from pharmacology, psychology, psychiatry, and so on and so forth. Same at Leuven Institute on Artificial Intelligence. It's I think now using experts from at least ten of the fifteen faculties, so that is a change. You all of a sudden are entering a completely new environment, but that is how we create skill and make a difference. We are not the only university doing that. We have a very close collaboration with University College London. What we are doing is actually in a very close, I would almost say not collaboration but a constant exchange of information between the two presidents and how we are evolving in that Endeavor, to become more interdisciplinary in nature. The way we are approaching that is, at the two institutions, almost exactly the same.

Interviewer: London. Yeah. Ok. Just two more questions about leadership. You've said a little bit about the institution already, but before we go there fully, your disciplinary background – how do you think it affects your work?

Rector: Yes, it does to a large extent. I have a background in sociology but then changed to economics and personnel economics, which brings me very close to management. I'm an organization scientist and that is extremely helpful. Having spent nine years as a dean in the faculty of economics and business makes you very familiar with budgeting, with the financials, simple accounting principles, risk management, the importance of how to deal with investment policies, infrastructure, and how to fund it – things like that. It without any doubt determines the priorities but also how you deal with them. It determines the language you speak and the strong focus on structure in the whole change of the university. Yeah, it's not only about agencies; also, structure is very important because it determines which agents will collaborate with each other. Yeah, there's a strong influence, then, and I'm aware of that.

Interviewer: How about your leadership team? How did you structure or organize that team, and how do you get the balance right between internally focused, externally focused, conservative people, creative people, managers – these kinds of different roles and personalities?

Rector: I have an executive team with eight vice rectors, which is quite large.

Interviewer: Large?

Rector: Yeah, and then the managing director of the university, who is extremely important. He's also leading the tech transfer office.

Interviewer: That's a COO/CFO type role? Registrar?

Rector: That's a COO/CFO type of person, but also an academic coming from the same faculty, and we started our careers on the same day and working in the same domain, so extremely close to one another. I always say within the university, this institution is led by two people. Not only by the president but also by the managing director. That is very well received.

Interviewer: Operations, money, HR?

Rector: Yeah. it brings together academic decision-making and infrastructure and money. In composing the executive team and selecting the vice rectors, I, first of all, went for a perfect gender balance. Very important in academia today, so there are four female and four male vice rectors. A good representation of all the disciplines within the executive committee is very important because in the end, the university is a bottom-up-driven institution. There is top-down decision-making. There is a certain level of compliance needed at the size of KU Leuven – twenty-two thousand employees, sixty thousand students – so you need a certain level of compliance. But being in balance within at least the larger faculties like engineering, medicine, economics, and business – it's very important. I selected a few of the vice rectors from those faculties and have a very good balance between people who are coming from different backgrounds. A few received their PhD in the US, a few others in Europe, so bringing to the table different types of academic backgrounds and familiarity with different systems, that's very important.

Interviewer: They're internally appointed?

Rector: Collegiality is very important for me, so I selected intentionally a few people who already knew each other very well so that you can immediately start with a strong group cohesion. We have an election-based leadership, so every four years, a director is elected in Leuven by all faculty and students and administrative staff, and so on. A few of them were also on my campaign board during the election period, so partners in crime so to say. But I made a very clear message from the very beginning that as of day one, the focus should be on the university and not on a political view of a team or a group that is now leading the university against other groups or coalitions within the university. I think we have a very, very strong loyalty today in most of the faculties, I can say. I think that's due to the fact that they were very well chosen. Subsidiarity is very important, so I only interfere if I think that a decision is going wrong, or I really disagree, or a decision is not in line with the strategic plan. But otherwise, at the size of this institution, you need to give them some leeway, some autonomy, and really translate that responsibility to the rest of academia and KU Leuven.

Interviewer: Just shifting away from leadership more to the institution, you've said some things already, but just briefly, given the time, what specific things do you hope to achieve in ten years based on the current reforms? What outcomes?

Rector: Remain where we are and even improve our position, and sorry for referring to the rankings, but they are important. They are not important in terms – I do not see them as an indicator of how we are doing in a competition. It's not about competing. It's simply what you also experience here in China. It is thanks to the very good rankings, the faculty – we are consistently ranked among the top fifty, and the top five or six in continental Europe, top fifty worldwide. So strong in tech transfer and innovation that we are capable of working together with the best universities around the world. We have a strong partnership with MIT, with Tokyo University, with so many top universities, and that is only possible thanks to the very good rankings, so keep trying to –

Interviewer: Do you see the rankings as changing maybe in ten years in terms of what they'll measure? Are you trying to work towards those?

Rector: Continental Europe is under pressure. We are doing very well. We are now in the world university ranking, so we improved from 48 to 45, always very close to that; and here in this beautiful city, things are changing so rapidly in Asia if you look at Singapore, China – Japan is kind of losing the feeling for what is changing in the world – but including maybe even Australia. Canada is doing very well and a few other countries, and we really need to make sure that continental Europe stays among the leaders of the pack in academia, so trying to secure that is very important. Further growth is extremely important, so we need to grow also in financial terms keeping the whole system together, because what is quite unique about KU Leuven is that all the operations are integrated in one legal entity. So the academic hospital, for example, is part of the university, not an affiliated teaching hospital. It is fully part of the university system, of course with a very strong financial firewall between the academic affairs and the hospital activities. But keeping that together in one system is very important.

Securing our campus operations is extremely important for the future of the university. We are always associated with the city of Leuven, but we have campuses in ten different cities in Belgium, meaning that you have to deal with ten different city councils in a complex country like Belgium with different communities, different types of government. So making sure that financial viability in the operations is good in all these places – so keeping the rankings, keeping the system together, financial viability of all the campuses – is very important.

Remaining a true university is of extreme importance, so combining an ambition for excellence with full academic freedom and combining fundamental, basic research, high risk without any direct material objective behind it – combining that with high levels of innovation and translation to society and to industry. Trying to balance all these different phases of the university's a very, very high priority, and balance is very important in that specific area, I would say.

Fifth, convincing the outside world of the importance of universities because.... Maybe not in China but in many parts of the world academia is coming under pressure because it's a very critical voice in society, not always very well received by the rest of the public voice. Strengthening legitimacy is for me a fifth, so making sure that in ten years, fifteen years, we still speak about universities in the same way as we do today, being unique voices in society which preserve the past and at the same time foster the new and the future. That combination – that's extremely important.

Interviewer: I'll just move to some questions about China and Tsinghua, and finally one last question about higher education more generally. What challenges do you think might shape Tsinghua's future?

Rector: I would say its success in further internationalization is very important for the future. It is doing extremely well. Very prestigious institution. Depending on the ranking, number one or number two in China, and mostly number one. Let's say most of the faculty is still Chinese, student body is Chinese. So that's for me a first challenge: making sure that you acquire the top talents, not only from within the country but also from abroad.

A second maybe is finding a good balance between excellence in research and being democratic and open to all layers of society. We have, for example, an open accessibility policy in Leuven which prevents us from refusing any students. So they are all welcome if they want to try. While here at Tsinghua and leading institutions in China, they select among the very, very, very best students. That's for me an open question whether that is a sustainable model in the long term. If you want to bring science to society, and make it useful to society, you have to make sure that not only the top elite gets familiar with the outcomes of it. Being open to society – I always compare the situation in Leuven being a top fifty institution, sixty thousand students – that's the same as all the undergraduate students of the eight Ivy League universities in the US. Yeah, so it's excellence by exclusion versus excellence by inclusion. Finding a balance between the two is also for the Chinese universities very important.

Interviewer: So I'll go to the last question. What change would you suggest big research universities should make to education to make sure that they best contribute to society?

Rector: In the segment of education, or through education influencing or impacting society?

Interviewer: Particularly through education as opposed to through the research function.

Rector: I would say remain loyal to the whole idea of research-based education. So staying loyal to the truth at its current status and as far as we know given the status of the science today. So grounding your education in your own research is for me very important, because it's a unique selling proposition of a university. Combining that with active learning, more activating forms of education, is a second very important one. And keep in touch with what is changing in the professional world and not being afraid of sometimes being led by changes in professional segments of society. Yeah, it's not only about the push sides – your research versus the content of your education. There's also a pull side – the demands in society. And that's not equally relevant for all disciplines, but it is highly relevant in those disciplines which are positioned in both professional and academic segments, like medicine, dentistry, engineering. Yeah, so those three elements are for me extremely important.

Fourth, trying to make a strong combination between the research basis of your education and what the Germans would call strengthening person skills and competencies and societal orientation of what you're offering. And especially that aspect is, I think, very important in today's society if you want to create strong citizens and responsible citizens for tomorrow's society.

19

PROFESSOR LILY KONG, PRESIDENT OF SINGAPORE MANAGEMENT UNIVERSITY, SINGAPORE

Interview background

Lily Kong from Singapore Management University visited Tsinghua University in November 2019 to discuss with Peng Gang, vice president of Tsinghua University, advancing interuniversity exchanges and deepening multifield cooperation. On 25 November 2019, Professor Hamish Coates of the Institute of Education at Tsinghua University interviewed President Kong.

Lily Kong, female, Singaporean, born in 1965, geographer, PhD, graduated from University College London. Since 2019, she has served as the president of Singapore Management University (SMU). Prior to serving as SMU president, she served as the provost and Lee Kong Chian chair professor of social sciences at SMU. Before joining SMU, she had also served as the vice provost (education), vice provost (academic personnel), vice president (university and global relations), dean of the faculty of arts and social sciences, dean of the University Scholars Program, and director of the Asia Research Institute at the National University of Singapore. In the nearly twenty-five years that she was a member of the Department of Geography, she developed a strong international reputation as a social–cultural and urban geographer. Her research focuses on social and cultural changes in Asian cities. She has won the Robert Stoddard Award, conferred by the Association of American Geographers, the Singapore Public Administration Medal (Silver), and the Public Service Star, as well as the Fulbright Scholarship and Commonwealth Fellowship.

SMU was founded in 2000. The university is Singapore's third public university and ranks 12th in the world in the 2021 QS World Specialist Universities Rankings. SMU has a School of Accountancy, the Lee Kong Chian School of Business, a School of Economics, a School of Computing and Information Systems, the Yong Pung How School of Law, and a School of Social Sciences. It has more than 11,000

DOI: 10.4324/9781003248286-21

FIGURE 19.1 President Lily Kong with Professor Hamish Coates

undergraduate and post-graduate students and nearly 400 full-time faculty. In 2013, SMU and Tsinghua University signed a memorandum of understanding to establish an academic partnership. To strengthen academic and educational cooperation, there have been exchanges of students between Tsinghua University's School of Economics and Management, and SMU's School of Accountancy, School of Economics, and Lee Kong Chian School of Business.

The interview involved the president and her personal background, leadership team, the president's university, Tsinghua University, Chinese higher education, and global higher education. President Kong touched on recruiting suitable talents for academic and administrative positions, managing administration and finances, creating space for faculty and students to focus on academic innovation, strengthening cooperation with industry, and forging future-focused programs (Figure 19.1).

The interview

Interviewer: You're a geographer by background. How do you think your disciplinary background affects your work as a leader?

President: I've reflected on that quite a bit. I think if I take a step back, geography has morphed a great deal over the years. The geography that I knew as an undergraduate – no, not as an undergraduate, as a high school student – was very much about mountains and rivers, and people ask me, "Is it going to rain?" and that sort of thing. The geography that has evolved over the years is much, much different than that. It is a very synthesizing discipline. It ranges from the dimensions to do with urban planning to human-environment interactions to climate change issues, so it's extremely broad. It's so broad that some detractors would call it an "imperialistic" discipline because it seems to be "colonizing" other disciplines. One can put a negative spin on it, or one can see it in a very positive way and I, of course, choose to see it in a very positive way. As a very synthesizing discipline, it draws from different disciplines, it's open to different conceptual ideas, different philosophical traditions, different methodologies.

The strength of the discipline is actually in being able to pull together diverse views and synthesize. That sort of thesis, antithesis, and synthesis kind of dialectical approach to things has been extremely helpful to my role as a university leader because it does require that there is a certain ability to draw from, to see things from, different disciplinary backgrounds, to be able to pull them together and to be able to make sense of diverse epistemologies and ontologies. I have felt particularly enabled by my own disciplinary training, and I have noted around the world that many university leaders actually have a geography background and we've talked about this. The University of Toronto was mentioned a moment ago at my meeting with Tsinghua University leaders, and Meric Gertler at Toronto is a geographer. I don't think it's an accident; I think it has something to do with the training and the disciplinary approach.

Interviewer: As you said, a very broad discipline. What sort of a geographer are you?

President: I'm a social-cultural geographer interested in urban issues. I study urban phenomenon and change. I've focused on Singapore in the main, and Asia more broadly. That again has been tremendously helpful because, as a university president now, I am extremely interested in getting our students out into Asia a whole lot more. That's partly informed by my own understanding of Asia and my own interest in Asia.

Interviewer: How do you invest your time, if I can put it that way, as a leader? Maybe in a week or a month, how do you see the investments that you're making?

President: Right. I was asked at my inaugural address, which I delivered at the start of this year, what kept me awake at night? There were two things that I identified. One was people, and one was money. I spend a lot of time on both those two things.

In terms of people, it's really about ensuring that we have the right people in place; whether it's in the faculty-academic side of the house, or the professional-administration side of the house. Finding the right people and making sure that they feel they have a developmental path. That they are coached, mentored, nurtured. Finding the right people and then ensuring that they have the developmental opportunities because the ideas of what to do in a university will come from them. I have no monopoly of wisdom on that. I can certainly have ideas, and I do, but really the power of a university is in the people whom I try to spend time on.

The second part of it is making sure that the university's appropriately resourced. That means spending time with fundraising. It means spending time with clarity about our financial model so that my colleagues then don't have to worry about that. They should be thinking about the great ideas – the things they want to do in research or in educational innovation. My job is to ensure that they have the resources with which to do that.

Very broadly, those are the two key areas. Of course, on a day-to-day basis, there's a whole lot more. Working with my colleagues to devise the appropriate policies to support their work, for example. And I don't trivialize that at all. It takes a lot of my time. Fundamentally, I think it's about people and resources.

Interviewer: Can I just ask, in a little bit more concrete sense, how do you give life to those two emphases during a week? That might not be an exact, or the best, unit of measurement. Meeting with students or meeting with faculty or faculty forums?

President: Just concretely, I ensure that I have my regular sessions with different categories of people on campus. Faculty, staff, students, alumni, board, advisory boards, industry partners. I've just about finished a year and one of the things I'm doing is sitting down with my assistant and saying, "Let's be sure that I hit all these different groups that I must spend time with." I meet with students, groups of students, probably about eight times a year. Outside of that, the students will have events that they invite me to, and that's separate, but I will make sure that I have these eight different platforms for meeting with different groups of students.

With faculty, I meet groups of faculty over lunch and it can be organized in terms of new faculty, faculty who've been promoted, faculty with particular research interests that I want to hear and understand what they're doing so that I can help to support their work. Just as an example, I met with a group that has an interest in researching different dimensions of the city. Urban issues. There were professors from sociology, geography, information systems, law, finance – all in the mix but all interested in the city. I think that's one of the things I can do which deans probably wouldn't do. Deans would work within their schools. What I can do is bring people from across the campus to forge the dialogues.

I meet with alumni once every two months as well, in small groups. I make sure I run through the schools. When I'm overseas, as I am now, I make sure that I meet alumni. Last night, we had our alumni in Beijing over to dinner. That's the people side of the house.

Of course, I spend a lot of time working directly with my direct reports, and there are too many right now because many of the professional services offices report directly to me. I'm just about to make a change with hiring a senior administrative person who will help oversee the day-to-day work.

Interviewer: How many people in your leadership team?

President: Right now, if I might just describe it, on the provost's side of the house, there are something like fifteen direct reports to him.

Interviewer: What is a provost at Singapore Management University?

President: A provost is the chief academic officer. In this case, he deals with all the academic programs, which is the educational programs and the research programs. That's the role I had before I took on the presidency.

Interviewer: PhD? Master's?

President: PhD, master's, undergraduate bachelor's degrees, and the research institutes and centres are under his purview.

Interviewer: Oh, all of the research, as well as the education programs?

President: Indeed. It's both research and education programs. We also have the continuing education programs part there. Then on the other side of the house are all the professional services: HR, finance, IT, campus infrastructure, safety, security, corporate relations, marketing. All of that reports indirectly to me right now. What I'm about to do is to appoint someone to oversee, help me oversee the bulk of that. Some of it will still report directly to me. If I were to think of maybe three to six months from now, depending on when the individual identified comes in, I would really have myself, the provost as the chief academic officer, and the senior vice president for administrative services as the three key leaders of the university. Then, there would be the vice provosts, the deans, and so forth.

Interviewer: You've taken a year to establish that?

President: I started with that thinking because I was working as provost as I said, just over three years, and had a good understanding of the inner workings of everything on the academic side of the house. I wanted to have a good direct understanding of the administrative side of the house. I took six months to really dive into that and I'm still deep in the weeds, but I started the search for someone to help me around about maybe four months ago. By the time the individual comes, I will have had probably a good year, or a good year-and-a-half, of really getting to know that side of the house. I found it tremendously helpful coming into the president's role from a provost's role because I really know the academic side well. I know the programs. I know the requirements. I know the research imperatives and ambitions, et cetera, very well. I hope to do that with the administrative side of the house, and then I can have people help me with those.

Interviewer: Ok, so you'll have basically two direct reports, or maybe two plus?

President: There will be more.

Interviewer: HR or something like this?

President: There will be two, plus a few. There are a few others that I will handle directly. The legal office I will handle directly, for example, because that's the board secretary, and I interface with the board. That's just one example.

Interviewer: When you have your leadership group meeting weekly, it would be just with that small number of people?

President: Yes. How it works is, well, right now it's me and the provost. In due course, it will be the provost, myself, and the senior person for admin. I meet with all my direct reports now on a monthly basis as a group, but on a monthly basis. At this point in time, I'm getting a firm grasp of everything that's going on. Then after that, I think I can step away a little bit more and be a lot more external facing as president. SMU was established with the help of Wharton and University of Pennsylvania and, therefore, it adopts an American structure and approach to things. In that context, the president has a significant outward-facing role, and it is something that I would transit a lot more to.

Interviewer: For the first year, your focus is on institutional matters, but now you'll start to look more intensively at government or business or international relations?

President: That's right. All of that. I'm already doing some of that; hence, visits like this which have the international dimension. But I think there's a whole lot more that I need to do with building relationships with business and industry, not just in Singapore but beyond, building relationships with government. And I'm hugely advantaged there because I sit on the Public Service Commission in Singapore, which allows me to know the public service well.

Interviewer: What's that?

President: The PSC is an independent, impartial body that has a critical role in the public service. We select and develop scholarship holders to become public servants, appoint senior public leaders, and maintain discipline, thus upholding integrity and impartiality. That means I have a good understanding of the public sector, and I know the public sector leaders across the portfolios. I sit on a lot of advisory boards and committees and councils of different government agencies as it is and have done that for many, many years now, partly because of my research expertise. I feel that of the three dimensions of relationships that I would like to and need to build –that's government, private, and international university sector – I have a good grasp of the government sector in Singapore. Likewise, the international university relationships: I spent seven years in my previous university, which was the National University of Singapore in precisely the global relations role, and have developed many good relationships and networks. Although with the passage of time, there's been a lot of change in university leadership, still there is a good base of relationships there. It is the business and industry sector that I think, particularly as a management university, I should spend more time on. Just as an example, next month I have organized for all the business chambers in Singapore to come and visit SMU to share with them our plans. The Australian Chamber of Commerce, Singapore International Chamber of Commerce, British Chamber of Commerce, et cetera. That community, I think, is where I'd like to spend more time.

Interviewer: Ok, the specific initiatives or developments that you're seeking to pursue may be in the future, now that you've got your administrative feet on the ground. Where are you going with that? Have you decided yet, or are you going to go through a process of consulting, or do you have some directions from government or council?

President: This was an advantage of having come through to the presidency from a provostship. In the last few months of my provostship, before I took on the president's role, I started consulting and I started having a series of discussions with different groups on campus, getting a sense of what their ambitions were but also their frustrations, et cetera. I then continued that into my first several months of the presidency, and I also established a few commissions, and what I called ideation tables that comprise colleagues on campus, as well as external stakeholder groups. People from business and industry and government agencies, to ideate around four key areas which I had identified and articulated in my inaugural address. I had identified these four areas through the original focus groups that I mentioned. The four areas, directions, are as follows. One, much greater industry engagement in our educational programs and our research. Two, a focus on innovation, which can lead to entrepreneurship, intrapreneurship, or, more broadly, developing change agents. The third is internationalization, and a fourth area we call integration, and that's integration internally but also integration with the city within which we are deeply engaged and in which we are located. I'll say something about each of those.

With the industry dimension, we've been going through a series of discussions on campus involving staff, faculty – not yet students – about where we see industry to be headed.

Interviewer: What's the horizon there: Singapore or Asia or Southeast Asia?

President: It's Singapore, Southeast Asia, and then Asia. What we've done is to look at what the government planning agencies have been looking at. We have had something called the Future Economy Council in Singapore, led by the deputy prime minister, thinking through what the directions with industry are. What does Industry 4.0 mean in Singapore? Where are the sectors in economy that are really going to make a difference in Singapore? What is the role of universities in supporting, if not leading, some of that? That's one piece. What we're hoping to do is to crystallize the areas that we would pay particular attention to, invest in for both research and education, and to develop ourselves as the go-to university for those areas that we choose.

Interviewer: Among Singaporean institutions or looking more broadly?

President: Among Singaporean institutions in the first instance. We have now converged on three areas that we will develop in concerted ways. The first is digital transformation – this includes the digital economy, understanding citizen and customer experience, impact of that transformation on everyday lives, and so forth. The second is sustainable living. This covers broadly issues from climate change to resource sustainability, but also sustainable aging, sustainable employment, and other societal dimensions of sustainability. We are concerned to help secure sustainable futures for the planet, for economies, and societies. Third, we have chosen to focus on Growth in Asia. What are the opportunities and challenges? What are the implications of growth?

Interviewer: Can international students study at SMU?

President: Yes.

Interviewer: How do they do that? Do they pay a fee?

President: They do. At the undergraduate level, most of the international students are actually subsidized by the Singapore government, though to a smaller extent than a Singaporean, but subsidized nonetheless. There are students who can opt not to take the subsidy and pay the full fees. The difference is that if somebody takes a subsidy, they are required to work for three years in Singapore post-graduation or with a Singapore-registered company somewhere else in the world. A student who is full-fee paying does not have to fulfil that obligation.

Interviewer: Any Singapore company in the world?

President: Any Singapore company in the world. We have ten per cent of our undergraduate population that's made up of international students. It could be a whole lot more, but we're limited by government policy just to ten per cent. That's just to make sure that we're catering to the demand from the Singaporean population. At the post-graduate level, master's and PhD, there is no limit. At the master's level, about seventy per cent are international students in that space. A lot from China, but not just from China, and of course in the PhD space, we have a high proportion of international students as well, probably about sixty-five per cent.

Interviewer: The contribution that you're doing, in terms of upskilling service provision or capability, would be through master's programs?

President: Yes.

Interviewer: For Indonesians or for Thai people who can pay that sort of fee?

President: Absolutely, but we have recently grown another wing, and that's skills upgrading that may not need a full master's degree. The Singapore government has led a national movement through what they call SkillsFuture. It's for the forty-year-olds, fifty-year-olds who need some upskilling and reskilling as the economy changes. The Singapore government has invested a lot of resources in that. Every adult Singaporean has received $500 which can be used for any course. At the same time, universities are encouraged strongly to get into the space of provision of short courses, and we get subsidized by the government if you need to develop your course and, well, the government subsidizes a lot of it. We've developed something called SMU Academy that, at the midpoint this year, would have had about twenty thousand unique individuals come and take short courses with us.

Interviewer: This is part of the continuing education school?

President: Yes. They could be doing courses on blockchain, which didn't exist when they were university undergraduates, or fintech or data analytics, or a whole bunch of other areas. Human capital development, technology, finance, service operations, business improvement, internationalization, and so forth.

Interviewer: How did you identify those areas?

President: We've done a couple of things. One is just in terms of the strengths within the university and two, what we assess to be the demand. We've shifted course along the way, just observing where the demand is. While we are very much known as a university strong in finance, starting as a management school, we thought that was where we really would make a big push, and we did, and we have a very healthy number there. The big explosion is in people who want to know the interface between finance and technology. Fintech, blockchain. How is it applied? We found that the largest areas are precisely in the interface between IT and business.

Interviewer: They're face-to-face provision; they're not online?

President: At the moment, all of them are face-to-face. We have experimented with some online versions, but we don't go fully online. At best, it is blended. We believe in that; it is very much the DNA of this institution to be much more personalized in our approach to education, starting with undergraduates. We make sure that that DNA pulls through our different kinds of courses.

Interviewer: You price it up, though, accordingly?

President: We price it accordingly. It might be up; it might be down actually because the price point in different markets differs, and we're just in the midst of a study of the market segments and the price points and the needs. As I've been visiting university counterparts in the region, and business and industry in the region, there is a strong demand for such courses.

Interviewer: They don't deliver a master's though. They deliver…?

President: They deliver certificates and graduate diplomas which can stack up. You can do an individual, stand-alone course, or you can do a number of those to stack up to what's in a certificate, and you can…

Interviewer: A certificate is a quarter of a master's maybe, and then diploma would be half a master's?

President: I don't remember the precise credits, but yes, it's a segment of a master's. Then, you can stack up the certificates into a diploma. Then if you do still more, you can stack up to a master's. Right now, what we're seeing is a lot of interest in the stand-alone courses and the certificates. A little bit in the graduate diplomas. It's too early in the day for us to see whether people are going to come back to stack up to a full master's.

Interviewer: From the Singaporeans or for…?

President: For Singaporeans, at this point in time. For the region, we started offering some courses but we're nowhere near ramping up, as the market demand in Singapore is so strong right now that we're catering to that in the main. Then we want to do the market study before we decide where we're going to really go.

Interviewer: What are the big challenges SMU is facing?

President: The big one is not unique to SMU but common to all the local universities. That's a declining cohort at the undergraduate level just because Singaporeans are not reproducing ourselves. Our fertility rate is at an abysmal 1.1. What it means is that the undergraduate population, over time, is going to decline. With government policy limiting international students at the undergraduate level, it means that the whole undergraduate cohort is going to reduce.

Interviewer: Might that change?

President: It could change. Depends on government policy.

Interviewer: The policy of many governments is just build more buildings and hire more faculty and generate more revenue. Singapore's taken a different approach.

President: Australia's done that very extensively. I think the challenge is a political one, as we see in many places. In the US, you would see a limit to the out-of-state students. In Singapore, the international students. The reason for that is that a very high premium is placed on university education, as in many Asian countries. The Singaporean parents' perception will be: if you have capacity to take in more students, why are you limiting the cohort participation rate to forty per cent, which is what it is. If they say you can take in another two thousand international students, why not take in more Singaporeans?

Interviewer: Why does the government place that block on the market of talent development these days? Maybe it made sense thirty years ago when families wouldn't contribute?

President: I actually agree with the government position. I don't know whether it should be forty per cent or fifty per cent, but I agree that if we open the doors too wide and there are too many graduates flooding the employment market, the value of the degree's going to drop. You're going to have degree holders who are bank tellers or…well, there won't even be bank-telling work because everything's going to be automated. We're kicking the can down the road as a country if we say, "Oh, come one, come all. Everybody has a degree." Then, the aspirations are built up for certain kinds of roles that the market cannot accommodate.

Interviewer: So it's to keep the labour market, to stratify the labour market service, so there's people who can try specifically for lower-tier jobs, if you like?

President: It's about assessing what the economy needs and delivering the education appropriately for that. I see the sense of this segmentation. Of course, who's to say what that magical figure should be? Forty per cent? Thirty per cent? Fifty per cent?

Interviewer: That comes from workforce projections and studies?

President: It does.

Interviewer: Basically, the universities are told what to do to service that need.

President: The universities are given enrolment targets.

Interviewer: Not catering for the fact that many Singaporeans would travel and work overseas.

President: The cohort participation rate does not include that proportion that goes overseas.

Interviewer: The main challenge is growing in ways that you can service, that don't dishonour domestic regulatory policies around student flows.

President: Yes. If there is going to be a declining undergraduate population, assuming the policy on international students doesn't change, then universities...

Interviewer: Is it ten per cent of a fixed number or ten per cent of the student number?

President: It's ten per cent of the intake target.

Interviewer: Ok, you can actually add more international students where you have empty seats in the room?

President: What happens is that a total target intake is assigned annually to each university, and ten per cent of that is for international students.

Interviewer: You don't have a problem filling space, so you would always have the requisite number of Singaporeans?

President: No, there has not been a problem filling space with the per cent requisite number of Singaporeans.

Interviewer: You won't lift people out of the vocational sector and shift them into the university?

President: We do have students who took the vocational education route who eventually make their way to the university.

Interviewer: Wouldn't the country keep the university numbers stable and import more people to service the lower end of the economy?

President: The importation is also a challenge because the watershed 2011 general elections were such that people are voting against the large influx of non-Singaporeans – of foreigners into the country. It's a delicate balance that the government is trying to keep in balance. Therefore, for us as universities, what we're looking to is to grow the post-graduate space, the master's space, and the continuing education space.

Interviewer: Are PhD numbers regulated or constrained?

President: They are.

Interviewer: By research funds and the like?

President: Yes. The master's is the only space where it's not regulated. The number of PhD students is regulated, and this is a recent constraint. The number of PhD students in each university is stipulated. The reason for that is because there was a huge growth in the last decade or so. A lot of these students were international students, with research scholarships, funded by Singapore taxpayers, and so there was a need to regulate. So the numbers have been stipulated, and within that, the proportion of international and Singaporean PhD students is also stipulated. Sixty-five per cent international, thirty-five per cent Singaporean. If you don't fill your Singaporean quota, you can't run away with your international numbers.

Interviewer: Got it. They're separate populations. My next question was about innovative social contributions, but it sounds like trying to apply the nation-building mission is front and centre of that. Then finding the slightly less regulated master's level to service the local regions. You can't actually service the local region through bachelor-level or PhD provisions. It's really master's or research projects.

President: Yes, and continuing education.

Interviewer: Oh, yeah, for profit. Let's turn a little bit now towards Tsinghua. What interests you most about Tsinghua?

President: Tsinghua, of course, has a strong reputation, particularly in engineering. What I've watched over the years is a growing attention to the arts, the humanities, as evident through the…. I forget what it's called now, the Tsinghua arts college?

Interviewer: School of Art and Design?

President: Art and Design. It used to be separate, somewhat separate, and then it's been brought into the fold.

Interviewer: Yes. It was a stand-alone college.

President: Indeed. Indeed. The rounding out of the university, if I might put it that way. Tsinghua attracts some of the best students in the country, and this is a very big country. The best are really amazing people. The quality has been extremely impressive as is its absolute commitment to that. Deep interactions and engagement with industry is also an area that we are ambitious to grow in and there are many things to learn from here. On this particular visit, we have particular missions. Collaboration in the law school and areas of intersections between law and technology. The work that's being done by my colleagues in research on aging populations. There are some specific areas where we can collaborate. Our accounting program has a joint master's in the CFO leadership space. These are specific program collaborations.

Interviewer: What challenges do you think would shape Tsinghua's future?

President: Hmm. That's a very good question. Size and tradition are double-edged swords. I know that from my own previous institution. A large institution is much more difficult to steer and change. Smaller institutions like the one I'm in right now, much more nimble. Not so many layers. Size and tradition. Tradition is a great advantage. History and tradition, where people say, "That's a venerable institution with its reputation, et cetera." Tradition is also very difficult to change. Sometimes in higher education, the need to be nimble is not to be underestimated.

Interviewer: How about Chinese higher education? What are your main impressions of it more broadly, across the system?

President: First, the massification of that over the years has been staggering. The number of graduates that the universities are producing is absolutely staggering, which has helped to power the economy but also brings its own social challenges. The ant colonies in Beijing, for example.

Interviewer: The "ant colonies"?

President: The ant tribes. The graduates who have poor employment prospects, are poorly paid, and are living in somewhat dire conditions.

Interviewer: Some may, in fact, be living underground, too, huh?

President: So the massification has been staggering, with its contributions and its challenges. Further, the massive resources that are pumped into some of the selected universities have been just astonishing. I have research collaborators in China. More often than not it's money chasing ideas. What else has struck me? The global ambitions, if you will. The pressures to publish internationally in SCI journals, SSCI journals, and so forth, that's really created a bit of a pressure cooker in the university system. I have had PhD students myself from China trying to get back into the Chinese system and the expectations of what they have to deliver in order to get their jobs are nontrivial. Those are some of the things I observe. The great ambitions that many of the universities have that have been enabled by the resources made available.

Interviewer: Where do you see this system going in the next thirty years? The current plan is to 2050, so where do you think China might be in terms of higher education by then?

President: I think some of the best universities in the world are going to be right here in China – the great advantage that many Chinese professors have is that they are much more bilingual than a typical professor in the US or UK, either just through their international activities or because they have returned from overseas.

They are able to navigate truly in a much more international way. When we say "international," over the last five decades, we've basically meant using the English language: the Anglophone world has dominated. In a truly international world, it's much more diverse than that and goes beyond the domination of Anglo languages. Many Chinese professors are going to be able to navigate that so much better. I see at the so-called international conferences the large numbers of Chinese professors who are attending. Within the country, the number of conferences internal to China, and the academic and intellectual discourses that are ongoing, are very vibrant themselves. These are people I see and know. There's a group of professors in China who are able to navigate both worlds. You don't see that as much in the US or elsewhere. I think in thirty years' time, some of the best universities in the world are going to be Chinese universities.

Interviewer: What sort of contributions do you think higher education should make during this period to broader or to the world? Research universities? Do you think that the role of the university will change?

President: Yes. I read recently an article, actually a report in *Times Higher Ed Supplement*, and what they'd done was to survey maybe two hundred university presidents around the world – for what they saw the changes to universities would be and the contributions of universities to the world. One of the things that I agree with, and I would have responded in the same way if I had responded to the survey, was that the greater involvement with the world of practice, whether it's industry or public policy, is necessarily going to deepen for the survival of the universities themselves. Because as governments and the public invest resources in universities, there is the expectation of return to society and economy. When that doesn't happen, universities will begin to lose the respect, the standing, in societies. The ivory tower of the university is not something that universities can afford. That's one area where universities, working closely with industry, business, government sectors, contributing back to society and economy, that's just going to be so important.

One of the things that the report mentioned, which gives me great cause for sadness, is the decline of the humanities, or I should say, the further decline of the humanities. I think we could not be more wrong if we allowed that. With automation, with artificial intelligence, with all the new technologies that Industry 4.0 brings, the new jobs created are going to be the ones that require human intervention in a way that machines can't. That means understanding the human psyche. That means understanding humanity. What is the humanities if not the study of humanity? I'm not suggesting that we should start producing a whole lot of graduates in history and literature, et cetera, but the education of an engineer, a scientist, a computer scientist, a doctor, must be done together with an understanding of the human being, the human individual and human societies. I would hope that universities would pay heed to that and play a leadership role in explaining that.

Interviewer: I feel like that the humanities is a substrate to the other more professionally oriented fields.

President: Yes!

Interviewer: Just one last question, if I may. If you could just pick one or two reforms to undergraduate education or doctoral education, what would you do? Without the constraints of your current university or your role.

President: There are two reforms at the undergraduate level that I have actually managed to introduce into SMU and scale up. We're in the process of scaling them up for the last three years, four years now. I firmly believe in them, and that's why I pushed to implement them. One of them is especially appropriate in a university that has the name "management" in it. One would imagine that we're producing professionals and, therefore, the emphasis and direction would be very much in producing the accountants, the lawyers, the business professionals, et cetera, and absolutely we would continue to do that. But at the same time, what I said a moment ago was that we should put a premium on introducing that core curriculum, or substrata as you called it, of education that's much more broad-based in the humanities or social sciences.

Interviewer: I think HKU has done that; the common first year.

President: We've certainly introduced a core curriculum that is very compelling, but more than that, we've recognized that the conversations generated in that core curriculum should go beyond the first year. We don't want students to say, "Well, let's get that over and done with." We actually want them to make the connections and linkages to the rest of what they learn in university. What we're trying to do is to, very intentionally in the classroom, make those connections. We had a capstone course for our business degree which entailed using the classics and asking the students to reflect on characters in the classics – to reflect on leadership and business leadership. So the challenge is, how to make those connections so that they're not disconnected parts of an education that the first part becomes a checklist of things that people have to tick off.

The other part is interweaving the world of academic learning and the world of learning from practice. The Germans have done that well with the apprenticeship system. Interweaving work and learning. We've started some work-study programs where our students, over four days a week, over six months, are interning with a company. One day a week, they're coming back to class, and it's in very specific programs that we have curated. Just to give you an example, we've tied up with Google Singapore. Our professors have worked with the Google professionals to develop the data analytics courses. The students then go and intern in Google partners like Grab and Carousel and so forth. They're interweaving the world of learning in the classroom and the world of learning at work. We've adopted the same arrangement in our health economics and management program where students are interning with SingHealth, which is the largest public provider of hospital care in Singapore. It's not in medicine. It's not in producing doctors or nurses. It's in hospital administration. Coming back full circle to the conversation

I had a moment ago in this room with Tsinghua colleagues about doing research on aging around the world, certainly in Singapore, we say the population is aging. We need more medical workers, by which we mean more doctors, more nurses, more radiotherapists, more physiotherapists. Not enough attention has been paid to the need for people who know how to run the hospital as an organization and a business. We've thus introduced health-care management, and our students are interning with SingHealth. They're sitting in meetings with the C-suites in the hospital sector, and they're taking courses co-curated with these people between the professors and the professionals in the classroom. That interweaving, I think, is going to be so important. While internships has, for a long time, been the main modus operandi, there is a risk that students do not adequately link what they learn academically and practically, so this is a way to help them bring what they learn intentionally together. That's what we're trying to do.

We've also developed something called SMU-X, which is a pedagogical approach where, essentially, it's consultancy with students working in multidisciplinary groups, and they're solving real-world problems. We have partners, "clients." It could be public sector, private sector, people sector, agencies, voluntary welfare organizations that are confronting a particular problem or challenge that they need a solution to. Our students, with supervision from a professor, will go over thirteen weeks and deliver something that is a solution or a perspective.

Interviewer: That's a full credit.

President: It's a full credit course.

Interviewer: It's structured at any point in the student's lifecycle, and it could be students from all three levels?

President: Yes, indeed. There are certain courses that are marked SMU-X. They are courses that would fulfil the curriculum requirements, but they're delivered in SMU-X style. We've grown that a great deal now, and so they're not just reading case studies, which has traditionally been the way.

Interviewer: Business might come to the university and say, "I've got a problem." Approach a particular professor. That professor would advertise for students.

President: Exactly.

Interviewer: Build up the capability and the students get experience. To capture your broad reform, which I'll take for bachelor's through to PhD, it's to get the broad, theoretical, classics-type thinking, professionally oriented thinking, and apply academic theory, method, and practice.

President: Indeed. I think that's a very nice summary of it. The academic learning and the practice learning interweave. Different platforms for doing that.

20

PROFESSOR FERIDUN HAMDULLAHPUR, PRESIDENT AND VICE CHANCELLOR OF THE UNIVERSITY OF WATERLOO, CANADA

Interview background

The former president and vice chancellor of the University of Waterloo, Feridun Hamdullahpur, visited Tsinghua University in November 2019 and had in-depth exchanges with Tsinghua University president Qiu Yong on strengthening cooperation in scientific research between the two universities. On 27 November 2019, Dr Liu Lu, a postdoctoral fellow at the Institute of Education at Tsinghua University, interviewed President Hamdullahpur.

Feridun Hamdullahpur, male, Canadian, born in 1953, engineering scientist, PhD, graduated from Nova Scotia University of Technology. He has served as the president and vice chancellor of the University of Waterloo from 2010 to 2021. From 2009 to 2010, he served as provost and vice president, and from 2006 to 2009 as provost and vice president of Carleton University in Ottawa. In 2013, he was awarded the Queen Elizabeth II Diamond Jubilee Medal for his outstanding contributions to education and innovation. In 2014, he was appointed a fellow of the Canadian Academy of Engineering. In 2018, he was appointed a special fellow of the Royal Society of Canada.

The University of Waterloo was founded in 1957 and is located in Waterloo, Ontario, Canada. It is one of Canada's most innovative research universities and it ranks among the top ten Canadian universities in various university rankings. It ranked 166th in the 2021 QS World University Rankings. The school is known for its Co-operative Education project, a model of government-industry-university-research cooperation, and an important driving force for regional economic and social development. The University of Waterloo and Tsinghua University have a long-term cooperative relationship. In 2005, the two universities signed an inter-school cooperation agreement and a student exchange agreement. The cooperation

DOI: 10.4324/9781003248286-22

FIGURE 20.1 President Feridun Hamdullahpur with Dr Liu Lu

between the two universities has covered quantum computing, mathematics, environment, and other fields. In 2018, the two universities decided to build a joint research centre for micro-nano energy and the environment.

The interview involved the president and his personal background, leadership team, the president's university, Tsinghua University, Chinese higher education, and global higher education. Key points included spending time on school construction, strategy formulation, and innovation, ensuring professionalism among staff and leaders, engaging people in strategic planning and institutional operations, and linking university education and research with the development of society as a whole (Figure 20.1).

The interview

Interviewer: The first question is about you. Where do you invest your time as a leader, as a president?

President: I invest most of my time in thinking, planning, strategizing about how we can make the university a more advanced university that students, staff, faculty will basically benefit from that more advanced study. That's where I invest my time overall, through a variety of different things: how, day by day, we can make the university a better place.

Interviewer: Do you invest any time managing people?

President: I do. My personal philosophy is to spend as little time as possible in managing that involves micromanaging, and spend most of my time in building, strategizing, and innovating. But there are times that, for a variety of reasons again, I spend more of my time in managing than I would like to. Those are the cases where if you don't do it, then you'll pay quite a bit for it. But ideally, I like to spend at least, if you want a hypothetical ratio, thirty per cent of my time in management and seventy per cent of my time in strategizing, planning, and building.

Interviewer: Good, interesting. So as we know, your background is mechanical engineering. How does your discipline background shape your leadership?

President: Yes, I think whoever is a leader will have to come from one discipline, and mine happens to be in engineering. I have degrees in both mechanical and chemical engineering. What helps me in my case, as an engineer, you have an ability to really have a good understanding of what the issue is, or what your conceptual design is. It gives me the ability to sift through really complicated issues and cases and have a way forward in my mind, and I have the ability to achieve that quite fast. Then again, it's all about teamwork and how you either build a team for this specific thing, or how do you distribute certain responsibilities and functions among the team members? That is basically how my engineering background helps me in my day-to-day job as president.

Interviewer: Right, so how are you using your technical knowledge to deal with challenges?

President: Yes, I don't, even though I'm still a very active researcher, and I believe I have many years of experience as an engineer. I make sure that I do not bring my own personal technical knowledge into addressing university-wide issues. I could've been a lawyer. I could've been a physician. I could've been a historian. Universities should have and must have expertise covering the entire spectrum of operations and I rely on those people as opposed to bringing my own subjective knowledge, which happens to be in engineering.

Interviewer: Can I ask another interesting question? How did you find it when you work with colleagues with social science backgrounds? What's the difference between these kinds of colleagues in social sciences and in natural science or engineering?

President: It's a must, absolutely, and we learn a lot from each other. To have an artist or people from arts or humanities or social sciences, basically, it deepens the conversation. They provide some very important angles or at least segments of a conversation that I wouldn't normally have myself, but they bring a very different perspective. The most visible one is the ability to think beyond concepts I would have considered myself, to think beyond what's readily available to me, and they're able to approach the "what if?" part of the question differently. Also, they're able to connect whatever we do to other big things. The most classical one, when I bring a subject of, let's say, connecting artificial intelligence to medicine and agriculture and other things, and they will say, "Well, there are also some ethical aspects," or "There are also human aspects, so then what about those?" Therefore, we're not coming out with initiatives that are only driven by technology or science. We're coming out with initiatives that are a lot wider and connected to political science or human rights, human behaviour, all of those things. It is absolutely a must, and I am very happy to have those kinds of people on my team, yes.

Interviewer: I believe you must have a very professional leadership team to assist you to deal with daily issues. What kind of balance do you think is important to find between people interested in performance, operations, these kinds of things?

President: Yes, so from my perspective, what you want to see happening at the university at every level must be demonstrated at the highest level at the president's office. If I expect the highest level of professionalism from everybody, from student services to food services to parking at the university, my office has to set an example. That's one thing. Number two, I do a lot of things. I talk to students. I talk to faculty. My day is filled with many things, and I will be totally lost, and many of the things that I do will be wasted if I didn't follow up, follow through some of those. I have a good number of people who ensure that what I will say to you one day, the following day I will not completely forget about it as if the conversation never happened. I have a position called chief of staff who is basically my right hand, right arm, in looking after the administrative part of what I do. It is done in a very professional manner that every time we have very well computerized sheets, items to follow, items in progress, and we go through them. There are others, for example, whose job is strictly to look after my calendar, making sure that everybody's desire to have a conversation with me or to meet with me to discuss some important things are addressed in a timely manner but at the same time manages my time extremely efficiently so that if I can't finish one meeting in seven minutes, I finish another meeting seven minutes sooner, and many other aspects. The president's office again, both from operational perspective and also professional perspective, has to set the highest example at the university, and I'm very happy right now that we're able to do that.

Interviewer: How many people in your presidential office?

President: It's a very modest number of five people.

Interviewer: So to what extent does the work of the leadership team focus on internal or external matters, or control or uncertainty?

President: They do both. As I said, even though it's five people, they coordinate with many of the internal stakeholders. They make sure that they work as a team. I'll give you an example. Say that I am going to host a group of people at my house for dinner, and these people could be industry people. They could be donors. They could be a lot of things, and my office is in control of what happens at my house, but they work with everybody else. Everybody who is involved makes sure that I have the right background, I have the right notes, have the right information, and

I know what the outcome should be from that dinner. It's not just to sit down and have a meal. It has a purpose, and then they make sure what will happen afterwards. It requires teamwork. Sometimes, they do it with internal people. Sometimes, they do it with external people. If I'm going to meet some government officials, they make sure that they work with their people and everything is well connected. Same as my visit here; that is coordinated in a fashion that involves a lot of internal people as well as external people here at the embassy, and all of those are controlled by the office again at the university.

Interviewer: Now, let's talk about your university. What specific cultures and traditions are important to your university?

President: Yes, our university is synonymous with innovation. It's a university where it differentiates itself from thousands and thousands of other universities because we're not prisoners of conventional thinking. We are able to think differently and that's how the university was created from day one, is how education should be, how research should be, how the two should be connected, and how we should progress as a university in the society and the world. That's how the university was created when there were many other universities around and they didn't need another conventional university. And so our DNA of the university very much just flashes out as a very innovative university, but it started out just with engineering, and then mathematics and computer science, and science and all of those came together. It may seem like in the beginning the university, even though very innovative, started out as a technology and science university. Now, it became a full comprehensive university with arts and environment and social sciences, everything along with its traditional strengths in engineering and mathematics and computer science.

Interviewer: Do any specific initiatives ensure the university achieves its innovation goals?

President: Absolutely, we call it strategic planning where we just completed one. What it means is the university does not see itself doing the same thing day after day after day, and it's very easy actually to be in that position by just building new buildings and modernize your classrooms a little bit and add more courses, so programs here and there and say, "Oh, well, we are keeping up to date." But for us, it is very important to connect ourselves with our past and with our future and how we'll be. Are we building a future that is important? To do that, go back to your previous question. How do we define ourselves? Who are we and how should we continue defining ourselves as a university that is very true to its core mandate, core characteristics? To do that, we talk to everybody, like students, staff, faculty, alumni, people outside the university. What their thoughts are, what their dreams are, what their imaginations will be. Then it's almost like a two-year process, a two-year-long process. Then you build a plan that will guide you for the next five years, and then you build another one. It's not just like having a book, a strategic plan of let's go to page thirty-six and see what it says. It is how you combine everybody's ideas, thoughts, dreams together and say, "This is the university we want to see five years from now," which differentiates itself from many others and stands alone as a unique, unconventional innovation university.

Interviewer: Did you do some student survey or questionnaire to ask students and alumni for the feedback?

President: We did, but we did more than that. We did close to fifty open sessions that people came to, either groups of fifty or sometimes over one hundred, and we sat in a room face-to-face and listened to them. We told them about certain things, but we listened to them. That is more important: to listen to them face-to-face.

Interviewer: How many students participated in that?

President: Probably about three thousand, yes, and then more either through online surveys or they sent comments. Our participation is very high. That's why when you have a plan like this, a lot of people will come and say, "Look, I have no idea what this plan is about. Nobody asked me." No, we asked every single person, and it was up to them to take part in it and a lot of them did. Therefore, when I say, "Here is our strategic plan," it is our strategic plan. It's not my strategic plan.

Interviewer: What kind of institutional challenges do you think the University of Waterloo is facing now, or maybe over the next few years?

President: Yes, so one common challenge that many institutions face is in our inertia or we stay in our comfort zone, don't want a lot of changes because for about one thousand years any university did more or less the same thing, teaching and learning and research. But there are hundreds, or now thousands, of different possibilities and permutations. To bring the sense of change, positive change, change for good is the most important challenge. To get people – those people are mostly faculty members, professors – to just take their minds off their day-to-day work and say that, as an example, I have been teaching physics for the past twenty years. This is what I do. Why don't I talk to people in the brain sciences or neurosciences and see if maybe we can combine something together? That's a change. That's a change in your mind, that's a change that takes people out of their comfort zone. This is what I know, is what I love. Now, gosh, now I need to figure out about the human brain or other things, but when you're able to combine those the results are spectacular. That is the challenge. The challenge is to get people to understand the value of positive change for the betterment of what they do, and for the good of whether it's society, or economy, or anything you can think of.

Interviewer: Another question that we're required to ask is what innovative contribution does the University of Waterloo contribute to society?

President: Many ways, every single one of our graduates is our contribution to the society.

Interviewer: Because of the cooperative plan?

President: Well, of course, cooperative education plays a very important role, but our objective is when you…of course, it cannot be done one hundred per cent. I wish it were, it could be. We tell our students, if your objective of coming to this university is just to get a degree and then get a job after the degree, probably you're really undermining or underestimating your potential. But if you're seeing yourself as leader, regardless of what you studied, computer science or physics or sociology, can you think of yourself as change agent? Can you think of yourself as a leader? Can you think of yourself as a disruptor that you don't need to wait for somebody else to come and do something and then you say, "Oh, I'll follow this?" If you think that you went to a university that provided you with absolutely the top excellent education, like the students here at Tsinghua or Waterloo, then why not? Why shouldn't that person be you? That thought whether it comes in the form of an entrepreneur, whether it comes in the form of a social activist, is our single most important contribution to the society. Then there are so many other more visible things, and either students, or faculty members, or research projects provide safe clean water to people in Africa, or they ensure that the food security is there. We talk about so many things to fight with climate change and many other things. Each and every one of what we do, including tremendous work in either quantum information, science, or physics, they are significant contributions to the society. And if you don't make that connection, I think you just become a very routine piece in this huge complex machinery.

Interviewer: I totally agree because the university must. They have a very strong connection with the society.

President: If you don't do those, many of our graduates will lose their jobs or functions to automation and artificial intelligence and robots.

Interviewer: What's the main impressions you may have about Tsinghua and China, especially Chinese higher education?

President: Yes, my first visit to China was in 1987, and my first university I visited was Zhejiang University, which where I went doesn't exist now. It's a brand-new university. We're a different campus. Tsinghua is synonymous to excellence to me, and not just in education but in scholarship and research, and again a very, very visible icon in China. And immediately when you say, "Excellent excellence in education and research," this is the university that comes to my mind first, and that's the reason why I keep coming back and forth. We have research partnerships. We have other partnerships. We have partnerships with many other Chinese universities, but Tsinghua has a very special place.

Interviewer: In the past few years, Tsinghua is trying to become more internationalized and has become a top university not only in China but also globally. From your perspective, how can Tsinghua best contribute to global higher education?

President: Yes. I think one thing that I take from my own institution that I…we are very careful in working with a very good, very good international partners that our both social, scientific, technological, and economic footprint will be much, much bigger if we are working with a number of other partners. Tsinghua is definitely one of them. In doing so, we are not necessarily too preoccupied by selecting our partners from "let's go to the THE ranking and work with da, da." They represent something. What we look at what will be the impact of this partnership? What will be the impact of this partnership to our students, to our researchers, and to our economy, to our industry, but to the whole world? I consider myself tremendously fortunate to be president of, in my mind, one of the best universities in the world. Same with Tsinghua is valid. What do I make the most out of this? How would the world benefit more if we do things together? How would the world benefit from what I do in Waterloo, Ontario, Canada? What would it mean to a person in the southern tip of South Africa? Believe it or not, those are a lot of the thoughts that go through my mind that I don't want my institution, or I don't want my time as president, to be wasted in worrying about the little things here and there, but a broader contribution. The best thing to do to build excellence at our institutions, excellence from research to excellence in teaching and learning, excellence in caring about other people, and how do we combine them that five years from now when you look, turn around and look back, say, "We have built something. We have built something that will stay, and others will be able to build on top of that." This is my understanding, my personal philosophy, of what excellence is. And I believe a greater degree of this is happening in Tsinghua as well. That's the reason why we are so keyed on establishing these partnerships.

Interviewer: Do you think Tsinghua has some kinds of challenges similar to University of Waterloo? What kind of challenges from your perspective, thinking about Tsinghua?

President: Yes, I don't have a lot of detailed information. For example, in the funding front, to me, our funding is very important. We have so many great ideas, initiatives, but they will not become a reality unless they are backed by funding and resources, and in our case, it's a challenge. We can't take anything for granted. In Tsinghua's case, for example, is funding a big issue? If it is, then it has to be very carefully factored into the university's planning to secure that funding. As I said, this is universal, that many professors, they are very happy and comfortable with what they do, and how do you get them to talk to each other? How do you get them to think beyond what they do today? Is this a challenge? Do you have an environment where people, faculties, students, graduate students, they come together and say, "Well, we have an idea. We have ideas that we could probably share with the administration." Those are the kind of challenges. The biggest challenge for me, and I believe it will be for Tsinghua, that to create an environment that is defying the status quo, the greatness of the status quo, and looking forward and say that, well, you look back ten years. This university is at a fabulous, fabulous place. We want to jump ahead ten years and look back and say that we are even at a much higher place.

Interviewer: What about the Chinese higher education, because Chinese higher education has already experienced a massive expansion in the last few years, so what about the future? Do you have any suggestions for Chinese higher education development in the next few years, especially the quality?

President: Yes, this is just an observation from my part. Chinese higher education, the number of universities, the number of university students, and the number of research projects, the sophistication, and excellence of those research projects, has just been fantastic. There is no resemblance, ok, between the time that I came here in 1987 and teaching at Zhejiang University, and systems that I knew one day they will be far ahead of it, and today there's a big difference. The Chinese, China, Chinese universities, in terms of quality and quantity, they leap forward like no other country, and the works gets done. What is missing in my humble observation is time for creativity, time for innovation that the made-in-China thought will have to be at the core of that. I think it's happening. I enjoy the presence of thousands and thousands of Chinese undergraduates, graduates. I think going forward, if there is without losing their native language ability is extremely important, but also there the fluency in, especially in, English and other languages will also be a very important factor for Chinese universities to really achieve their next level of status.

21

PROFESSOR THOMAS F. HOFMANN, PRESIDENT OF THE TECHNICAL UNIVERSITY OF MUNICH, GERMANY

Interview background

In October 2020, Thomas F. Hoffman, president of Technical University of Munich, attended the online signing ceremony of the flagship partnership memorandum between Tsinghua University and Technical University of Munich. On 12 November 2020, Professor Hamish Coates of the Institute of Education at Tsinghua University conducted an online interview with President Hoffman.

Thomas F. Hofmann, male, German, born in 1968, graduated with a PhD from the Technical University of Munich, Germany. Since October 2019, he has served as the president of the Technical University of Munich. He has served as the editor-in-chief and member of the Editorial Board of journals such as *European Food Research and Technology*, *Molecular Nutrition and Food Research*, *Chemosensory Perception*, and *Agricultural and Food Chemistry*. President Hoffman won the German Chemical Industry Award and the Young Scientist Award from the Agricultural and Food Chemistry Branch of the American Chemical Society (ACS). He has received the 2013 Annual Research Paper Award of the *American Journal of Agricultural Chemistry and Food Chemistry*, the US Agricultural and Food Chemistry Application Award, and other awards from the ACS.

Founded in 1868, the Technical University of Munich is a member of the German TU9 Alliance. It was also selected as one of the first three German Elite Universities by the German Research Federation. The Technical University of Munich ranks in the forefront of various world university rankings. For example, it is ranked fiftieth in the 2021 QS World University Rankings and forty-first in the 2021 *Times Higher Education* World University Rankings. The Technical University of Munich has nurtured many Nobel Prizes, Leibniz Prizes, and other top award winners. It has close ties with many famous European companies in scientific research, education, and production, and continues to send into society

DOI: 10.4324/9781003248286-23

FIGURE 21.1 Professor Thomas F. Hofmann

Source: Thomas Dashuber, Technical University of Munich.

a large number of outstanding talents. The school advocates internationalization and has scientific and educational cooperation relationships with nearly a hundred universities across the world.

The interview involved the president and his personal background, leadership team, the president's university, Tsinghua University, Chinese higher education, and global higher education. Professor Hofmann discussed vision setting, supporting people and building communities, institutional structures, spurring innovation and spin-offs, and repositioning universities within changing knowledge ecosystems (Figure 21.1).

The interview

Interviewer: Where do you invest your time as a leader?

President: Primarily to present the strategic vision of the university as a whole, like the TUM Agenda 2030, which we released about one and a half years back to define the nature and future for TUM, but also to relay to members of our TUM family the future goals and the shared values we have. Particularly also, to encourage people around the university to think out of the box and cross-connect between the different departments and schools in order to tackle the really important challenges that are waiting at the intersections of disciplines. Finally, I think to represent the interests of the university in politics and political decision-making in the state of Bavaria, as well as being engaged as a leader in our major alliances, regional and local alliances here. Because TUM is very strongly rooted also in the local ecosystem, but also internationally to our alliance partners, academic partners but also industrial partners.

Interviewer: Ok, so a fair amount of vision setting and outreach, both of a political nature, but also building connections and engagements. Would I have that right?

President: Right.

Interviewer: Could you give us an example of a specific day. I don't know that anything is typical this year, but say yesterday? What does your diary look like this week, for example? We try and get very specific. Otherwise, everyone says "vision setting."

President: Yesterday, we finalized the fundraising activity. We just signed the contract for a new institute on building and construction, and it was a fifty million Euro fund which we will receive in order to build up this new institute. That is also a part of my work, to be heavily engaged in fundraising in order to support the strategic vision of the university. For example, integrating AI technologies into our really strong architecture and construction faculty is one of those. That's why we also look for extra funds to support those ideas. That's one of my major activities as well.

Interviewer: Ok. You're a chemist or a chemical engineer, or both?

President: Chemist.

Interviewer: How do you think that affects your leadership? Does it have any effect, or has it had particular shaping factors, or makes no difference?

President: My background for strategic study of the university as a whole?

Interviewer: In terms of your role as president and your disciplinary background, is there a connection there?

President: No, I don't see a real connection there. The only thing which is important is that, even in my times as an active chemist, I was always a person who had most fun cross-connecting my expertise to those of other scientists of other fields. Not only cooperation between chemists, but chemists to the medical faculty, to the life science faculty, et cetera, or even into other fields. I think this type of mindset is what I try to bring over more intensely into the university as a whole, but not especially because I'm a chemist. I think it's just more this interdisciplinary mindset that I experienced, that I just got over the last fifteen to twenty years, and that I will bring over more intensely into the university as a whole. I think it's quite independent whether I would be a chemist or a physicist or an engineer.

Interviewer: Ok, that's helpful. There seem to be two different perspectives broadly. One is it matters enormously. The other is, as you say, as you get more senior, you develop more generic leadership capabilities. You did say at the end if you were in the STEM fields. I presume if you're in the arts and humanities it could be different in terms of your capacity to talk to faculty members at TUM, yeah. Ok, let's go then to the unique experiences we have in 2020. I'll just ask you some basic questions because the situation is changing day by day all around the world. We're doing another project where we're trying to look at hybrid learning around the world and quick transformations that we've all found ourselves in this year after waiting so long for computers to finally deliver. You said the campus is open, but you've basically got some students who can study off campus online, and some who are coming in to do studios or labs or clinicals or things like this. Is that correct? It's a hybrid arrangement. Can you just give us a bit of an overview of what that involves at this stage?

President: Sure. I think what you said is completely right. It's because TUM is also a rather international university, so we than one-third of our students are not from Germany, and that means that also due to travelling restrictions, it's just not possible that all the students come in. What we learned is that after the first shutdown we had in Germany in March and April, at that time, most of the students really were at home, were not in Munich. Most of the students used the time during the summer season where the situation became better to come back to Germany. We have a lot of students from China, for example, here in Munich currently. They experience, so to say, a hybrid then, of digital performance – this is what they do from home – and really on-campus experience where we at least want to bring, to a certain extent, students in small groups to the campus.

That's particularly important for the freshmen students, for the first semester students. If you come to the university and you do not know either your colleagues or any other members, it is really a challenge. That's why we said we particularly want to support the first semesters and the transfer students, to be sure that they become a member in this university community so that they get to know their colleagues in the semester, that they at least meet once in a while their professors and so on. This is then supported and complemented by digital courses. Also lab courses, for example, in chemistry and biological or engineering lab courses. They take place in a physical form on campus.

Interviewer: Ok, so do individual faculty make the decision about what's on campus, what's online, or is it more at the faculty level, or is it an institutional level, or do you have a code system?

President: No.

Interviewer: Is it arranged by day or by location? Do you have a university-wide committee?

President: Yes, we have a university-wide committee when it comes to the hygienic regulations and what are the frame conditions, for example, to have practical courses: how many students can you have in a course, depending on the size of the room, and so on? This is done centrally, but then we have flexibility also on the department level. At least what we said is that, for example, for first semesters, they should have a priority when it comes to which students can use the premises here on campus. This was, so to say, steered centrally. The same thing is that lab courses definitely should be done physically, although we have some virtual lab courses available, but it's not the same. It's difficult to substitute, and that's why those courses that cannot be substituted we offer physically, and this is managed by the departments and the professors. That is working out very well, but we don't steer into the edges of the university and say to each and everybody what she has to do. This is not what we do. We just give the frame for it, what the expectation is, and then we get feedback and see which mechanisms work well and don't work so well. Then we can reshape it. This is working quite nicely.

Interviewer: My knowledge is mostly of Berlin, but the students don't live on the campus; they live in the community.

President: Right.

Interviewer: Yes, so they're actually coming in and out of the campus in a selective way and living in the community and student residence, so they're involved in the community. They're not on a campus facility, a locked campus facility.

President: Some are living at the campus, and some live in the city centre, for example, depending on where you are. TUM is a multi-campus university. We have five campuses. Depending on where you are, they then take the subway so that's a ten-minutes ride, for example, from Munich to our main campus. Yes, exactly.

Interviewer: Ok. Did you have a plan for this, or you developed this plan in March, shall we say? You had some kind of risk plans but you had to pull them together for this particular crisis?

President: Oh, in March, April, and May, students were not allowed on campus. At that time, there was really almost a close-down of the university campus. Not scientifically. The scientific labs still were operational with post-docs and PhDs. They worked in tandem, in a tandem operation style to be sure that you have the physical distancing, but students were not allowed on campus. The last semester, summer semester, was purely digital. This semester, the winter semester now, is more hybrid, still a lot of digital and will keep on to the future digital courses, but it was still primarily digital. But we have also had substantial presence on campus. That's different from the last semester.

Interviewer: I do want to talk about the future, but I'm just trying to get a sense of the present. Just a little bit about last year and the year before. Did you do online learning at all?

President: Yes.

Interviewer: In any meaningful way, or was it just around the edges? You could actually do some courses fully online, or it was half and half?

President: In the past, what we had was, I would say if you quantified it, I would say that probably twenty per cent of our courses were available digitally. They were backed by physical courses. The students could, for example, go to the campus to listen to the professor, and then at home or wherever could listen to the same course again in a digital format, like a redundant system: twenty per cent. Now and for the last semester, the summer semester, we ramped up digitally to probably really almost one hundred per cent. It was a major endeavour, but the student feedback – so we also did evaluation, so we evaluated the courses by student evaluations – and we got most of the courses very nice feedback. In particular, also now know much more about what type of formats, digital formats, are more efficient in education than others. We use this feedback now also to reconfigure what we are doing now in the winter semester.

Interviewer: That's exactly the direction I want to go. You've basically been forced to scale from twenty to one hundred per cent online. [Laughter.] I don't think any of us want to live online one hundred per cent of the time.

President: No.

Interviewer: You then say, ok, we can reverse engineer what we do in the future, what we've done in the past, and do the future a bit differently. What are you doing? What's going to stick in the future? What would you change? What are you going to keep? How are those decisions being made? What are the implications, I guess, for how you do education and teaching? I'm guessing that most of your faculty had some experience teaching online, but clearly logging into Zoom is different to actually doing a proper job. You actually need a different set of skills. What are you going to do into the future? Do you have enough clarity on that yet, or are you still having committees and doing experiments and waiting to see what winter brings and all this kind of thing? What do the next three years look like?

President: What we will change in the future is that, for example, the large-scale courses, so with about five hundred students, for example, first-semester mathematics and engineering, for example, those type of courses we will offer digitally in the future, and probably even only digital. That will be backed by smaller courses that bring from these cohorts smaller groups together that work more in a challenge-based project type of style to support, and to further experience, what they learned in the digital course. I think these large cohort programs, lectures, they will be taught digitally even in the future and then use the time they have on campus more for physical interaction, bringing students and teams together with the professors. This is the strategy we are following.

There are consequences, for example, because it means, do we need in the future that number of these large lecture halls? We have a lot of large lecture halls for thousands of people, for example. Definitely, we need some of those, but do we need that in this number? Don't we need also smaller groups, smaller formats where we can bring the teams in a co-creation space together, even between the disciplines, for example? I think this is what we are currently discussing. What is the consequence on the infrastructure of the university as well? It's not only on teaching format. It's also connected to how the future infrastructure will look like.

Interviewer: Related to that, how about staffing needs and the level of staffing, and the cost of duplication online and on campus? Instead of a full professor teaching first-year maths, you might have a person like that videoing the resources once, and then having more low-level staff give local support to students, for example. Have you analyzed the productivity implications of all of this, or is it too early? I guess you don't want to duplicate everything. That's very expensive.

President: No, we do not want to duplicate everything. In the past, we duplicated. Our digital formats were duplicated with presence formats. For those large-scale lectures, we will not duplicate that in the future because we will use then our presence time. And also the space we have – because the space is more limited somehow for smaller student cohorts, bringing them in teams together, and have the very large-scale lectures probably exclusively in a digital format.

Interviewer: Ok. Re-engineering a bit teaching and learning and social experiences, if you like, which then has some staffing implications. I don't know how easy it is to redo staffing in a German university, but probably like most, it's not that easy. You can reskill people over a period of years or redeploy them to do different things, or give them more research time, but the infrastructure also has an implication. Are there any other major consequences in terms of the next twelve to eighteen months, do you think, in terms of change at TUM?

President: At twelve months? I think twelve months is a very short time when you think of infrastructure change. For next year, next twelve months, and because we are now in the middle of the winter semester, we hope that even in the following summer semester, so summer semester 2021, that we will come back to a much higher degree of physical presence again on campus. I'm still fully, one hundred per cent, convinced that in the future, leading universities, our physical universities, are places perhaps of physical exchange between people and students and scientists, although this will be much more than in the past supported by digital programs. I don't see any university taking leadership in the future that will be primarily a digital university without strong physical interactivity. I think the physical interactivity is exactly what a university is all about, but it needs to be much more complemented and strengthened by digital programs. We started, or just launched, an edtech lab, an education technologies lab, where we really also developed new learning technologies that we bring into future education programs. It will be, I think because of the campus experience, for students to be inspired because they meet the professors, see these wonderful role models, but also the exchange they have between the different disciplines. This is so important for their personal growth and their motivation to find their way into the future that I cannot believe that can be taught digitally. I think you need the campus experience for that. It will be, much more than in the past, supported by digital means.

Interviewer: Yeah. Education is basically a human thing.

President: Exactly. Yes, there's a social component to it as well.

Interviewer: Yes, as in meeting your spouse, for example. An important dividend, I believe. You've gone through the broader implications for higher education, which is my next question. We will come back to elite universities, or prestigious or global universities, but where do you think the challenges and opportunities lie for higher education in and amongst all of this change? What are the major problems, if we focus on the problems because I guess everyone talks about the good stuff?

President: I think that one of the challenges is to be sure that universities manage to create this community spirit. This is also what I hear from some of the companies. Some of the companies at the moment, they complain that due to really a massive home office offerings, people stay at home not just for several days, and they come back to the campus, and they again work from home. You don't have this type of segmented presence on campus, but really, if you are in a home office for several weeks or months, we will lose some community spirit. This is important, to build a corporate spirit we always say, a TUM family that we all fight for and work very hard every day to improve the university as a whole, to improve the skills of our students, to improve our scientific performance, et cetera, et cetera. I think if this disconnected type of working today, which is digitally connected but not physically connected in the long run, I would be afraid that we may lose some of this community spirit, which I think is crucial for a global university. There are also some positives. For example, we did quite intensively use the time, this new time through COVID-19, to connect with other universities in Europe – with EuroTech Universities Alliance partners, EPFL Lausanne, and some other partners we have here, also Imperial College – to open some of our digital courses to their students. They opened their courses for our students. It means that, for example, if you are a student at TUM and you study certain programs, and there may be an interesting lecture at Imperial College or EPFL in Lausanne, that our students can get access to that to get an additional skill. Many of our programs are similar, but nevertheless, universities have some distinct differences, some specialties that may be interesting also for other students. If we use this also in the future, say through these digital means now, we can expand the horizon for our students. I think that is definitely an opportunity which we should take. That's probably a positive thing, and a negative thing, if you want it.

Interviewer: That's great. Ok, turning to TUM specifically now, can you give us a sense of the specific cultures and traditions which are important to TUM?

President: I think what TUM since several years stands for is that we are in constant change. It has the agility to react quickly to changing frame conditions. I think the frame conditions are changing all the time. There are scientific challenges, sure, and also today with the crisis, to be able to react quickly, and not only to react but to use these new frame conditions also to even catalyze, for example, certain changes that probably we should have done five years back. It's this entrepreneurial mindset that the university has to identify areas of opportunities and then try everything to exploit those opportunities. Also, it's the integrity of our community, of our partners. It starts from students to professors, to our alumni, to the alumni network that is truly global, and our partners in industry. Yes, I think these are two very important things.

Interviewer: Ok, so given that culture and tradition, what specific reforms do you plan? I know you didn't plan many of the transformations this year, but what specific reforms do you plan in the next, maybe, three or five years?

President: The university is in a historical transformation at the moment. We started some years back with completely reforming our faculty recruitment, but this is ongoing. We started about eight years back with the tenure track. That helped the university a lot to really be much more attractive for top people from all over the world and helped us in particular to internationalize. For example, we now recruit about forty per cent, almost fifty per cent, of our faculty from other nations. That leads to, in particular, if you compare TUM with other German universities, massive internationalization of faculty and students.

Interviewer: Within Europe or outside Europe, anywhere?

President: All over the world. Then, I think the biggest change we have currently is to move from the traditional system of faculties – faculty means more or less departments – into a school system where we have a matrix structure of larger schools, and cross-connecting through schools' integrative research centres that then focus on major challenges on, so to say, transdisciplinary approaches in order to tackle larger challenges. We changed from a very stiff, segmented system of individual, disconnected departments into this matrix system of schools and cross-connecting integrative research centres. We are on a good way to do that. The first schools have been founded. The first IRCs, Integrative Research Centers, have been founded. This process will be finalized completely in about two-and-a-half to three years.

Interviewer: Were you motivated by financial, strategic, research – what were the main drivers for that? I'm sure you wanted to optimize everything, but what was the main or the proximal stimulus for that major reform? Secondly, you mentioned something about tenure and faculty and global recruitment. How do you see the faculty, not just the workforce structure or the job structure, but are you going to start getting more people from industry or from different sorts of backgrounds other than government, for example? How do you see the workforce changing to suit that different model?

President: When it comes to faculty recruitment, I am fully convinced that we need a good mix of people with an industrial background, in particular engineering, but also with young tenure track professors coming in with strong new theoretical foundations, with new approaches, and bringing those together. So practical experience for some of the faculty members on the one hand, and the really scientific, top-notch, more basic research initiatives – bringing those people together.

I think this is the key. I think future engineering – at least in the past, Germany recruited many professors from industry. If you ask me, I think too many. That was the reason why sometimes the universities in Germany were very strong in collaboration with industry because of the natural bridges, so to say. That's fine. You need to keep that, but it's not enough anymore. We need all the new inspiration by new people coming, really, from a scientific track record but bringing those together in teams where you bring not only the different disciplines together but also the practical experiences and the practical needs and really where the needs are on the other hand with new approaches. I think this is a critical mass we have to build up.

Interviewer: What were the main drivers for these major reforms?

President: The major reason is not money because you just mentioned that. No, it's not financial reasons. It's primarily, how can we increase the scientific performance of the university to really bring out disciplinary strengths we have and work together in interdisciplinary teams? More a collaborative innovation approach. How can we support that? What we learned is that in the former system, sometimes we needed lots of activation energy to bring the people from different faculties together. With the new system, we see that already we have obviously a much lower barrier to cross the own research fields and to enter into new areas joined with other colleagues. I think that was probably the major reason. There are some others, but this is probably the major reason.

Interviewer: You sort of said, "This is what we want the institution to be contributing," and then worked backward from that to think about the easiest way of getting people together to solve or address those needs.

President: Without losing disciplinary strength: that is the point. We do not want to have interdisciplinary generalists. We want to have disciplinary deep divers with an open mindset for interdisciplinary collaboration. What we need, we need structures that support this type of cross-connectivity.

Interviewer: Just to be clear, that's obviously on the management research side, but that also then flows onto teaching and the expectations of graduates.

President: Yes exactly. Teaching is actually the same thing because I think the skill profile you need today, or probably in ten years, in fifteen years, the skill profiles are changing. Definitely you need, in a distinct discipline, you need deep-dive knowledge. There's no doubt about it, but this is not enough anymore. You have to learn the interdisciplinary connectivities of your field into others. You have to get the skills to communicate with other disciplines. There's a new culture, also a cultural aspect of collaborative spirit, that needs to be taught to our students, and this is not going to happen if you only teach the students in individual, segmented departments.

Interviewer: Ok. On to the next focus area of the interview, which is about global higher education generally. What do you think characterizes or distinguishes global universities? How would you distinguish a global university from a non-global university?

President: In particular, I think how attractive the university is to get best people from all over the world. Students, faculty, a university that is locally rooted. I think each global university needs to be rooted in a local ecosystem, very strong foundation. This gives the university its strength to branch out internationally and to be on eye-level in alliances with other strong places, with other strong partner universities, and have the joint ambition to really tackle major global challenges we have, not only local minor things but really tackle those major challenges. I think this is what I at least see as very important. To be attractive for the world, that's for me a global university. Even some as in our case to also have physical presence in other countries and other continents because this also helps a global university then to attract new people from all over the place, finding new partners in industry, or even in the governments, to help also solving local problems in other countries. That's, for example, one reason why we have our alliances in US, in Brazil, in Singapore, et cetera, et cetera.

Interviewer: What specific things do you think could or should be done to boost the research and innovation potential of these universities? You've talked about the internal restructures and the like, but clearly these universities, as you just said, are playing a much greater role in the community, in world affairs. As I'm focusing here on the link between the university and ecosystem, if you like, what is that ecosystem, and how should universities change it? What do they need to change themselves? I'm looking beyond government policy here.

President: I'm a strong believer that in the future it will be not necessarily the competition between institutions that counts. I think what is important is it will be the competition between ecosystems, between metropolitan regions. And that's why I think global universities with global ambition will need to do everything to generate local synergies, first of all, even with other universities. For example, here in Munich, we have two really excellent universities: the technical university and the LMU, our sister university. We always have been strong competitors in the past, and we need to be competitive. We want that because this is our drive. We have an everyday drive to be better than the other. That's true, but our strategy needs to be collaboration. This is, I think, important to generate local synergies because together in certain areas, like in astrophysics or in quantum sciences because both universities are very strong, we can generate a Munich ecosystem around quantum technologies. This is why Munich is in Europe here number one in quantum technologies because we bring all our forces together. We call this One Munich strategy. We try to bring on certain core areas of expertise where we think we can take a global leadership. We will bring our experts together, and that includes not only academic institutions. It includes global enterprises. Munich has the major strategic advantage that many of the large global enterprises with their headquarters are in Munich. We have seven tech companies with headquarters here. Seven others just moved in. We have a lot of the IT, biotech, and automotive mobility industry, we have sitting here and several others.

Then, we have the advantage that Munich is developing to become a hub for B2B high-tech companies, start-ups. TUM alone: we produce about seventy to eighty tech start-ups every year, with several unicorns which really grew massively over the last years. To bring those people together around core areas of technologies so that we have fundamental research in certain areas, and that goes all up the innovation pipeline to reach the market at the very end. I think that will be a key for the future for a global university: to be so attractive to get the best people from all over the world coming to Munich, and then to cross-connect with other places. That's the reason why, for example, we entered into a flagship partnership with Tsinghua just in recent years: because we think although Tsinghua is, with Beijing and with Shenzhen, such a place to bring, to bundle, forces in certain areas like in added manufacturing. We can jointly take really global leadership in those fields, and this is how I think global universities will work in the future. Local strength, and then cross-connect to the best in the world.

Interviewer: Just one more question about global universities and then a final question about Tsinghua. Given what you've just said, I couldn't imagine a worse set of indicators than the current set of university rankings for not just understanding what the operating environment is, but really guiding it forward into the future. What could we replace the current information discourse with if I can put it that broadly? How would you actually give concrete quantitative life in terms of policy indicators? How do you give life to what you've just said? Is it by measuring regions, not universities? Is it by looking at things other than patents in terms of contributions or social initiatives? How do we measure that stuff?

President: I'm not sure whether I got your question. How to measure the success of this community building?

Interviewer: Currently, everyone thinks that some universities are the best universities in the world because they publish papers in a small number of journals.

President: Oh, I get your point.

Interviewer: That might've been good twenty, thirty years ago, but there's no relation to what you just said. How do you demonstrate what you've just said, I guess, is the short question?

President: I think it's too easy to measure the performance of the university only by looking on publications. It's very important, no doubt about it, but I think even if you look at the current rankings, most of those rankings are still focusing too much on the classical, traditional parameters. It's much more than that. Look to the engineers. Why is the engineering industry in Germany, why are they very strong? We educate top people, the top education that goes then into industry, and that is also why it brings us up in some of the global important rankings, for example, to a place number six worldwide. That's important. If you look to the medical doctors, we need top medical science, yes? That reflects in papers, but on the other hand, even important for our university hospital is, for example, to be really an outstanding place for surgery, for example, and really medical craftmanship. You will not find that in any of those rankings.

You can go through many of those parameters where we more and more say publications alone is too short-minded in order to measure the success of, or let me say the societal impact of, a university. For me, it's important that universities of the future, and I think that will become even more important, will have a measurable impact in society, maybe in people education, maybe in developing new technologies that are then used in industry and really goes into application. So not got stuck in the lab somehow and never will reach the daylight. This needs to be, I think, rethought.

Interviewer: Ok. That's very helpful. I think there's the next twenty or thirty years of our job in the field of higher education studies, so thanks for that very ambitious and meaningful research agenda. What interests you most about Tsinghua?

President: I think what is really interesting to see is really that Tsinghua can look back to a remarkable development in recent years, becoming one of the leading universities within quite a short time. In particular, what I know at least from the communications we had so far, is also the sense for interdisciplinary cooperation and understanding, collaboration within the university as a whole. I think it manages that very well: concrete relations. Finally, probably also the role Tsinghua plays, or can play, in the future – even more when it comes to the university's broader social responsibility or societal responsibility. I think these are three pillars where I see Tsinghua on an excellent track.

Interviewer: Thank you. Just two more things, and then we'll let you go to your next meeting. Very much appreciate your time this morning. Any other things you'd like to add based on what we've talked about? Any final points?

President: What is the role of universities in supporting start-ups, in building ecosystems also with deep tech start-up families, so to say? You can see major cultural differences between the continents. In Germany, start-ups in the past were not, I would say, in the major focus of any university. It was primarily teaching and research, and that's it. TUM, about fifteen years back, started to really build up lots of programs from entrepreneurial education to networking to whatever, so massive programs, and that finally worked out that TUM today is very successful. This is still not enough. We have to do everything we can, not only to come up with nice papers. We need them, definitely. No doubt about it. But this should not stop there. We need to bring our technologies more efficiently to society and to our businesses. For example, we now initiate a new program which we call TUM Venture Lab Network. We span a network of venture labs across TUM in order to form these ecosystems on deep tech areas; for example, a venture lab on quantum technologies where we bring the industry start-ups and our faculty capacities together. We have the same for manufacturing and another one for energy research, for example, so to build critical masses around that generates capability for our scientists and students to go into the start-up or realize the start-up ideas. But also capability for other start-ups of other countries coming to this community because they will benefit from this ecosystem that is developing around a core field of expertise. That's probably one of the latest initiatives we just have started.

Interviewer: How do you know if that's working? Is it the number of spin-offs, or the amount of money, or the amount of people working, or the amount of building space?

President: Yeah, we usually count the numbers of start-ups that are still surviving after five years, and then in particular, the number of workforce they generate. That's important for us. Definitely, we also look on the funds they are raising; yeah, sure. But I think the number of workforce, that's important for us.

Interviewer: Excellent. Thanks so much for sharing your expert and unique insights. I really appreciate it.

PART 3

Guiding insights

22
PERSPECTIVES ON UNIVERSITY LEADERSHIP

Foundation steps in a global project

The research has contributed initial insights that help presidents understand their peers and their work, deepen international engagement and collaboration, inform development of presidents, and serve conceptual and empirical foundations for future international research. Indeed, learning about global university presidents is becoming more important given the changing political economy of higher education in many countries whereby the locus of power and responsibility is shifting from systems to institutions, emphasizing the work of university leaders. It is particularly the case, of course, that global university presidents are operating in 'post-systemic' ways.

This book has revealed initial insights from an ongoing research project which is analyzing the complex and shifting roles and functions of global university presidents. The book has focused on presenting the ideas and telling the stories of presidents, in their own words. These words are unique. They reveal precious insights from the vantage point of the presidential office and delve further to show how presidents think and feel about their role and the major issues they confront.

These stories make a timely, timeless, unique contribution to higher education and the world. The important roles played by both education and research have become very clear in 2020. Higher education is the cradle of so many futures. There remains an urgent need to know more about what it does and its futures. It is especially important to learn about higher education in China. Chinese higher education has grown very large and continues to open up, to globalize, to strengthen, and to create new wealth for the world. Especially during times of uncertainty and transformation, the views of top global leaders are vital to deeply understand the complexity, strength, and contours of academic partnerships and contributions.

DOI: 10.4324/9781003248286-25

This book concentrates on the presidents' own words, but it is helpful to analyze major themes emerging from the 'data.' Doing this provides a conclusion to the interviews and helps signpost further developments.

Highlight themes and quotes

Complexity, contrast, and change characterize how presidents lead major universities. Sustained research helps find the deep structure underpinning each of the topics touched upon in the interviews and uses concepts and frameworks to construct broader research contributions. Here, we summarize highlights.

While interviews flowed freely around defined topics, they generally began by reflecting on the presidents directly. Recent analysis has probed this facet of the interviews (Liu et al., 2020). Presidents come from a range of backgrounds, and there is not one single 'recipe' for leadership. Fundamentally, however, presidents are characterized by a leadership orientation, scholarly excellence, cross-cutting generalized competence, and the capacity for reflective development. Presidents take many 'steps into the presidency.' Key considerations include career profiles, academic pedigree, leadership experience, political skill, and the capacity for continuous growth.

The following quotes capture these facets of presidential careers:

> My disciplinary background is that I am a space scientist, so I'm a geologist who studies rocks from Mars, and meteorites, and the moon, and things like this. It's kind of an odd background, but space exploration by its nature is very team-based and very interdisciplinary. I think of my experience – I worked at NASA before I was a college president – and I know that if you have really big goals, if your goal is to send people to Mars, no one person can accomplish that goal. You have to bring people together with many different backgrounds and many different experiences to be able to achieve big things. I think that is how my own background tends to play into this work in that I am very comfortable trying to bring teams of people together to address grander challenges.
>
> (Laurie Leshin, Worcester Polytechnic Institute)

> The thing that lawyers and engineers have in common is a need to engage with the realities of the world to some extent.... I think there is this sort of dialog between what it is we want to do, what the realities are, how we respond to those realities, how do we build processes, how do we build institutional structures, how do we find a different way of doing something when something doesn't work.... Those are the kinds of things lawyers do. It's a very kind of practical orientation. I think what lawyers and engineers in academia have is this ability to bring together the kind of theoretical qualities – and some of them very academic qualities, the importance of

thought at some level – with a sense of practical realities, and how do you get people to work together?

(David Leebron, Rice University)

As the interviews convey, university leadership teams play important and growing roles in how presidents run large and complex institutions. These teams range in size and composition, and three to seven people typically report directly to the president. The interview data affirms the importance of achieving all kinds of balance in these teams. Fundamentally, presidents play the core role in university leadership teams, helping to compose and guide them. For instance,

> To have an artist or people from arts or humanities or social sciences, basically, it deepens the conversation. They provide some very important angles or at least segments of a conversation that I wouldn't normally have myself, but they bring a very different perspective. The most visible one is the ability to think beyond concepts I would have considered myself, to think beyond what's readily available to me, and they're able to approach the "what if?" part of the question differently. Also, they're able to connect whatever we do to other big things…. [W]hen I bring a subject of, let's say, connecting artificial intelligence to medicine and agriculture and other things, and they will say, "Well, there are also some ethical aspects," or "There are also human aspects, so then what about those?" Therefore, we're not coming out with initiatives that are only driven by technology or science. We're coming out with initiatives that are a lot wider and connected to political science or human rights, human behaviour, all of those things.
>
> (Feridun Hamdullahpur, University of Waterloo)

> I'm not a micromanager. I give the broad general direction, and then I trust people to get on with the job. I'm very fortunate to have very capable people doing that. The specific system within which I function is not like the American presidential system, that when I come in I bring my own team. You inherit a certain number of people, and they have defined terms.
>
> (Wim de Villiers, Stellenbosch University)

> Collegiality is very important for me, so I selected intentionally a few people who already knew each other very well so that you can immediately start with a strong group cohesion. We have an election-based leadership, so every four years a director is elected in Leuven by all faculty and students and administrative staff, and so on. A few of them were also on my campaign board during the election period, so partners in crime so to say. But I made a very clear message from the very beginning that as of day one, the focus should be on the university and not on a political view of a team or a group that is now leading the university against other groups or coalitions within

the university…. Subsidiarity is very important, so I only interfere if I think that a decision is going wrong, or I really disagree, or a decision is not in line with the strategic plan. But otherwise, at the size of this institution, you need to give them some leeway, some autonomy, and really translate that responsibility to the rest of academia and KU Leuven.

(Luc Sels, KU Leuven)

Our vice presidents of finance and administration are focused more on the operations of the university. Our vice president of advancement is focused on fundraising and external relations. Our academic leadership, again, is balanced between the internal operations of academics and making sure that we are keeping up with those external trends. We talk about it a lot, this need to balance between near term and long term, and internal and external. It's something a leader does, to hold those balances, to be checking, "Are we balanced correctly? Are we too far one way or the other?"

(Laurie Leshin, Worcester Polytechnic Institute)

One of each president's main jobs is to design the university's future, and the interviews revealed a substantial amount about progress, reforms, challenges, and initiatives. The topic of institutional status and position invariably arose, alongside the need to build internal institutional strength and differentiate in competitive global markets. International positioning is particularly important for accessing top staff and students, and increasingly for delivering contributions to multilevel communities. Internally, most presidents have embarked on various structural and personnel reforms, with several doing so in response to external opportunities and constraints, and others putting incentive funding in place. It is important to define 'grand challenges.' Despite their strength and status, few institutions could be characterized as 'standing still.' Indeed, guiding a productive, 'positive restlessness' seems key to steering their universities into novel and often challenging waters.

Key insights into university reforms include the following:

[W]ithin Sciences Po, there are two or three things that are key in terms of the institutional culture. First of all, multidisciplinarity at all levels of training. We feel that it is important to exchange disciplinary viewpoints in order to enable our students to gain a true understanding of the complexity of the world…. The second thing is being open to the world. And so the internationalization that has been going on for at least twenty years, and even a little more, is also very central to the way we see ourselves as having to learn from the rest of the planet and having to teach our students to be aware of what's happening out there. The third thing, in terms of culture, is mixing at all times. Mixing theory, that is to say, science with practice, because we aim at training young people who will take up positions of leadership in the world five, ten, twenty years from now.

(Frédéric Mion, Sciences Po)

[W]hen we did our recent strategic plan, we looked around at the world. We said, well, actually there are different ways to extend our reach and impact. And so we've put as a priority developing online degree programs. For example, we have one in place now at the Business School, and a second will launch in the fall in computer science. Well, they're fully online with opportunities, I would say, to come to campus and participate. But they're fully online, and both of them are at, or close to, the price point of the residential programs.

(David Leebron, Rice University)

[W]e are working on the visibility of things we care about at WPI, enhancing our reputation around project-based learning, so we started something called the Center for Project-Based Learning at WPI where we invite other universities to come and learn from us. After fifty years of working on projects, we really know how to incorporate this into a higher education curriculum. In the past five years, we have served one hundred and thirty other universities which have sent teams to participate with us in the centre, and collectively they serve 1.3 million students a year. It's a way to have an impact on a lot of students in higher education with what we are passionate about – project-based learning.

(Laurie Leshin, Worcester Polytechnic Institute)

University finance is a closely guarded, complex, and important facet of institutional leadership in higher education. It is an area in which presidents have unique, even privileged, perspectives. It is an area where old truisms prevail, accounting norms are defied, and macro- and microeconomics blend with international politics and local instincts. Presidents' words have much to offer regarding university finances. Highlights included the following:

[T]he one thing I wish I had known, which I have realized, is the brute economics of running a university.

(Stephen Smith, University of Exeter)

And for a university in our type of society, acknowledging that we live in different systems and they are differently funded, we are pretty clear that going forward, an aging population will cost so much to look after that governments will find it difficult to find all the money necessary to run top universities. We, therefore, need to move to a situation where our graduates become so successful that they will one day say to our university, "You did really well by me, I have done very well, I would now like to help the university stay successful and to help fund the university through philanthropy."

(Peter Høj, University of Queensland)

They (the government) were just elected. They ran on a mandate to balance the provincial budget in four years without raising revenues. No increase in taxes. That is, it's all going to be cuts…. We have an approved budget.

All the assumptions may be invalid. We'll have to manage that very, very quickly. Then, in February, there will be another provincial budget, which will be for the 20/21 budget year. That's the one where we'll probably have the more significant reductions.

(David Turpin, University of Alberta)

Talk is often about ideas, buildings, products, and complexities. But fundamentally, education is about people. People are usually separated into categories based on what they do, financial relationships, who they are, or life or career stages. Each university embraces a hugely diverse community, often a microcosm of society at large. Binding and sustaining these diverse communities are keys to institutional performance, nature, and presence. On this core theme the presidents noted the following:

We decided to raise the importance of teaching quality and innovation in our promotions criteria to be more equivalent to that of research performance – now you really have to be good at both to get promoted in most circumstances. I'm very proud to say that of all eight research-intensive universities in Australia…UQ easily has the highest student satisfaction. In that sense, I say we are a most comprehensive university because we are good at both teaching and research across virtually all disciplines.

(Peter Høj, University of Queensland)

The biggest challenge occurs around, let's say, hot topics like artificial intelligence, and it is recruiting the best professors available. There is international competition, and we are not recruiting from other universities.… We are recruiting from industry and, for example, when we talk about artificial intelligence, we have to recruit from Google and Facebook. The salary level for these colleagues in industry is so high compared to what we can pay as a professor's salary. So I think this is really a challenge for us, not always being behind what industry is doing.

(Ulrich Rüdiger, RWTH Aachen University)

Being global means being international, and managing relations, people, and funds beyond the nation state. Major universities are invariably tightly linked to governments, but they transcend political or national interests in many ways. Science, education, expertise are marshalled within states but inherently transcend or transverse national boundaries. Often, pushing such boundaries is core to a university's role and identity. International relations are core to a global university, as presidents' remarks illustrate:

One of the things we do with the partners we work with, increasingly, is have significant professional service interactions.… [C]olleagues at other universities around the world can come to see how we operate, we come to see how they operate, then it's much more than just a leader. I mean, if a leader changes, the focus changes. So we're trying to build more organic relations with not just academic staff and students but systems.

(Stephen Smith, University of Exeter)

I think universities do have this unique position and capacity to build collaborative endeavours, even if our governments are having conflicts and deep disagreements. Universities have been a kind of fifth or sixth estate, something in which even state universities have been recognized as having some independent role in creating a kind of global mindset in which we work together to address and think about common problems. I do worry about the barriers that the political states can sometimes put in front of that, whether that's barriers about the transmission of information and collaborating in certain fields, or the movement of peoples.

(David Leebron, Rice University)

We are a global university. This year, we will launch what we're calling the Global School, based on this project work and building upon it to continue to offer opportunities for us to engage in new ways around the world.... We do not have physical infrastructure in other countries. We have many, many relationships, and our faculty travel with our students when they go to these other countries. That's the infrastructure we have – our relationships.... [W]e're very excited about where the Global School can take us because right now we might have a student team in three or four different countries working on something about transportation or health care or sustainability. We can start to bring together those individual experiences and do something more collectively.

(Laurie Leshin, Worcester Polytechnic Institute)

Major universities have complex, deep engagements with governments. Many institutions contend that their funding, horizon, composition, and role go beyond national or political borders to serve larger professional or scientific mandates. Basically, however, every university is anchored by a national regulator, framed within a national education and research ecosystem, and infused with a particular culture. The importance of government and government relations was recognized by presidents:

[U]niversities, I think, can bridge political divides and reach out to areas that our countries may have difficulties with. Universities can often collaborate. For example, academics in Israel collaborate with academics in Palestine because to them the partnership matters more than the politics.

(Nancy Rothwell, University of Manchester)

> [T]he role of the president is to help modify the external environment to benefit the mission of the institution so that there's a receptor capacity out there so that as the environment changes, it changes to help facilitate us and the accomplishment of our mission. That involves meeting with government officials – locally, provincially, nationally, and internationally. It involves meeting with members of the broader community, whether that is the business community, people in industrial sectors.
>
> (David Turpin, University of Alberta)

Global university presidents provide really important expert insight into Tsinghua University and Chinese higher education. Tsinghua University and Chinese higher education have grown remarkably in recent decades, touching many facets of academic and global life. These 2019 interviews signal that Tsinghua University is seen as a flagship institution playing a vitally important role in higher education affairs. It is recognized as a leader within China in terms of reforming key areas such as faculty work, academic standards, education reform, and doctoral program development. The presidents recognized tough challenges Tsinghua University will face as the world becomes characterized by more nationalism, commercial innovation, and technology boundaries. Each president, of course, brought different experiences and relationships with them to their meetings. One was a Tsinghua alum, another had been visiting China for decades, for others, it was the first visit. All remarked on growth, innovation, and the need for sustainable global engagement among leading universities.

Finally, the interviews tapped into presidents' views on global higher education. Scarcely two decades ago, higher education was, like most sectors, far less globalized than it is today. Through their leadership, many of these presidents have sponsored globalization by producing global graduates and, of course, through global research networks and contributions. Though the interviews were conducted in 2019, the presidents each foresaw emerging international headwinds and reconfigurations. Accordingly, they saw a larger and broader future role for universities. These sentiments have proved correct, with the time since the interviews revealing the important socio-economic rejuvenation role these large public institutions must play.

Reference

Liu, L., Hong, X., Wen, W., Xie, Z., & Coates, H. (2020). Global university president leadership characteristics and dynamics. Studies in Higher Education, 45(10), 2036–2044.

23
PROSPECTS FOR LEADERSHIP PRACTICE AND RESEARCH

Moments for change

Reflecting on university presidents' insights on leadership reveals prospects for higher education practice, policy, and research. The ideas of individual presidents presented throughout this book have been affirmed, integrated, and extended in global conferences on higher education contexts, innovations, and futures. Drawing on two international university president conferences, in this final chapter, we extract insights regarding university presidents' roles and contributions, the challenges they face, and approaches to cultivating future leaders. As Liu et al. (2020) note, studying presidents' experiences and ideas reveals the need for more systematic development of future presidents, for major research into 'what works' in higher education, and for global governance.

These ideas and sentiments were echoed and reinforced in dialogues between university leaders in 2020 and 2021. These influential meetings convened university presidents during times of major crisis and change, enabling them to clarify shared ideas and perspectives.

The 2020 Tsinghua and UNESCO special dialogue was convened to focus on education during and beyond the pandemic. Among other guests, the special dialogue was attended by fourteen university presidents from the Australian National University, Imperial College London, Peter the Great St. Petersburg Polytechnic University, Politecnico di Milano, University of Buenos Aires, University of Cambridge, University of Chile, University of Exeter, University of Malaya, University of Nairobi, University of Toronto, University of Washington in St Louis, Waseda University, and Yale University.

Presidents affirmed the need to ensure sustainability and continuity of education provision. There was much focus on the nature and limitations of emergency online learning. The shock arising from the pandemic also triggered broader analyses,

DOI: 10.4324/9781003248286-26

including training of teaching staff, sharing of IT infrastructure and expertise, quality assurance, and ensuring marginal groups of students retained access. Presidents remarked on the lack of preparedness of higher education institutions to react to this grand challenge and at the same time the rapid redirection to online learning. They agreed this was a global problem, requiring universities both to work together to create solutions for their own activities and to enable them to serve others.

The April 2021 Global University Leadership Forum was convened as part of a broader Global Forum of University Presidents. It was attended by one hundred representatives from thirty universities and nineteen countries. Eighteen university presidents reflected on three core questions emerging from the analysis of the interviews presented in this book. These questions explored presidents' work, external challenges, and leadership development.

The first topic focused on the role and contribution of university presidents. President Xia Wenbin of China's University of International Business and Economics pointed out that to build China's new liberal arts talents, presidents needed to serve the national interest, serve social needs, and foster openness, innovation, and tolerance. Humanities disciplines need to deploy teaching strategies which develop creative, empathic, and broad-minded talents. Tokyo Institute of Technology president Kazuya Masu observed that innovation lies at the core of science and engineering universities: these universities must contribute to society's technological development and also cultivate interdisciplinary graduates. Christian Lerminiaux of ParisTech in France noted presidents play an important role in leading their institutions conduct of scientific research and innovation, talent training, and social contribution. The duty of universities is to train imaginative future business and social leaders who have impact. Universities must lead global digital transformation around research, learning, and teaching. President Tim van der Hagen of Delft University of Technology in the Netherlands reflected that presidents should focus more on serving society, investing in greater inter-university cooperation, developing new paradigms, and spreading common values across national borders. President Laurie Leshin of Worcester Polytechnic Institute in the United States advocated that university presidents must capably transform their institutions in ways that honour past engagements, present challenges, and future opportunities; concurrently, presidents need to leverage their schools' advantages for positive social impact.

The second part of the Forum focused on challenges university presidents face in promoting the development of global higher education. Michael Wesley of the University of Melbourne pointed out that boundaries between countries should not become an obstacle to the pursuit of knowledge. Universities are internationalist institutions existing in national communities. This emphasizes innovative partnerships for progressing frontiers. Scholars need to collaborate in exploring ways to spread and share knowledge. Universities need to actively establish cooperative relations and promote the extension of knowledge boundaries. President Hideo Ohno of Tohoku University in Japan counselled that to fully respond to global challenges, universities must both look within and cooperate with local governments, other universities, and society. David Gann, pro vice chancellor of Oxford

University, said the university president's mission is to solve challenging problems, like saving more lives through technological innovation. At the same time, the core of education is to cultivate people – universities must help lead the next generation to establish correct values. President Bernd Huber of the University of Munich in Germany considered universities should serve the world and gather all forces to contribute to society. The responsibilities of the future university also include cultivating the next generation to quickly respond to challenges, adapt to growth in student numbers, and cultivate students with future skills.

President Chris Day of Newcastle University in the United Kingdom pointed out that universities are vital to the development of human civilization. With a shared vision of making humans better, and the planet a better place, universities should bear the responsibility to promote the establishment of transnational and cross-cultural partnerships. President Andrei Rudskoi of Russia's St Petersburg University of Technology observed that to realize the university's social mission, it is necessary for universities to initiate cooperative alliances through cooperation between the world's leading universities, thus providing information on major global issues. Vanessa Scherrer from the University of Paris contended that the internationalization of universities must meet four conditions: namely, to have international influence, to have global appeal, to become a hub for global cooperation, and to award degrees to students around the world. University presidents should promote the interdependence of universities around the world, especially in promoting cooperation in personnel training, so as to cope with the challenges of the future. They must adopt the attitude of helping each other because all are in the same boat.

The Forum theme focused on how to train future university presidents. President Aiji Tanaka of Waseda University in Japan noted that university presidents needed to have integrity and vision for the future, understand challenges, and clearly discern knowledge development needs. C. Raj Kumar, president of Jindal University in India, conveyed a view that universities need to establish an integrated framework, and find a balance between scientific research and teaching through continuous experience accumulation. University presidents need to demonstrate academic independence, lead by example, and cultivate and transmit good values. University of Brunei's Joyce Teo Siew Yean noted future university presidents must deal with life after the pandemic, challenges from digital transformation, and reforms of traditional operating models. They must establish an educational and scientific research environment that enables full development of leadership and innovation and promotes growth of a new generation of university presidents. Erik Lithander, vice chancellor of the University of Bristol in the United Kingdom, considered that in addressing common global social problems, future universities should devote themselves to finding solutions. They must consider sustainable development of universities and their impact on local communities. University presidents need to be flexible, provide academic leadership, and lead socially at home and abroad.

Combined, these ideas convey consistency across university contexts, cultures, and countries. They reveal universities engaged with big social problems and prospects, playing formal and formative and core roles in crafting innovative and impactful solutions. This means re-engineering disciplinary, institutional, professional, and historical arrangements. It affirms the importance of university partnerships in a changing world, including hosting trusted and confident global/borderless networks, and working across boundaries in synchronized transnational institutions. Of course, this means inspiring the next generation of learners, most particularly by setting conditions which help people fulfil their own potential. This means building the academy, attracting excellent people who can lead, and inspiring contribution. Overall, this means a shared momentum for raising the voice of universities in the world.

Future developments

In conclusion, it is helpful to look forward and portend productive futures for this field of leadership research and development.

The interviews reveal the need for much more systematic development of future presidents. Every leader spoke to this point, so much so that it formed a major part of the launch Forum. Part of this doubtless involves formal training. Experience and broader cultivation are also key. Current presidents certainly have central roles to play in such development. So too do university governors and those responsible for selection arrangements, including faculty or broader stakeholders where elections are held. Prioritizing leaders who rise through academic ranks sends one message – engaging leaders with broader sectoral and social experience sends another.

There certainly remains a need for major cross-institutional, if not cross-national, research into 'what works' in higher education. Nearly all presidents revealed legacy employment and academic models were stretched and needed reform but that besides consultants, they lacked clear and credible guidance on reform options. Looking at university leadership teams, and how presidents govern them, is a topic of growing relevance. Holding 'international rankings' as a dominant criterion for success is insufficient, and the leaders spoke of many more complex goals and successes. University harmony and, increasingly, community contribution, are of growing focus, reinforcing the need to study how different leadership arrangements enable these outcomes.

The presidents' insights affirm the need for global governance of core facets of higher education. Various commercial firms, such as publishers and rankings agencies, have grown to play a de facto role in this regard, but these are manifestly inadequate. With such great transnational research and student exchange, there is a growing need to ensure clarity and alignment among academic standards, to confirm comparability of teaching and research and leadership competence, and to provide greater clarity around funding, quality, and networks.

While reasonably accepted in conversation, this project exposes the need to clarify what 'global university' means, not just semantically but in practical ways. This triggers broader discussion about the nature and reach of different types of universities. Are national universities from small countries as global as smaller universities from larger economies? How do different missions and sizes and research rankings nuance what is 'global'? Are there many 'globals' or just one? A little light could be shone on this matter by exploring governance, in terms of what is being governed, but there is value in more immediate analysis.

Finally, given the unprecedented change being experienced by higher education since 2020, there remains an unambiguous role for conducting more research on presidents. Every president remarked on this project's unique value. These interviews helped build community among the presidents, gather unique insights, and bring out opportunities for partnership and reform. These ideas can be lost in highly polished corporate documents. The sit-down interview remains a key means for understanding important facets of higher education.

Reference

Liu, L., Hong, X., Wen, W., Xie, Z., & Coates, H. (2020). Global university president leadership characteristics and dynamics. *Studies in Higher Education*, *45*(10), 2036–2044.

INDEX

Printed in the United States
by Baker & Taylor Publisher Services